The Hermeneutical Theory
of Paul Ricoeur

B
2430
.R554
K46
1983

The Hermeneutical Theory of Paul Ricoeur

A Constructive Analysis

David E. Klemm

Lewisburg
Bucknell University Press
London and Toronto: Associated University Presses

© 1983 by Associated University Presses, Inc.

Associated University Presses, Inc.
4 Cornwall Drive
East Brunswick, NJ 08816

Associated University Presses Ltd
25 Sicilian Avenue
London WC1A 2QH, England

Associated University Presses
2133 Royal Windsor Drive
Unit 1
Mississauga, Ontario
Canada L5J 1K5

Library of Congress Cataloging in Publication Data

Klemm, David E., 1947–
  The hermeneutical theory of Paul Ricoeur.

  Bibliography: p.
  Includes index.
  1. Ricoeur, Paul. 2. Hermeneutics—History—
20th century.   I. Title.
B2430.R554K46   1983   121′.092′4   82-22708
ISBN 0-8387-5041-9

Printed in the United States of America

Contents

1	Introduction	9
	Purpose and Procedure	9
	Summary and Thesis	15
2	Ricoeur's Place in the Tradition of Hermeneutical Discussion	18
	Schleiermacher and Dilthey	18
	Martin Heidegger and Ontological Hermeneutics	27
3	The Development of Ricoeur's Thought	45
	The Evolution of Ricoeur's Thought from Reflective Philosophy into a Hermeneutical Phenomenology	45
	Ricoeur's Notion of Expression	61
	Expression as Object	62
	The Process of Expression and Understanding Expression	66
	Subjective Conditions of Expression	69
4	Ricoeur's Hermeneutical Theory	74
	The Nature of Discourse	74
	Theory of Text	82
	Text as Object	82
	The Process of Textual Understanding	90
	Subjective Conditions for Understanding Texts	102
5	The Religious Dimension of Text and Understanding	109
	Ricoeur on Religious Language and Theological Hermeneutics	111
	A Second Attempt to Specify Religious Language	121
	A Formal Analysis of Religious Texts and Theological Hermeneutics	133

6 Appropriation of Textual Meaning and the Question of Truth	140
The Object of Appropriation	143
Appropriation as Event	147
Subject of Appropriation	153
Ricoeur's Proposal for Ontology	157
Religious Appropriation and the Question of Truth	159
Bibliography	177
Index	181

The Hermeneutical Theory
of Paul Ricoeur

1 • Introduction

Purpose and Procedure

In this volume I propose to present a systematic analysis of Paul Ricoeur's hermeneutics. But beyond that, the aim of this work is to construct a possibility, which Ricoeur himself has not recognized, for defining what is specifically *theological* hermeneutics within Ricoeur's philosophical hermeneutical program. For Ricoeur, hermeneutics basically has to do both with a theory of how the understanding can have immediate acquaintance with the sense or meaning embedded in textual signs and with a theory of how signs in texts that do not immediately yield their meaning can be deciphered so as to render that meaning to understanding through explicit mediation. The task of this work, then, calls initially for a systematic analysis of what it means to understand texts in Ricoeur's theory, and additionally for a more specific delimitation of a dimension in the understanding process that can be designated as a "religious understanding" (to which a theological hermeneutics can by definition be said to refer).

This task of delimiting a theological hermeneutics within Ricoeur's general theory does not treat hermeneutics as an isolated subdivision of theological science, in this case one having to do with development and application of rules for scriptural exegesis. To specify theological hermeneutics within the framework of a general hermeneutical theory is, rather, to contribute to what is called fundamental theology, in that it establishes conditions of the possibility for a type of thinking that can be designated as theological thinking. That this is so is clear from the fact that any possible revelation or disclosure of ultimate meaning and truth can, in the nature of the case, be intelligible only if it appears as a meaning carried by a sign. Fundamental theology must include theological hermeneutics, and theological hermeneutics is necessarily part of fundamental theology.

With respect to the organization of materials here, I intend to heed Paul Tillich's dictum that such thinking should be systematic in form. According to Tillich, systematic thought must display semantic rationality, logical rationality, and methodological rationality.[1] Semantic rationality involves the necessity for exactness in the use of terms and concepts to avoid ambiguity. Logical rationality has to do with the consistency of ordered assertions made through division and combination of concepts within the body of thought. Methodological rationality concerns the justification of the specific way assertions are arrived at and put forward. Such a justification, it seems to me, must be given with respect to the *unity* of the systematic thinking.

By the *unity of systematic thinking*, I refer to its characteristic of having thought proceed out of a single principle, which can be clearly stated. By following the principle, the whole range of relevant topics is generated in an ordered and potentially exhaustive progression. The sign of completeness in the system is the return to the starting point by following the principle. For reasons that will become clear later, I propose to think systematically in this work, but not to set out the lines of a closed system. It is my intention to think through what is called the hermeneutical process, and to do this so that a theological dimension is set forth. But this procedure would not warrant a closing of the circle formed by following the principle. Let me elucidate this more closely.

The hermeneutical process, or the process of raising hidden meaning to clear understanding, as we shall see below in detail, is a *linguistic process* through and through just because language in the broadest sense of that word, is the medium for human experience and thought. That is, since the *thinking* process on the one hand and the process by which we *experience* reality as it is given to us on the other hand both take place in the medium of language, therefore the process of understanding, which connects the activities of thinking and of the experiencing of concrete realities in the world, is also a linguistic process. The process of understanding, in other words, as a basic form or structure in which the self is related to the world, must be seen with reference to two other basic relations to the world: (1) the relation of our forming definitions and abstract concepts, and (2) the relation of our having concrete experience of things (as in perception, for example).

Ricoeur's position, which is shared with his dialogue partner in hermeneutics, Hans-Georg Gadamer, is that language is the medium in which both our abstract thinking and our concrete experiencing assume definite shape and are determined as thought or experience *of* something and not another thing. Understanding is the process that synthesizes the perceiving-experiencing on the one hand and the thinking on the other. Understanding discovers sense embedded in signs because understanding is the process by which the concrete percept, the physical reality as sign, is connected with an abstract thought or concept to render an understood meaning. The meaning with which understanding is immediately familiar (or which must be laboriously mediated) is a connection between thought, which on its own is independent of experience, and experience, which on its own is independent of thought. Thoughts (e.g., the definition referred to by the term *tree*) and percepts (e.g., the thing designated by the term *this* when pointing to a tree) are both linguistically fashioned. And the connecting activity, the understanding process, is also a process that is actualized in the medium of language.

The basic linguistic unit of the understanding process is the sentence, for in the sentence we have the paradigm for the original separation *(Ur-teil)* and conjunction of what is immediately understood as a unity of percept and concept. For example, in the sentence "This is a tree," what is expressed in the relation between subject and predicate is the separation and conjunction of a percept ("this") with a concept ("tree") by means of a copula ("is"). What was immediately understood *to be* a tree is expressed in its identity (the percept and the concept are somehow the same) and in its difference (the percept and concept are also distinct). Between the two and functioning as identity of the identity and difference is the copula *is*. The connecting copula is the locus of the meaning discovered in a physical sign by applying abstract thought. What we understand immediately or struggle to understand mediately is marked in the grammatical unity of the sentence by the finite form of the verb *to be*, which is co-thought in any intelligible English sentence as the grammatical correlate of understanding. Our access to what we understand (or misunderstand) as the meaning of a sign is limited to the use we make of the verb *to be* in its finite forms as a connector between thought and percept.

The hermeneutical process is essentially a linguistic process, and hermeneutics is necessarily tied to the philosophy of language since the connections that are made in acts of understanding are always linguistic connections. I should also note at this point that the relevance that a hermeneutical philosophy of language has for theology today is analogous to the relevance that metaphysics or first philosophy had for the philosophical theologies that were systematized up until the time of Kant's critique of metaphysics. This is so because what is understood when we understand the meaning in a sign, as is indicated by the grammatical locus of the understanding in the copula, is precisely the *being* of the thing signified.

The being of something can be designated here, for the sake of a preliminary grasp of what is to be developed herein, as the connection between the universal concept or thought-determination and the particular percept or experience-determination. Understanding is the activity or process by which we are referred to the being of things.[2] For this reason, hermeneutics has an intrinsic ontological dimension. The hermeneutical process is a linguistic one, and the direct object of attention for hermeneutical philosophy is language. But the content of our understanding, when we understand the meaning carried by linguistic signs, is being.

Now it follows that a systematic treatment of the hermeneutical process as outlined in Ricoeur's theory must display methodological rationality by showing, in the first place, that the systematic principle to be followed is itself basic to the "linguisticality" of the understanding process. The linguistic process through which we understand the being of things, other people, and ourselves, minimally involves the elements of speaking or expression and hearing or listening. The derived forms of these two basic elements are writing and reading. The linguistic process, then, must initially encompass (1) the moment in which meaning is verbally expressed in order to communicate that meaning to one who listens understandingly, and (2) the transition from spoken to written forms of language, which communicates meaning to one who reads understandingly, and (3) the understanding and appropriation of the expressed meaning.

We can say that description of a linguistic event includes the fact that, on the one hand, someone pushes out (ex-presses, *ausdrückt*) a meaning by conjoining and separating in language (or at least in gesture) a thought and percept (e.g., "This is a tree"). And, on the other hand, someone receives or takes in the sense by seeing that connection between general thought and particular percept. On a more refined level an account of the linguistic process must include description of what takes place when spoken language is fixed in textual form and thereby released from the interlocutory situation, so that the meaning inscribed there can be uncovered by anyone who can read and decipher what is objectified in the linguistic signs, and thereby appropriate the sense of the text.

If this linguistic process is unraveled in a certain way in order to display a sequential pattern that is abstracted from the ordinary process in which each element is engaged more or less simultaneously, we can sketch an identifiable path as follows: it is the pattern of the self going out of itself (into language) and returning to itself (in appropriation of meaning), but never completely. The starting point is the moment of utterance as such. As soon as one speaks and expresses a sign-sense, the silence of absolute self-identity, the pure identity of the "I" with itself, is broken. Through speech, the "I" who was silent and purely with itself falls into existence. The absolute "I," which in silence is unconditioned by linguistic determinations, posits itself in speech as "this one here," the existential self. Any utterance whatsoever implies a speaker who is "this one here" by virtue of having placed the "I" of prelinguistic absoluteness into the world for a possible hearer. To say "This is a tree" is to say "I am here speaking and this is a tree, nothing else."

The very first moment, then, of the linguistic process is the self-positing of the "I" as "this one here," which is presupposed in any expression. But if we look more closely it is evident that the moment of expression presupposes another element. The self as "I," the point of origin of thinking and speaking, does go out of itself and empty itself, as it were, into the matter of speech by saying, "I am this one here who says. . . ," thus distancing itself from itself. But "this one here who says. . ." is, strictly speaking, *not* the "I." The "I" as absolute point of origin of speaking and thinking is indeed disclosed through linguistic utterance, but it is also concealed, because the "I" who hears or who speaks again (whether it is that of the same person or not) is always identical with that absolute point of origin. The "I" is systematically elusive just because it is the originating point for thinking and speaking and can never be brought into view. The "I" does empty itself into the matter of speech and objectify itself in linguistic expression, but it retains its universality over against that concretion just by changing its position and timing (if it is another person who hears and responds and thus connects the absolute "I" with "this other one here") or at least its timing (if I am speaking or thinking to myself and respond to my own utterance). The "I," then, goes out of its initially "blind" or "empty" silence in speech into a kind of self-alienation as it posits its existence in the world through expression, and that is the first moment of the hermeneutical process.

The second moment of this linguistic process is the further distancing of the self from itself in the transition from spoken to textual language. The written text also presents the concrete positing of an "I" as "this one here," but it does so in a form that permits the text and the self-understanding carried with it to be torn from the original setting of its composition and readership. Textual meaning clearly is susceptible of greater estrangement than spoken meaning and provides special problems for the understanding process by which the "I" who reads can appropriate in self-awareness the possibility of being a human self as revealed and concealed in that text.

The third and final moment in the linguistic process as seqentially abstracted here would be the return of the self to itself through understanding and appropriation of the meaning of being a self-in-a-world that is pushed out and concretized in language. In this moment the "I" who reads or hears and understands recognizes the meaning of being concretized in the text as a possibility for *me* to be, and appropriates the mode of existence expressed there as a possibility for this "I". The self here returns to itself; the alienated meaning of being a concrete embodied self is taken up into the life of a self-positing "I." The silence at the end of this process, the silence of one who hears or reads and understands, is not the "empty" silence that is the silence of the "I" in its initial self-awareness; it is rather the "full" silence of comprehension.

The assertion here is that the linguistic process, which minimally includes speaking, writing, hearing, and reading, can be reduced to the process of the self going out of itself and returning to itself, which can be marked out in the three moments just described.

Put to work as a systematic principle, the "self goes out of itself and returns to itself" can be used to generate the set of topics that need to be treated in a systematic account of hermeneutics. But the principle, as I said earlier, does not permit the delineation of a closed system because of some characteristics of language as the medium of the hermeneutical process. Language is *historical* through and through, which means that it comes into existence through the creative capacity of people who are situated in time and place and who are thoroughly influenced by their situation, and it develops and changes in the course of time until it ceases to be a living historical language. The importance of this is that linguistic meanings are transformed by their use in history. Old meanings become sedimented and are lost, and new meanings emerge through the meaning-creative potentiality of language. As a language develops, new ways of understanding ancient expressions can always emerge from behind the limits of what is currently understood. The linguistic process is open-ended and future-oriented. The absolute "I" has an infinite ability to engender and receive meaning through the historical medium of language, so that it can be said that the "I" is always "on the way to language."

Summary and Thesis

I propose in the second chapter to place Ricoeur's hermeneutical theory in the context of some dominant historical influences on his thought. The organizing theme is that Ricoeur's hermeneutics has its uniqueness in combining two previously disconnected lines of thought in the hermeneutical discussion. The methodological-epistemological line prescribes specific methods of interpretation of texts based on analysis of the conditions of the possibility of the understanding process as we actually use it. This line runs from Schleiermacher through Dilthey to Ricoeur. The ontological hermeneutics of Martin Heidegger, on the other hand, presents a line of thought that harks back to themes in Kant and Fichte in working out an interpretation of the being of man and its connection to temporality, and drops interest in defining principles for textual exegesis.

Ricoeur combines these two lines insofar as he pursues the methodological issue for the sake of its ability to shed new light on the meaning of the being of man in its temporality. The emphasis here will fall on Heidegger's thought, since Heidegger sets the contemporary context within which Ricoeur has submitted his contribution.

The first part of the third chapter will trace the evolution of Ricoeur's thought toward hermeneutics. Ricoeur came to the contemporary hermeneutical discussion as one whose concern was with philosophical anthropology and whose method can be characterized as a post-Husserlian phenomenology modified by Kantian limits. Ricoeur justifies his turn to hermeneutics by showing an inner necessity in this style of reflective philosophy that impels it toward hermeneutics. But he never forsakes his unique method of phenomenology even as it becomes "hermeneutic phenomenology." When the implications of hermeneutics for philosophical anthropology and even ontology are drawn, Ricoeur relies on the phenomenological method developed prior to his hermeneutic turn, which will be given consideration here.[3]

The second part of the third chapter begins the systematic treatment of Ricoeur's hermeneutics with an inquiry into the meaning of linguistic expression in the broadest sense for Ricoeur. Expression is treated first in the analysis of Ricoeur's hermeneutic theory because it is the first moment in the hermeneutical process defined above.

The fourth chapter follows the hermeneutical process of the self's distancing itself from itself by tracing the transition from spoken expression to written text. Ricoeur's mature hermeneutic theory takes its bearings on the theory of text as the true locus of the hermeneutical problem and the place of greatest density for a philosophy of language that hopes to reveal something about the being of man. In this chapter Ricoeur's concept of poetic text as a sign carrying sense and signifying an extralinguistic referent will be considered in detail.

The fifth chapter has three parts, all focused on the specifically religious dimension of text. With entrance to the religious aspect of textual meaning, the self finds its extreme moment of self-distancing through language just where it discovers the possibility for recovering, through religious understanding, the meaning of being a self.

The first part inquires into Ricoeur's position on the religious text. For Ricoeur, a religious text is a type of poetic text in that it displays the metaphoric ability to refer to a possible mode of being. What is unique to a religious text is the presence of certain "limit-expressions," which function to extend the reference beyond a possible mode of being to the open horizon of ultimate and religious concern. As a matter of practice, Ricoeur identifies the category *religious text* with the Bible.

The second and third sections of the fifth chapter develop in two steps the constructive intention of this analysis: to show that Ricoeur's general theory of interpretation contains a possibility for defining theological hermeneutics that is unnoticed by Ricoeur. In the second section the distinctions among sign, sense, and referent, with which Ricoeur has constructed his theory, will be shown to suggest a second way of defining religious language. The thesis proposed in this section is that the "mode of being" that Ricoeur claims is the referent of a poetic sign/sense can itself be understood as a sign with sense that refers to the source and origin of meaningfulness to which religious understanding responds. This added level of signification defines the religious dimension of text.

In the third section a second but related thesis is set forward.

The sign, sense, referent relations are considered for the purpose of formal articulation of a typology of texts that permits identification of religious texts outside the Bible (and nonreligious texts within it), irrespective of content. The thesis is that religious texts are signs carrying a figurative sense that fully presents the referent there together with the sense and without hiatus between them. Theological hermeneutics can then be articulated as the interpretation of religious texts with the aid of existential-ontological language.

The sixth chapter treats the topic of appropriation of religious textual meaning for Ricoeur. At this stage the hermeneutical process reaches its aim: the actualization of the intention of the text through transformation of the self-understanding of the reader in the event of appropriation. The distancing of the self from itself is overcome as the estranged meaning is made one's own. With appropriation, Ricoeur's effort to develop methods for interpreting texts is brought to its completion with reference to the lived experience of the reader. And it is at this stage that the implications of Ricoeur's hermeneutic theory for philosophical anthropology and ontology are drawn. The key components of his contribution to these two areas are those of the investigation of the poetic imagination as one of emergent meaning, and the discernment of the dialectical principle of "being as."

With the completion of the description of hermeneutical process in appropriation, the project returns to its starting point, but at a higher level: appropriation prompts new expression, but from a self that now understands itself as one engaged in the ongoing hermeneutical process of striving for authenticity through appropriation. But the return to the starting point is not the closing of a circle. Hermeneutical awareness of the self as constituted *through* the event of appropriation, is awareness of the finitude of the self and its understanding of being. The hermeneutical circle is thus perhaps best thought of as a spiraling process by which the self comes ever more deeply into itself by comprehending the limits of being a self in a world.

2 • Ricoeur's Place in the Tradition of Hermeneutical Discussion

Schleiermacher and Dilthey

The word *hermeneutics* has its origins in the Greek verb *hermēneuein* and the noun *hermēneia*, which have three directions of meaning: to express/expression, to interpret/interpretation (in the sense of "to clarify by commentary"), and to translate/translation.[1] The basic meaning is "to bring to understanding" or "to mediate understanding" with respect to the various forms in which understanding can be a problem.

The hermeneutical problem of mediating the unfamiliar into understanding is of course not a new one or an isolated one, but is rather as old as language itself and has assumed diverse guises. For example, the hermeneutical problem was posed in antiquity with the need to interpret messages of the gods, to deliver religious and moral commentary upon the Homeric epics, to develop a philosophical doctrine of rhetoric, and to achieve normative application of authoritative texts. Judaism was confronted with the hermeneutical problem in the task of interpreting the law through its sacred Scripture. So too did the early Christians have to translate the kerygma into the Greek world and to express the relationship of the New Testament to the Old. Medieval Christianity made a hermeneutical decision to bring scriptural exegesis tightly under the wing of Church tradition with the schema of a fourfold meaning in Holy Scripture (historical, allegorical, moral, anagogical) and was opposed at the hermeneutical level by the Reformation principle that the Scripture interprets itself without need of tradition as a norm.

At the end of the eighteenth and the start of the nineteenth century, however, with the rise of classical philology and the historical sciences, the hermeneutical problem took a new turn. Prior to this time the problem was always conceived as a localized one, in which a decision was made to treat *this* text in a certain way. But with the initiation of historical consciousness in the nineteenth century and its recognition that all thinking and expressions of language are historically conditioned by a changing cultural context, the problem of hermeneutics opened up. Certainty with respect to any interpretation now had to rest on a reflexive and general description of expression and understanding as it actually happens rather than on the assumption that some one attitude or approach to a text would ensure immediate and undistorted comprehension of the intention of the text. The hermeneutical problem could no longer be restricted to the specialized task of defining the meaning of a certain text within a tradition, but was transformed into the general problem of securing the conditions of the possibility of understanding at all so that principles of textual exegesis could be derived from them.

The force behind the universalization of the hermeneutical problem in the nineteenth century is that of the central position accorded to the power of *critique* as the recognition of the infinite capacity within the human spirit to dislodge the meaning or being of whatever may appear as self-evident. As Robert Scharlemann puts it:

> Critical consciousness, which has become more and more at home in the thinking of Western peoples since the time of the Enlightenment, is characterized by the fact that it feels as untrue any immediate relationship to actuality. What is true is only that relation to reality which has been mediated by an answer to the question whether the phenomenon really is what it presents itself to be. With critique consciousness takes final leave of the condition in which it can simply accept things as they actually present themselves.[2]

Critique, as it is defined above, is closely tied to the spirit of the Kantian "Copernican Revolution" in that it implies the shift from the naive assumption that objects are realities in themselves to the critical view that objects represent appearances for the situated viewer.[3]

Schleiermacher, who should be given credit as the first to move hermeneutical discussion to the level of general theory, developed his theory on the soil of critique.[4] He recognized that once critical method was given free rein, no historical documents, including the Bible, could be read any longer with the immediacy of precritical belief. Schleiermacher's theory addressed this situation with an attempt to isolate a description of understanding as it occurs in conversation where immediacy of meaning still reigns.[5] The central task for Schleiermacher's general theory of interpretation was to work out principles with which to mediate critically that situation of immediate understanding where it does not happen on its own, namely, in dealing with the text-tradition. The assumption was that in dealing with ancient texts, misunderstanding occurs as a matter of course and that understanding must be achieved through interpretation.[6] The aim of interpretation is to reconstruct the circumstances in which understanding is again direct and uninhibited.

With this aim of overcoming the cultural distance recognized by historical consciousness and of restoring immediacy of understanding through hermeneutical theory, Schleiermacher sets a theme that is carried on by his late-nineteenth-century successor, Wilhelm Dilthey, and then in the twentieth century in somewhat modified terms by Paul Ricoeur. What is common in this line of theorists who work out exegetical principles is the desire to accept the legitimate results of radical forms of critique, while working beyond them to restore fullness of meaning in what Ricoeur calls "second naiveté." In Ricoeur's words, "the time of restoration is not a different time from that of criticism; we are in every way children of criticism, and we seek to go beyond criticism by means of criticism, by a criticism that is no longer reductive but restorative."[7] Whereas immediacy of belief has been irreducibly lost in critique, hermeneutics in Schleiermacher, Dilthey, and now Ricoeur aims at mediated immediacy of meaning through the conviction that "by *interpreting* . . . we can *hear* again."[8] The common hope is that "beyond the desert of criticism, we wish to be called again."[9]

Schleiermacher conceived this goal in highly psychological terms, and his view had considerable influence throughout the nineteenth century. Since Ricoeur has fashioned his program in such a way as to depsychologize Schleiermacher's Romantic hermeneutics and its revival in Dilthey's work and in this way to overcome "the extreme perplexity on the part of the founder of modern hermeneutics," it might be helpful to review briefly the proposals of Schleiermacher and Dilthey.[10]

Central to Schleiermacher's theory is the contention that the object of interpretation, the linguistic expression (taken in the broadest sense to include text and living speech), has a twofold reference: to the objective meaning in the context of the entire language and to the specific thought in the entire life of the speaker or author.[11] The combination of these two elements in the linguistic expression demands in turn the combination of two methods of interpretation: *grammatical interpretation*, which focuses on the common language itself in order to grasp the linguistic usage of the author so that the text may be placed in its linguistic contexts,[12] and *technical* or *psychological interpretation*, which aims to gain full understanding of the author's individual style as the way he sets his experience and thought into language.[13]

An expression is considered by Schleiermacher to be a thought that has been concretized from out of an infinity of linguistic possibilities and that refers to a series of linguistic contexts: contexts set by words in a sentence, sentences in a paragraph, paragraphs within a work, works within a genre, and so on. As such, the expression *(Ausdruck)* is the product of an essentially free, individual, and artistic thinking *("das künsterlische Denken")*, which externalizes itself *("sich äussert")* in a given language. In the end, the meaning of the expression can only be approximated in the understanding by feeling,[14] since what is most important about the expression as an aesthetic construct is the original experience behind the thought that is expressed.[15]

The basic aim in understanding a distanced written expression is to reverse the act of generating the expression, to reproduce the productive moment in such a way that we "understand the text at first as well as and then even better than its author."[16] This is to be achieved by creatively coordinating the grammatical and technical-psychological methods so as to make conscious much of what the author himself could not have known. Each of the two methods is pursued dialectically along the "hermeneutical circle," so that meaning is sensed with increasing depth and precision by referring it from part to whole, expression to context, and back again from whole to part.

In grammatical interpretation the procedure is governed by two canons that define the circle in language: (1) Meanings are to be determined in their individuality through feeling the sense of word-meanings in currency at the time the author wrote;[17] (2) Each passage must be considered as the peculiar shaping of a single meaning through the reciprocal relation between it and the context of the work.[18] Grammatical interpretation presupposes knowing the language as the author knew it at his moment in history. It clears the way for an intuitive grasp of the subjectivity of the one who uses the language to express his individuality.

In technical-psychological interpretation the goal is to uncover the theme of the work as the impelling motive behind the author's expression through divinatory and comparative methods. Here the hermeneutical circle is psychologically inscribed: (1) The divinatory method aims at the transformation of the interpreter into the author so as to gain an immediate grasp of the author as individual.[19] (2) The comparative method subsumes the author under generic types and seeks out distinctive traits.[20]

Interpretation of a work is completed when the results of grammatical interpretation agree with the results of technical-psychological interpretation.[21] Success in the former is dependent upon linguistic sensitivity and mechanical skill, whereas success in the latter is dependent on one's ability to know other people.[22] Both of these presuppose that "each person contains a minimum of everyone else," and that understanding is thus possible by comparing others with oneself through a basic "divinatory" skill that reaches the act of thinking and the life-experience of the other person.[23]

Although Schleiermacher never wrote a systematic treatise on hermeneutics but left only notes, a lecture compendium (1819) with marginal notes (1828), and two speeches before the Prussian Academy (1829), he founded modern hermeneutics and decisively influenced his successor in hermeneutical theory, Wilhelm Dilthey. According to Dilthey's interpretation of Schleiermacher, the most significant contribution from Schleiermacher was the suggestion that hermeneutics is the methodical development of the process of understanding, which occurs, at basis, through the psychological transposition of the interpreter into the mental processes of the subject behind the text.[24] For Dilthey, psychological transference into the life of another person is retained as the real basis of hermeneutic theory, but Dilthey preserves this feature of Romantic hermeneutics in a changed intellectual situation with an altered problem.

Between Schleiermacher and Dilthey several upheavals had taken place that account for there being a new set of requirements placed on hermeneutical theory. In the first place, the late nineteenth century saw the rise of history as a science of the first rank under the leadership of von Ranke and Droysen, and indeed Dilthey can be considered as the last and most sophisticated theoretician of the historical school. But in the second place, the late nineteenth century witnessed the collapse of Hegelian philosophy, which had exerted tremendous influence on the *Geisteswissenschaften*.[25] Positivism and empiricism were ascendant in philosophical circles with the demand "that the mind take as its model for all intelligibility the sort of empirical explanation current in the natural sciences."[26]

Reflecting on these developments, Dilthey saw the task for hermeneutics as providing epistemological foundation for the *Geisteswissenschaften*. In order to reply to positivism, Dilthey attempted to endow the sciences of culture with an epistemology and a methodology that could justify the historian's claims to objective knowledge. Dilthey pictured his work as running parallel to Kant's, whose *Kritik der reinen Vernunft* gave epistemological foundation to the *Naturwissenschaften*, but irreducible differences between the *Geisteswissenschaften* and *Naturwissenschaften* prohibited a simple return to Kant.[27]

According to Dilthey, we possess a primordial acquaintance with reality, and this is the proper object of the human sciences. This acquaintance is prereflective, a participatory "inner lived experience" *(Erlebnis)*.[28] Natural science, in contrast, methodically abstracts from *Erlebnis* to produce an "outer sensory experience" *(äussere Erfahrung)*, which it takes as its object.[29] Kant had regarded the mind and external reality as irreducibly discontinuous, and therefore inquired after a homogeneous "third thing" that could stand between and join them. But Dilthey saw that there is always already an immediate and intimate relationship between the mind and the expressions of human *Erlebnis* that characterize the *Geisteswissenschaften*, because "die geschichtliche Welt ist immer da, und das Individuum betrachtet sie nicht nur von aussen, sondern es ist in sie verwebt . . . (the historical world is always there, and the individual not only views it from outside, but is woven into it)."[30]

For Dilthey, *Erlebnis* can be defined as the immediate experience of the possibility and necessity of relating the self to the world. As such, it is prior to reflective consciousness and the forms of conceptual awareness, although it is permeated with immediate awareness *(Innewerden)* and intellectuality *(Intellektualität)*.[31] Awareness is always present in life through mood *(Stimmung)* and feeling *(Gefühl)*, so that life can be said to be ordered to reflection.

The outer sensory objects of natural science are to be explained *(erklären)* by showing causal connections in the sensory manifold. The expressions of the common inner world of *Erlebnis*, on the other hand, are expressions of meaning, which we do not explain, but understand *(verstehen)*. The critique of historical reason must work out the epistemological procedure of *Verstehen* in order to secure the objectivity of the *Geisteswissenschaften*.[32] For this task Dilthey turned to hermeneutics, where he sought the central trait of understanding in the psychological part of Schleiermacher's program. For Dilthey,

> every science of the spirit—and by this Dilthey meant every knowledge of man implying some historical relation—presupposes a primordial capacity to place oneself into the psychical life of others. In natural knowledge, in effect, man only reaches those distinct phenomena whose fundamental thingness escapes him. In the human order, on the contrary, man knows man; no matter how foreign the other man may be to us, he is not alien in the sense of the unknowable physical thing.[33]

In Dilthey's estimation, hermeneutical theory performs the functions of establishing the conditions of the possibility of understanding historical expressions and of determining principles for exegesis. For Dilthey, the hermeneutics of written expressions form the objective and scientific layer of understanding and provide specific rules for explication of texts.[34]

According to Dilthey, written expressions are always *Lebensäusserungen* (expressions of life), in that they emerge out of an individual existence as it is involved in the whole of life *(Erlebnis)*.[35] As such, the expression is always an irreducible individual[36] that refers to the interconnectedness of everything in the life from which it arose.[37] Written expressions, then, not only are transparent to the individual existence of the author but also intend meanings. These meanings refer to the network of relations that Hegel called "objective spirit," namely, the common heritage of language, law, morals, art, and so on. Dilthey called these interconnecting cultural contexts *Zusammenhänge*.[38]

To secure the objectivity of written expressions of life in historical texts, Dilthey made use of Husserl's definition of expression as it appeared in the *Logische Untersuchungen* of 1900. Following Husserl verbatim, Dilthey calls an expression *(Ausdruck)* "jede Rede und jeden Redeteil sowie jedes wesentlich gleichartige Zeichen (every speech and every part of speech as well as every essentially similar sign)." Then, paraphrasing Husserl, he adds, "und diese Ausdrücke unterscheiden sich von Zeichen anderer Art dadurch, dass sie etwas bedeuten. . . . Sofern der Ausdruck sich so auf eine Gegenständlichkeit bezieht, meint es etwas (and these expressions are distinct from signs of other kinds through the fact that they signify something. . . . Insofar as the expression refers in such a way to an objectivity, it means something)."[39]

Under this doctrine, expressions are signs that carry an ideal meaning in the sense that they rise above the flux of life to serve as media of reference to things, events, processes, states of affairs, and so on. Because life objectifies itself in fixed expressions that are open to being understood, the historian is able to understand not only the private *Erlebnis* of the author but also the universal realm of objective spirit.[40]

Historical understanding for Dilthey is in the end a spiraling process of grasping the inner life of individuals ever more deeply with respect to relatively general and ever-widening, encompassing, cultural contexts. Expressions of life in texts are to be grasped as referring both to the objective cultural spheres and to the inner power of the individual.[41] Only acquaintance with the common cultural world will allow individual texts to be understood with sophistication, so higher understanding relies on expertise in the *Geisteswissenschaften*. But in the final analysis the *Geisteswissenschaften* themselves are founded on the basic art of understanding, which is achieved through empathetic transposition (*hineinversetzen*) and which makes possible reliving (*nacherleben*) and reconstruction (*nachbilden*) of the historical experience.[42] For Dilthey, the highest art remains that of transposition of the self into the other self as expressed through texts.[43] Psychological transposition through shared *Erlebnis* is the basis of understanding, and understanding finds its fulfillment in the successful art of empathy with "ein Wiederfinden des Ich im Du (a self-recognition of the I in the you)."[44]

The relevance of the preceding summary of the hermeneutical reflections of Schleiermacher and Dilthey for the analysis of Ricoeur's work that is to follow is that Ricoeur places his own hermeneutical theory in direct line with the intentions of Schleiermacher and Dilthey even while he argues against the psychological emphasis of Romantic hermeneutics. Ricoeur stands in the line of thought represented by Schleiermacher and Dilthey because he, as were his predecessors, is concerned with the development of a general theory of interpretation (after the breakup of Romantic hermeneutics) based on a description of the process of ordinary understanding and with special applicability to the interpretation of texts.[45]

Like Schleiermacher and Dilthey before him, Ricoeur offers an "epistemology of interpretation," as he puts it, and contributes to the debate over method in the interpretative sciences. In that sense Ricoeur's view of hermeneutics is that it belongs to the epistemological field defined by Schleiermacher and Dilthey.[46] What distinguishes the execution of Ricoeur's hermeneutical theory from the theories of Schleiermacher and Dilthey is that his program is founded on a sustained reflection on the nature and function of language and that he drops reference to psychological transposition.

But Ricoeur's theory is charged with a special task greater than that of setting forth a canon for exegesis even while it includes it. This task is the dominant intention of Ricoeur's thought: to present a philosophical anthropology in response to the question "What does it mean to be human?" For Ricoeur, hermeneutical theory is important, not just for legitimation of the inescapably interpretative sciences, but also and primarily for its potential to disclose something about the being of man.[47] Ricoeur has always implied that his contribution to the theory of text-interpretation was offered in hope of a "better understanding of man and the bond between the being of man and the being of all beings."[48]

In this latter concern Ricoeur goes beyond the Schleiermacher-Dilthey problematic and joins a second line of thought, which runs from Kant through Fichte and Heidegger and which has a primary concern with the being of the self as revelatory of being as such. Ricoeur belongs in this line because his interpretation theory was engendered out of the conviction that in a certain significant sense man *is* language, and that, since writing is the full development of language, the laying out of the principles of textual meaning may uncover something that points to the being of man and ultimately to being itself.

To see Ricoeur's connection with this second line of thought, through which he makes a contribution to philosophical anthropology and ontology, I shall trace the outlines of the basic contemporary work in this area—Martin Heidegger's *Sein und Zeit*. In Heidegger's work no reference is made to the problem confronted by Schleiermacher and Dilthey: the construction of principles to govern textual exegesis. Interpretation is rather primarily conceived as interpretation of human being. Ricoeur's position in the whole hermeneutical discussion is defined by the fact that in his theory he combines the two previously disconnected lines of thought outlined here.

Martin Heidegger and Ontological Hermeneutics[49]

With the publication of *Sein und Zeit* in 1927, a decisive new stage in hermeneutical discussion opened up. With one stroke the primary meaning of hermeneutics was disjoined from the problem of the development of principles for textual interpretation and reconstituted as the interpretation of existence, a *"Hermeneutik der Faktizität."*

Ricoeur interprets it this way: If the first movement from the localized handling of hermeneutical problems to the working out of a general hermeneutical theory by Schleiermacher was inspired in the climate of critique and the Kantian "Copernican Revolution," the second great movement from epistemology (Schleiermacher-Dilthey) to ontology (Heidegger) can be called a "second Copernican reversal, which will relocate the questions of method within fundamental ontology."[50] The question is no longer "How do we know . . . ?" but "What is the *mode of being* of the one whose being *is* to understand?"

Heidegger self-consciously takes over the term *hermeneutic* in *Sein und Zeit*, but not to use it as did Schleiermacher and Dilthey to refer to the theory of textual interpretation *(Auslegung)*. *Sein und Zeit* leaves that issue untouched and considers it a derivative one, at least a step removed from the more basic kind of *Auslegung*. Heidegger's sense of hermeneutic is *ontological*, in that it pertains to the interpretation in existentialist concepts of the understanding of being that *Dasein* has already laid out *(ausgelegt)* publicly in its world through its discourse *(Rede)*.

Ricoeur for the most part agrees with the ontological turn signaled by *Sein und Zeit*.[51] It is true that Ricoeur parts ways with Heidegger in deciding to retrieve the task of Schleiermacher and Dilthey to work out the epistemological-methodological side of hermeneutical theory, and in that way to provide what Heidegger neglects, namely, a theory that tells how textual understanding is possible and how methods of interpretation can be prescribed from basic principles. Ricoeur's motives for this include the wish to present an "organon" for exegesis, a foundation for the historical sciences, and the basis for arbitration between rival interpretations.[52]

Ricoeur thus takes a "long route" in hermeneutics through semantics and theory of the text rather than the "short route" of Heidegger, who turns hermeneutics into an ontology of understanding. Yet ultimately he shares Heidegger's goal—to think the meaning of being by way of hermeneutics. Ricoeur hopes that he will finally contribute to Heidegger's ontological project by carrying methodological discussion successively by stages to its ontological implications.

Ricoeur clearly places his own work within the goals established by Heidegger and proclaims his intentions to think forward the epistemological-methodological project of Schleiermacher and Dilthey for the sake of its potential to add to the ontological project of Heidegger. As he says:

> It is the *desire* for this ontology which animates our enterprise and which keeps it from sinking into either a linguistic philosophy like Wittgenstein's or a reflective philosophy of the neo-Kantian sort. My problem will be exactly this: what happens to an epistemology of interpretation, born of a reflection on exegesis, on the method of history, on psychoanalysis, on the phenomenology of religion, etc., when it is touched, animated, and as we might say, inspired by an ontology of understanding?[53]

Before we consider Ricoeur's theory and the contribution it makes to the interpretation of *Dasein* and ontology, let us look more closely at what Heidegger conceives hermeneutics to involve.

The question to which Heidegger devoted lifelong commitment is the *Seinsfrage*, the question about the meaning of being. Hermeneutics enters his discussion because his exposition of the *Seinsfrage* demands an interpretation of *Dasein* as the place where being is manifest.

According to Heidegger an obscurity and forgottenness surround the meaning of being, though it is the most fundamental word and thought in the language. The philosophical dogma asserts that inquiry into the explicit meaning is superfluous because (1) it is the most universal, and hence the most empty of concepts, (2) it is undefinable as highest genus, and (3) it is used with self-evident meaningfulness in everyday occurrence.[54] But this dogma only shows the need to explicate the meaning of being. Heidegger says that there is no clarity as to the basis ontological difference between *Sein* and a definable *Seiendes*, and it is commonplace to assume that the quiddity or definition of the *Seiendes* is its being, when such is not the case.[55] In the midst of this oblivion, nonetheless, everyone understands what is meant when one says "the sky *is* blue," or "I *am* happy."[56] We do possess a preontological understanding of the meaning of being, even while we lack an explicit concept. Heidegger's intention is to think the meaning of being, and in *Sein und Zeit* this is undertaken through a hermeneutic of *Dasein*.

Throughout the history of metaphysics, being is thought as supreme being conceived as the sum total of positive predicates. As a post-Kantian philosopher, Heidegger recognizes that this view is no longer tenable. Heidegger must instead follow the transcendental line of inquiry into the conditions under which being can be known, and thus win assurance that the many beings that are to be questioned with respect to their being are reached as they actually are. But such *a priori* conditions of the possibility of ontology are themselves modes of the kind of being we are as questioners. Therefore the being that we are is the one reachable as it is and is selected as the entity to be questioned. The *Seinsfrage* is to question *Dasein*—the being that we are—with respect to its being because

> es ist . . . dadurch ontisch ausgezeichnet, dass es diesem Seienden in seinem Sein *um* dieses Sein selbst geht. Zu dieser Seinsverfassung des Daseins gehört aber dann, dass es in seinem Sein zu diesem Sein ein Seinsverhältnis hat. Und dies wiederum besagt: Dasein versteht sich in irgendeiner Weise und Ausdrücklichkeit in seinem Sein. Diesem Seienden eignet, dass mit und durch sein Sein dieses ihm selbst erschlossen ist. *Seinsverständnis ist selbst eine Seinsbestimmtheit des Daseins*. Die ontische Auszeichnung des Daseins liegt darin, dass es ontologisch ist.[37]

> It *(Dasein)* is . . . ontically distinguished in that this entity *(Dasein)* in its very being is concerned about being. It therefore belongs to the very being-constitution of *Dasein* that it has in its being a relationship to being which is itself one of being. And this means further that *Dasein* understands itself in its being in some manner and explicitness. It belongs to this entity that with and though its being, being is open to it. *Understanding of being is itself a defining characteristic of the being of Dasein*. The ontic distinctiveness of *Dasein* lies in the fact that it *is* ontological.

Fundamental ontology is to be pursued as existential analytic of *Dasein* because *Dasein* has a preontological understanding of what it means to be in understanding itself as an existential possibility to be or not to be itself. What *Dasein* essentially *is* is determined by its existence, and as existent *Dasein*, it understands what it means to be the one it is.[38]

The path to fundamental ontology seems to be cleared. According to Otto Pöggeler, that path involves these steps: (1) Interpret the elements of the structure of *Dasein*'s being in order to make explicit the preunderstanding that *Dasein* has of *Sein*, (2) uncover the one *ground* of the various modes of *Dasein*'s being as that upon which *Dasein* projects its modes of being, and (3) articulate that ground in such a single explicit meaning of *Sein*.[59] I shall attempt to lay out a sketch of these steps.

In the first place, Heidegger's analysis of the structure of the being of *Dasein* indicates that care *(Sorge)* is the being of *Dasein*.[60] That care is the being of *Dasein* is made possible by the peculiar set of relations that make of *Dasein* a clearing within being: *Dasein* designates *a being* (the one I am), which has understanding as its primary *mode of being*, and which understands *being*. Subject, activity, and object are mutually reflective, hence a place of manifestation, a clearing within the obscurity of being.

With respect to the subjective aspect, to say that care is the being of *Dasein* means that the self is concerned about itself in the world and that the self relates itself to the world in care. This is shown in the everyday concern-filled dealings *(Besorgen)* with what is ready at hand and in the everyday language that displays that concern.

As an activity, the care making up the being of *Dasein* is basically evident in the understanding process. The understanding process here is an elementary projective thinking that connects two other thought-relations between self and world: formal thinking and perception. Understanding makes the connection between the universal concept at our disposal and the particular percept revealed in a sentence such as "The sky is blue." That is, the understanding makes the ontological synthesis that connects entities through its activity of concern.

The object of *Dasein*'s care, then, is a connected entity, the result of the ontological synthesis, and a being. But—and here the circle making up *Dasein*'s being comes back on itself—in making the ontological connections that constitute the objects of care, *Dasein* synthesizes itself as a living connection between the universal "I" as the point of origin and agent of connecting and the particular "this person here in the world" who is determined by the relation of care. The being of *Dasein* as care is understanding what it means to be the one it is on the basis of a preunderstanding of being. And since understanding is always a synthesis of a datum (a given reality) with thought, the being of *Dasein* is marked by a thoroughgoing finitude. *Dasein* is finite in its "facticity" or situatedness: the understanding process is limited by the reality given to experience. Yet *Dasein* is open to the infinite at the same time in its potential in every moment to reconnect given reality with meaning in thought.[61]

So far I have outlined the sense in which Heidegger says that the being of *Dasein* is care. I should like to articulate more specifically the elements of this structure, but first I shall show how Heidegger's hermeneutic of *Dasein* is a continuation of a line of thought with roots in Kant and Fichte, and thus provide added clarity to the structure of the self as Ricoeur conceives it.

By transforming the field of hermeneutics from reflection on the methodology of the human sciences to explication of the ontological ground on which any system of sciences may be built, Heidegger connects the hermeneutical problem with the classical proposals by Kant and Fichte to show the ground of the sciences through analysis of the structure of human thinking and experience. Of importance here are Kant's deduction of the transcendental ego and Fichte's description of the self as a *Tathandlung*.

The intention of Kant's first critique, within the context of asking how synthetic *a priori* judgments are possible,[65] is to acquire transcendental knowledge of the dimension of objectivity constituted by the necessary conditions of the possibility of acquaintance with any object whatsoever. According to Kant, the knowledge of objects that we do possess presupposes both the sensibility that receives intuitions *(Anschauungen)* through the *a priori* forms of intuition (time and space), and our understanding *(Verstand)* that orders the manifold of intuition through application of *a priori* and empirical concepts. Experience of an object, then, presupposes synthesis of concepts and intuitions. And since the manifold of sensation is spread out through time, experience of a unified object that perdures through time presupposes a transcendental appreception or "I think" that is aware that it is aware of the object as synthesized through time.[63]

The transcendental ego or reflexive subject is the dimension of the self that applies concepts to intuitions and thereby orders the flux of appearances into coherent objects of experience. So too it assigns the experience to itself in the unity of a single consciousness that can identify the experience as *my* experience.[64] Now since sensibility and understanding, intuitions and concepts, are different, the transcendental ego must in turn have acquaintance with some third thing, intermediate between the two and homogeneous with each, by which to combine them. This third thing is the transcendental image: as an image of an object in general it fits the abstract quality of the concept, yet as an image of this specific kind of object it fits the concrete quality of intuition.

The conditions necessary for the construction of such an image are set forth in the chapter on schematism, in which Kant deduces the faculty of the transcendental imagination as capable of producing the image for a concept according to a synthetic rule. That rule is the *schema*, the representation of a universal procedure of imagination in providing an image for a concept.[65] This schema is a product of the pure productive imagination as it allows me to produce the image whereby I can recognize, for example, this four-footed animal as a dog.

Heidegger's work in *Sein und Zeit* picks up this Kantian problem of schematism in that "understanding" *(Verstehen)* in Heidegger, as a primordial projective thinking that is ontologically prior to any scientific thinking, stands in the same place as the transcendental imagination in Kant. Just as the imagination mediates between concept and intuition in Kant by providing an image of what connects the two, so for Heidegger *Verstehen* as projective thinking is directed toward the being of what is thought by throwing ahead what is between concept and percept, universal and particular.

One difference between Kant on the transcendental imagination and Heidegger on understanding is that whereas Heidegger calls understanding the basic mode of *Dasein's* being, Kant cannot on his epistemological principles identify the presupposed "I think" of transcendental apperception as a being. The transcendental ego is deduced as a necessary condition of the possibility of knowledge, yet it is itself unknowable for Kant just because of his claim that knowledge of an object always involves a synthesis of concept and intuition.[66] Since all intuition for Kant falls under the spatial-temporal forms of sensibility, and the "I" is neither in time nor in space, no intuition of the "I think" is possible. Reflexive awareness that I am is unaccountable for Kant, and he merely obscures the problem when he calls it a *Vorstellung* that is *"ein Denken,"* not *"ein Anschauen,"* when his system allows only for sensible intuitions and not for intellectual ones.[67]

A decisive step beyond Kant in reflecting the being of the self was taken by Fichte in the *Wissenschaftslehre* of 1793, in which Fichte deduces the basic concepts on which a system of the sciences can be founded from the activity of a transcendental "I" that posits itself as limited by what is not-I. Whereas Kant claimed that we must presuppose the activity of reflexive awareness but cannot intuit that activity as a being, Fichte thought that he had advanced the true Kantian doctrine with his claim that the "I think" is the most accessible part of knowledge, the determining ground of existence with which we are acquainted through an intellectual intuition.[68] Self-consciousness is not limited to a condition of conscious experience, but rather is what determines *(bestimmt)* everything in consciousness.[69]

According to Fichte, the structure of the self can be deduced from the laws of logic as forms of pure thinking. The law of identity presupposes the element of what we may call "pure being" in the statement "I am I," which always accompanies identity. The law of noncontradiction presupposes the element of nonbeing or opposition expressed in the statement "opposed to the I is nothing that I am not," which is implied in any statement of difference. And the law of definition presupposes the element of finite being expressed in the assertion "in the absolute 'I' there is opposed to a divisible not-I a divisible 'I.'" Altogether, the self bears the structure of "I am I" not as dead identity, but as the identity of the identity and difference of the infinite reflexive self and the existential self in the finite world that is counterpoised to it.

For Fichte, the structure of the self is a two-in-one of "I [the original point of thinking and doing] am [yet am not exhausted by] this existential self here." And this structure of the self can be intuited through an intellectual intuition of the disproportion between what the self *should be* (and ideally is) as transcendental activity and what the self is in its *actual* self-world relations. The task is to level that discrepancy by seeing all objective appearance *(Erscheinung)* as illusion, and the shining-in *(Schein)*, through that appearance, of the absolute "I" as true content.[70]

The twofold self of Fichte's system, which includes the pure *activity* of thinking by the "I" that connects existential self and world, is also designated as *a being* in that the "I" places itself here in the world and falls into existence constantly in joining concepts to intuitions. The self has the structure in which "Handlung und Tat sind Eins und eben dasselbe; und daher ist das: *Ich bin*, Ausdruck einer Tathandlung (Activity and deed are precisely one and the same; and therefore '*I am*' is an expression of a deed-doing)."[71] The self as *Tathandlung* strictly speaking exists both as posited self here and as always in the process of coming into existence without ever being able to do so completely as the absolute "I" and point of origin of thinking. The self is infinite activity and finite being at one and the same time.

When this is put in Heidegger's terms, we can see the same structure of *Tathandlung* in *Dasein*. For Heidegger, the "I" that understands being through its connecting activity is itself also an existing being that is there. It is also a connection between the particular self in the world and the universal "I." Heidegger, however, can be distinguished from Fichte. He draws a more complete description of the existential structure of *Dasein* by focusing on *Verstehen*, *Befindlichkeit*, and *Rede*. More important, Heidegger opens up the temporality of the self in a way not anticipated by either Kant or Fichte. I shall save further discussion of the temporality involved here until I discuss the meaning of the being of *Dasein* for Heidegger. First the basic elements that make up the structure of *Dasein* will be sketched out.

Heidegger uses the term *existential* (as opposed to *concept*) to denote an element of the ontological structure of *Dasein* and a category of human being. We always find ourselves already in some determined situation, which we then strive to understand. Therefore the first existential to consider is *Befindlichkeit*, which means "the relatedness to beings one already finds oneself in." *Verstehen's* first task is thus to orient us in a situation and to discover its possibilities.[72]

Befindlichkeit is the ontological name for the dimension of *Dasein's* being that is attuned to being through mood. It thus indicates both *die Gestimmtheit* and *die Stimmung*.[73] Through mood *Dasein* is always brought before being as there; it finds itself in a place, attuned to being, and endowed with a certain voice *(eine Stimme)*. *Befindlichkeit* defines *(bestimmt)* the self and discloses *Dasein* in its "thrownness" and projection through mood. Mood here does not designate a mere affect, but a fundamental mode of *Dasein's* being that is always permeated by understanding, the second existential to be mentioned here.

Just as *Befindlichkeit* is always permeated with understanding, so too *Verstehen* is always attuned in mood.[74] Any act of understanding is localized in a situation that *Dasein* finds itself in, but *Verstehen* is the more basic mode of the two because *Verstehen* has the sense of *"etwas verstehen"* or *"etwas können"*—to be able to do something—and the basic element of *Dasein's* being is that it *is* able to be what it is. *Dasein* is its *Seinkönnen* insofar as *Dasein* understands how to be the one it is, as exhibited in its ability to deal carefully with things in the world for the sake of its own being.

Heidegger's *Verstehen* has the unique quality of being the projecting activity by which *Dasein* throws forward a possibility for it to be. Heidegger says, "Das Verstehen hat an ihm selbst die existentiale Struktur, die wir den *Entwurf* nennen (Understanding has in itself the existential structure that we call projection)."[75]

This activity of projecting has at least two forms. I project both the being of an entity (as when I understand preontologically what the possibilities are when a tree is pointed out) and the being that I am (as when I form an image of myself as one who constructs self-world relations in different but intelligible ways). Heidegger's *Verstehen* is ontologically prior to what Dilthey articulated as *Verstehen* in its distinction from *Erklären*. Both of these epistemological projections rely on an elemental ability to imagine a possibility and an outcome. If I explain a ship's movement in the current, I already project the possibility of the current's causing that movement. So too if I understand a decision of Bismarck, I already project the possibility of making that decision in certain situations. Heidegger's *Verstehen* isolates the ontological structure that is the condition of the possibility of each particular act of understanding.

The primary sense of interpretation *(Auslegung)* is defined by Heidegger with respect to the existential-ontological sense of *Verstehen*: interpretation is *die Ausbildung des Verstehens*, in which what is already there in understanding as a project is explicitly worked out in terms of itself. The understood thing is interpreted as that thing. For Heidegger,

> das im Verstehen Erschlossene, das Verstandene ist immer schon so zugänglich, dass an ihm sein "als was" ausdrücklich abgehoben werden kann. Das "Als" macht die Struktur der Ausdrücklichkeit eines Verstandenen aus; es konstituiert die Auslegung.[76]
>
> that which is disclosed in understanding, the understood thing, is always already accessible, in such a way that its "as what" can be explicitly indicated. The "as" makes up the structure of the explicitness of the understood thing; it constitutes the interpretation.

If interpretation makes explicit what is already laid out in an understanding of something preontologically, then interpretation is never presuppositionless, but is always guided by the content of the prereflective project: "Die Auslegung von Etwas als Etwas wird wesenhaft durch Vorhabe, Vorsicht und Vorgriff fundiert (The interpretation of something as something is essentially founded through fore-having, fore-sight, and pre-understanding)."[77] In this way, what is understood in interpretation is, strictly speaking, the being of that thing:[78] some connection is made between percept or feeling and a concept so that the object is understood to be in this or that way.

The understood thing is always grasped in its being, however, with respect to the meaning co-grasped in the same act of understanding. Meaning, itself an element in the ontological structure of *Dasein*, is that against which and in view of which something is understood as something. It is that "worin sich Verständlichkeit von etwas hält.... *Sinn ist das durch Vorhabe, Vorsicht und Vorgriff strukturierte Woraufhin des Entwurfs, aus dem her etwas als etwas verständlich wird* (in which the intelligibility of something maintains itself.... *Meaning is the goal upon which something becomes understandable as something through projection. This goal is structured through fore-having, fore-sight, and pre-understanding*)."[79]

Co-original with *Befindlichkeit* and *Verstehen* is the existential *Rede* or discourse. *Rede* is an element of *Dasein*'s being that provides the place of the openness of *Dasein* as being-in-the-world: one who understands himself and entities in the world on the basis of a situation as a possibility to be. *Rede* for Heidegger is the area of *Dasein*'s disclosure and has a "worldly" rather than a psychological manner of being:

> Wenn die Rede, die Artikulation der Verständlichkeit des Da, ursprüngliches Existenzial der Erschlossenheit ist, diese aber primär konstituiert wird durch das In-der-Welt-sein, muss auch die Rede wesenhaft eine spezifisch *weltliche* Seinsart haben. Die befindliche Verständlichkeit des In-der-Welt-seins *spricht sich als Rede aus*. Das Bedeutungsganze der Verständlichkeit *kommt zu Wort*.[80]

If discourse, the articulation of the intelligibility of the "there," is an original existential of openness, and if openness is primarily constituted through being-in-the-world, discourse must also and essentially have a specifically *worldly* mode of being. The attuned-through-mood intelligibility of being-in-the-world *expresses itself as discourse*. The totality of significations of intelligibility *comes to word*.

Heidegger grounds language or speaking in *Rede* or discourse as the articulation of the *Verständlichkeit* of the *Da* of *Dasein*, and thereby depsychologizes language. The Schleiermacher-Dilthey heritage of language as the externalization of the experience of the empirical subject is overturned here in the existential analytic.[81] When *Dasein spricht sich aus*, it discloses the full sense of its "being-in" *(mitsein)* the world, since *Dasein* is always already "outside" itself in care for things in the world when it speaks. I should like to reserve further discussion of the worldliness of discourse for a later stage of this work, which will pertain to the notion of "textworld" in Ricoeur. At present I shall limit myself to the description of the elements of *Rede*.

According to Heidegger, *Rede* includes "das Worüber der Rede (das Beredete), das Geredete als solches, die Mitteilung und die Bekundung (that which the discourse is about [the talked about], the said as such, the communication, and the making known)."[82] This list could be expanded to this fuller scheme: Someone says something about something to someone for the sake of making something known somewhere.

These elements of *Rede* are not ontic properties of language but are rooted in the mode of being of *Dasein*. They are all present, whether the utterance of *Dasein* takes the primary form of a "mitteilend bestimmende Aufzeigung (communicating, makingdefinite, pointing out)" or the derived form of *Urteil*. In the former and primary case, the thing spoken of is placed or understood in the mode of being of *Zuhandenheit* or readiness-at-hand. When I speak of something that is ready at hand, like a tool, speech points out the tool in its being as I put the tool to use within the world.

The derived form of *Aussage* in the form of judgment *(Urteil)* indicates another kind of self-world relation. In an assertion such as "The hammer is made of iron and weighs x grams," I no longer communicate the view *(Umsicht)* I have with respect to things in the world for me about which I express care, but I rather place the hammer as separated entity in the mode of being present at hand *(Vorhandenheit)* over against an isolated subject.

Whether we speak of *Aussage* as *Aufzeigung* or *Urteil*, however, the condition for the possibility of either is the element of the structure of *Dasein* that Heidegger calls *Rede*.

So far I have given a brief account of the elements that make up the being of *Dasein*. As being-in-the-world, the being of *Dasein* is care as it is manifest through *Verstehen*, *Befindlichkeit*, and *Rede*. The next step for Heidegger is to show the meaning of the being of *Dasein*, the goal *(Woraufhin)* of *Dasein*'s understanding as an "ability to be" the one it is. Heidegger intends here to treat the structure of *Dasein* as a set of signs carrying meaning and hence open to interpretation. Ontology can be conceived as hermeneutic of *Dasein* just because for Heidegger *Dasein* has the character of a sign pointing to a sense. Now what is the meaning of the being of *Dasein*?

According to Heidegger, temporality is both the meaning of the being of *Dasein* and also that in which the as-structure of understanding and interpretation is grounded.[83] What *Dasein* understands in knowing how to exist as itself is always *time* as the meaning of its existential projects. This reference to time can be explained by showing the connection to the meaning of the self in Kant and Fichte already described above.

Kant deduced the faculty of transcendental imagination, which can mediate between intuitions and concepts by virtue of its ability to produce the image for a concept on the basis of the schema as a synthetic rule for the production of images. For Kant the fundamental problem of schematism most importantly concerns the schemata of pure concepts that underlie all empirical concepts, and that cannot be brought into any generalized spatial image but must determine the form of inner sense (time) and thereby of the senses in general. The schemata of pure concepts determine the pure image of time as a succession of moments and the form of all intuition.[84]

Schemata for pure concepts are rules for determining time transcendentally, and they are thus the true and sole conditions under which such concepts acquire relation to objects and possess significance.[85] For example, the schema of the pure concept "reality" is "being in time," that of "negation" is "not-being in time," that of "substance" is "permanence of the real in time," that of "cause" is "rule-governed succession in time," that of "magnitude" is "number as the unity of successive addition of like units," which is due to the generation of time itself in the synthesis of the intuitive manifold.[86]

Time for Kant is both the pure form of objectivity as such (as the form of inner sense), yet also the source of all objectivity in that the transcendental ego in some sense generates time in synthesizing the manifold. I must generate time to know an object, yet what I know as an object of perception is at basis time. Kant raises the problem of time by seeing that time is somehow basic to the ontological synthesis since, in the last analysis, what is schematized *is* time. But Kant does not pursue further this question as to how the being of the self is connected to time. Heidegger, on the other hand, brings just that question into focus.

The way in which Heidegger concentrates on the connection between the being of time and that of the self departs dramatically from the view of time in the speculative idealism of Fichte and Hegel, as Heidegger points out explicitly.[87] For Hegel, the being of temporal succession is the atemporal eternal now, which is always the no-longer and not-yet, the elusive source of arising and passing. Hence the problem for Hegel (as well as Fichte) is to show how the absolute and atemporal "I" or *Geist* falls into time and empirical reality.

Heidegger transforms the problem from that of connecting the infinite "I" with the finite and temporal self by claiming that the *Geist* or infinite "I" does not "fall" into time, but originally exists as the *temporalizing of temporality*. Time is not the eternal now as signal of the timeless freedom of the "I," but is *my finite timing*. The "I" temporalizes its activity in that the "I" always already sees, acts, thinks, and feels temporally and sequentially. The "I" temporalizes its perceptions, feelings, thoughts, and actions through the process of understanding. And in understanding the meaning of the being of objects, persons, processes, and itself, *Dasein* understands being as temporal or sequential. Thus the temporalizing of human activity by the "I" discloses another dimension of the finitude of *Dasein*, namely, that the "I" and the being of beings toward which understanding is directed are in the end unthematizable because conditioned by temporality. The uncovering of temporality signals the recognition of the finitude of *Dasein* and of being. And since the "I" always understands time finitely as time-in-order-to, the real issue for *Dasein*'s understanding of its own possibilities to be is whether time is seized authentically or inauthentically.[88]

Now what would it mean to say that in understanding and knowing how to exist what we understand is always time in the sense of "my finite timing"? To put it differently, what would it mean to say that time is the meaning of the being of *Dasein*? For Heidegger it means that the act of existing, which for *Dasein* is "to understand," is always temporal. Care, as the connecting activity by which being-in-the-world synthesizes entities, persons, events, as well as itself as *Dasein*, is temporal through and through.

The temporality of *Dasein* can be pointed out more exactly with reference to the existentials already discussed. *Dasein* cares for things, events, and persons in the world for the sake of its own meaningfulness. Its caring activities always display temporal modes. The "I" of "I am this one here in the world" who projects possibilities to be *(Verstehen)* is *future*-oriented. The "here" or "Da" of *Befindlichkeit* is always *past*-oriented, in that it is always already situated in and attuned to a place. And the "am" of "I am here" (*Rede* as the articulation of *Verstehen* and *Befindlichkeit*) falls into existence as the disruption of authenticity.[89] These three temporal *ecstases*—future, past, and present as modes of *Dasein*'s standing out within the horizon of time—are structurally unified so that each implies the temporalizing of the other.[90] The dominant mode of time, however, is the future, because it is connected to *Verstehen*'s character of *Entwurf*.

Understanding is grounded in the ecstatical unity of temporality in that each of the temporal ecstases belongs to the whole structure of temporality since, as Heidegger puts it: "Zeitlichkeit zeitigt sich als gewesende-gegenwärtigende Zukunft (Temporality times itself as the future which makes present through the having-been of the past)."[91]

For Heidegger the temporal unity of the ecstases is also a unity of horizon or world. Whether one deals with the prereflective care *(Besorgen)* with things in *Zuhandenheit* or with objects as *vorhanden*, or whether one looks directly on the being of *Dasein* in hermeneutical reflection, one always has *a priori* understanding of the world or context of meaningfulness as the horizon of the temporalizing.[92] The world as such, of course, is an existential of *Dasein* and is therefore neither *zuhanden* nor *vorhanden* nor reflexively constructed, but is itself temporalized in the temporality of *Dasein*. The ecstases of timing in which *Dasein* is "outside" of itself are always contextual and worldly.[93]

The place where the ecstatic-horizonal unity of temporality is open for interpretation is *Rede*. Discourse as logos makes understanding possible just because it lets something be seen *as* something through its pointing out. And as the medium of articulation of *Verstehen* and *Befindlichkeit*, discourse permits the retention and anticipation that make possible the synthesis of something as something. Language is the openness of *Dasein* in the sense that in *Rede* the meaning of the being of *Dasein* is disclosed.

The two basic modes of *Dasein*'s being, as revealed through the temporality of *Dasein*'s *Rede*, are those of authenticity and inauthenticity. It is no accident that Heidegger first discusses the inauthentic mode of being directly after his analysis of "*Da-sein und Rede: Die Sprache*"[94] and under the heading "the everyday being of the '*Da*' and the falling of *Dasein*."⁹⁵ The inauthentic mode of being shows up in language through the tendencies toward gossip (*das Gerede*), curiosity (*die Neugier*), and ambiguity (*die Zweideutigkeit*), through which *Dasein* expresses loss of itself and surrender to the acquired opinions of *das Man* (the anonymous "they" of public opinion).

With respect to the temporal modes of *Dasein*'s being, the division between authentic and inauthentic being can be displayed as follows. The language of inauthentic *Dasein* resists its temporality and forgets that it is responsible for its own timing and merely "awaits" (*Gewärtigen*) its future as something that ineluctably comes *to* it. Inauthentic *Befindlichkeit* is expressed in the language of forgetfulness (*Vergessenheit*) with respect to the past. In the present, everyday *Dasein* merely submits to the inauthentic situation as *Gegenwärtigen* (the time in which things are made present).

The language of authentic *Dasein*, on the other hand, times *Verstehen* as creative anticipation (*Vorlaufen*) of the future (in particular by recognizing *Dasein*'s own death and finitude). *Befindlichkeit* is timed authentically as recollection (*Wiederholung*) of the past. And in the present moment, *Dasein* exhibits authenticity when it takes over the moment (*Augenblick*) with the insight that penetrates to an understanding of what the situation demands.⁹⁶

Heidegger's description of the authentic present as the penetration into the demands of the moment is not limited to understanding a possible mode of timing my present activities. Heidegger's analysis of the temporal structure of *Dasein* allows us also to see how *Dasein*'s insight may penetrate to a grasp of the *whole* of Dasein as care. This possibility of understanding the meaning of the whole of *Dasein*'s being is opened through anticipation of the "end" of *Dasein* in death. For death is the possibility for me to be that finalizes my past, cuts off my future, and invades my present as the perspective from which *Dasein* is seen in its wholeness and conclusive meaning. According to Heidegger,

> Der Tod ist eine Seinsmöglichkeit, die je das Dasein selbst zu übernehmen hat. Mit dem Tod steht sich das Dasein selbst in seinem *eigensten* Seinkönnen bevor. In dieser Möglichkeit geht es dem Dasein um sein In-der-Welt-sein schlechtin. Sein Tod ist die Möglichkeit des Nicht-mehr-dasein-könnens. Wenn das Dasein als diese Möglichkeit seiner selbst sich bevorsteht, ist es *völlig* auf sein eigenstes Seinkönnen verwiesen. So sich bevor-

stehend sind in ihm alle Bezüge zu anderem Dasein gelöst. Diese eigenste, unbezügliche Möglichkeit ist zugleich die aüsserste. Als Seinkönnen vermag das Dasein die Möglichkeit des Todes nicht zu überholen. Der Tod ist die Möglichkeit der schlechthinnigen Daseinsunmöglichkeit. So enthüllt sich der *Tod* als die *eigenste, unbezügliche, unüberholbare Möglichkeit*.[97]

Death is a possibility of being that each *Dasein* must itself take over. With death *Dasein* stands before itself in its *ownmost* potentiality for being. This possibility concerns nothing less than the being-in-the-world of *Dasein* as such. Its death is the possibility of no longer being able to be there. When *Dasein* stands before itself as this possibility it is *fully* referred to its very own potentiality to be. All relations in it to other *Daseins* are dissolved when *Dasein* stands before itself in this way. This ownmost, nonrelational possibility is at the same time the most extreme. As potentiality for being, *Dasein* is unable to surpass the possibility of death. Death is the possibility of the utter impossibility of *Dasein*. Thus death reveals itself as the *ownmost, nonrelational, unsurpassable possibility*.

As the ownmost, nonrelational, and unsurpassable possibility, death is an element of *Dasein*'s facticity that permeates and focuses the whole of life. Death is "ownmost" in that it is a unique possibility that reveals in a heightened way how existence is characterized by *care* for one's individual being and world. Death is also "nonrelational" and "unsurpassable" in constituting an untransferable and ever-present possibility. Death is the possibility of no longer existing that one necessarily assumes as soon as one is; and, among possibilities, it radically raises both the question of the meaning of life and the question of identity. When inauthentically viewed, death is seen anonymously and externally: sooner or later "one" must die—but for the moment, not yet! Death is inauthentically construed as "something in general" that is abstracted from lived experience. But when authentically seized as a present possibility for me—the possibility of my impossibility to be the one I am— death discloses the individual and unique character of existence in that it brings me back to the self that is my own, to the self as *finite freedom* within the project of connecting a world as a context of meanings.

In projecting the possibility of death, *Dasein* is displaying care. As a real possibility for being, death is grounded in the being of *Dasein* as care.[98] Only a being who is concerned about what it means to be can project the possibility of death. And once anticipated as a present possibility, death provides the standpoint from which to grasp the wholeness of *Dasein* in its *meaning*. If the open background, the "upon which" of my projections and choices, is present as the horizon of death, I may understand the urgency of my choices and actualize the authentic possibilities through which I may achieve wholeness. Understanding existence as temporal and finite, the "I" of *Dasein* is set free to make the authentic choice as an expression of the wholeness of being. Anticipation of death focuses *Dasein* on the meaning of being: existence is temporal and finite but open to new meaning.[99]

We now reach the threshold of the final step of Heidegger's hermeneutic of *Dasein*. If Heidegger has articulated the being of *Dasein* as care, and then has shown that the ontological meaning of care is temporality, then what success does he have in specifying the single explicit meaning of *Sein* as time? If the various self-world relations—*Befindlichkeit* and *Verstehen* articulated in *Rede* either authentically or inauthentically—are read as signs that point to their single source in temporality as well as to the *Woraufhin* or the goal of the various projections *Dasein* makes, does Heidegger manage to make explicit that source and goal of *Dasein*'s understanding into a single concept of being?

It is well known that Heidegger failed to make the transition from the interpretation of the meaning of care as temporality to an interpretation of the meaning of being as such. According to Otto Pöggeler, temporality cannot serve as first principle by means of which the modes of *Dasein*'s timing are made possible.[100] As first principle, temporality is no entity but times itself finitely in the modes of future, past, and present.[101] But then the problem of thinking the meaning of temporality emerges through this aporia: If temporality is to be thought as first principle grounding the differences between the various modes of being on which a system of the sciences could be built, this principle cannot itself be thought of as temporal. From the other side, if the investigation into fundamental ontology is to be considered a historical one, it cannot appeal to temporality as its basis. There is an incompatibility between temporality and the grounding principle.

Heidegger hoped to take the being of *Dasein* as a sign pointing to being as such as the leading meaning of the various modes of being. This was the warrant for calling his work a hermeneutic of *Dasein*. And indeed he was able to show that *Dasein*'s being is a sign that points to being. But by the end of the published portion of

Sein und Zeit, he had come to see that the leading meaning of *Dasein*'s being is a sign that cannot be interpreted: "Das Zeichen bleibt ohne Deutung (The sign remains without interpretation)."[102]

Given this inability to move from analysis of *Dasein* to the meaning of *Sein*, after 1927 Heidegger explored a second starting point in which he hoped to let the medium of language and its revealing power show the signs of *Sein* to *Dasein*. As we shall see below, Ricoeur forms his hermeneutical theory in full awareness of the plan and outcome of Heidegger's program. As was Heidegger, he is interested in the interrelation of the being of man, the being of time, and being as such. He wants his hermeneutics to contribute to philosophical anthropology and ontology. But in light of the impasse from *Dasein* to *Sein*, and fearful of loss of contact with methodological thought in moving from the revealing power of *Sein* in language to *Dasein*, Ricoeur elects the "long route" through philosophy of language and semantic theory to seek for the ontological and anthropological implications of a return to the problematic of Schleiermacher and Dilthey: How to give theoretical foundation to the interpretation of texts?

3 • The Development of Ricoeur's Thought

The Evolution of Ricoeur's Thought from Reflective Philosophy into a Hermeneutical Phenomenology

Only relatively lately has Ricoeur undertaken to write a comprehensive hermeneutical theory based on a philosophy of language. Prior to his hermeneutical turn, Ricoeur made a lasting contribution to the French phenomenological movement in the first volume of *Philosophy of the Will, Freedom and Nature*.[1] He also produced essays on social thought, politics, historical theory, and Christian faith, as well as on various themes in existentialist and phenomenological thought.[2] Ricoeur's work contributes to a wide range of important topics.

A unifying theme, however, runs through Ricoeur's work prior to and through his concern with hermeneutics, giving coherence and identity to the whole. Ihde and Rasmussen rightly express that theme in the question "What does it mean to be human?"[3] Ricoeur's work is best characterized as a contribution to philosophical anthropology, and his recent publications in hermeneutical theory are no exception. Ricoeur's hermeneutical theory enters the thick of current discussion of normative principles for exegesis and theory of text, but it does so because text and textual understanding present a space of openness in which a relatively clear trace of human being can be discerned. Ricoeur has turned to hermeneutical theory in part because he has become convinced, with Heidegger, that "man is language,"[4] in the sense that language is the openness of *Dasein* and reveals a relationship to being.

In this section I shall not present an account of Ricoeur's philosophical development except where it is directly relevant to the justification and execution of hermeneutical theory. I propose to sketch an outline of Ricoeur's modification of Husserlian phenomenology as a method with which he could pose his central question, and to analyze briefly the application of that method to the theme of human fallibility in part I of volume 2 of *Philosophy of the Will*. This major work, entitled *Fallible Man*, immediately precedes Ricoeur's turn to hermeneutics in the second half of that same volume of *Philosophy of the Will*, *The Symbolism of Evil*.

In *Fallible Man* Ricoeur shows how far a pure reflection on human being can proceed until it reaches an aspect that cannot be reflected directly. For Ricoeur, this point is reached where thought attempts to follow the transition between fallibility and "fault" or the state of already fallen existence. Since that transition is an irrational one, reflection on the meaning of being human from within the actual condition of existential disruption must turn to a second starting point. The demand for this new starting point marks Ricoeur's adoption of a hermeneutic of linguistic expressions as a way of deciphering the selfhood that is bound up with the condition of fault. I shall summarize below the evolution of Ricoeur's thought to hermeneutical theory in this way and shall indicate why Ricoeur argues that the turn to hermeneutics is justified by the intentions of reflective philosophy before I proceed to the main task of this chapter. That task is to begin the systematic study of Ricoeur's hermeneutical theory with a description of his notion of expression as it emerges from his early hermeneutical philosophy and continues to remain in place as a basic term throughout the development of his mature hermeneutical proposal.

The influences that set Ricoeur on his own philosophical path were initially those of Gabriel Marcel, his teacher, and Edmund Husserl, father of phenomenology. From his study with Marcel, Ricoeur was exposed to reflection, conducted in Socratic fashion, on the great themes treated by Marcel in his writings: the primacy of the "I am," the decentering of the *cogito* within being, the mystery of concrete being, the experiences of despair, anticipated death, and hope, and the like. Ricoeur attributes to Marcel his early interest in the existentialist subject matter to which he would apply his own methods.[5]

But if Marcel gave Ricoeur the substance of his philosophy in this way, Husserl's writings on phenomenology contributed the formal method. From Husserl, Ricoeur received the inspiration and some tools for a systematic approach in philosophy, which Marcel lacked. Like Marcel, Husserl placed the question as to the meaning of phenomena in central position, and he turned attention to the "things themselves," that is, to the content of lived experience. But unlike Marcel, Husserl worked out exacting methods for approaching the problem of meaning, and Ricoeur was eager to acquire them.

For Ricoeur, Husserlian phenomenology is most importantly a method based on the doctrine of intentionality, which defines consciousness as consciousness *of* some object, namely, the correlation of name and perception, a signification and an intuited fulfilling of the intention. Phenomenology methodically describes objects of consciousness and correlative acts of intending. This method is called "phenomenological reduction," and it proceeds through these steps: (1) the *epochē*, in which one suspends belief in the existence of the object, and (2) the *eidetic* phase of reduction, which includes intuition of the essence of the phenomenon (its mode of appearing) as it is constituted by the transcendental ego. The aim of the descriptive method is to exhibit the elements and the relations between elements that make up the structure of the phenomenon as an intended object of consciousness related to an intending subject. Ricoeur's work from the beginning has taken the style of a noematic analysis in Husserl's sense of phenomenological reduction, in which one reads the object, person, event, or expression for the correlate structure of consciousness.

Ricoeur considered the phenomenological method to be independent of any metaphysical program, and any extension of method into ontology he held to be inappropriate to the goals of phenomenology. Yet this is what Ricoeur saw in Husserl's own development after *Logical Investigations:* the reduction became less and less method and more and more ontology.[6] In Ricoeur's estimation, in the *Ideas* (which Ricoeur translated into French with commentary) and *Cartesian Meditations* Husserl turned his back on the phenomenology of signification. Husserl made a "metaphysical decision" to replace description of phenomena appearing *to* consciousness with "egological" description, in which the meaning of what appears is said to be constituted *in, by,* and *for* consciousness.[7] The result was a full-blown "idealism," a hypostatization of the reflexive subject as the one in whom self-world structures are constituted. The error of Husserlian idealism rests on two false claims.

The first of these is the claim made by the later Husserl that perception has an indisputable primacy in consciousness.[8] In taking this position Husserl retreated from his earlier view that consciousness is a balanced synthesis of speech and perception, meaning and intuitions. Husserl thus made perception the ultimate foundation of consciousness. But by doing so, Ricoeur thinks, Husserl trapped himself. For reliance on perception drove him back to naive realism. And he could save himself from the errors of naive realism—errors he had himself exposed in articulating the idea of phenomenological reduction—only by enriching realism with the doctrine of idealism that the percept is constituted in, by, and for the transcendental ego.[9] The turn to perception fed the idealist tendency. From Ricoeur's perspective, such a role for perception overlooks the historicalness of the language and thought to which we already belong in binding any perceptual appearance. It also neglects the ontological structure of *Verstehen* that Heidegger articulated in *Sein und Zeit*. All understanding proceeds out of a structure of anticipation in which the object is initially grasped in the *Vorhabe*, *Vorsicht*, and *Vorgriff* that participation in a historical linguistic tradition makes possible. There is no such thing as a presuppositionless interpretation, and the Husserlian claim that we have such a grasp of perceptual evidence is an illusory and vain one.[10]

The second error that Ricoeur thinks brought Husserl to his "idealist" distortion of phenomenological method is the claim that the ego is the best-known entity. Husserl thought that, unlike perceptual objects, the ego is not given through *Abschattungen*, "perspectival profiles." Consequently it is purely immanent and without transcendencies. Husserl concluded that the ego is the place of fullest intuitiveness.[11] According to Husserl, self-knowledge is indubitable for that reason and can serve as ultimate foundation for knowledge of the object. Ricoeur, in contrast to Husserl, invokes Heidegger. Section 25 of *Sein und Zeit* shows that the ruses of self-consciousness are cleverer than those of the thing.[12] The self is more unknown to me than any object of nature could be because in self-knowledge (and knowledge of others) inauthenticity clings to the deception that *Dasein* is itself, when as a matter of course *Dasein* takes its sense of self from the anonymous *das Man*, the "they" of "they say . . ." Psychoanalysis and the critique of ideologies that stem from Nietzsche and Marx provide ample documentation for the doubt expressed in Heidegger's question as to the *Who* of *Dasein*. Selfhood is a task to be accomplished against the tenacity of inauthentic self-consciousness, not an indubitable starting point for a perceptualist phenomenology.

In order to resist the tendency toward "idealism" in Husserl while protecting the central doctrine and methodological significance of phenomenology, Ricoeur has modified Husserlian phenomenology by invoking the notion of "limit-concepts," which he finds in Kant. Ricoeur has preserved the Kantian distinction between reason, understanding, and sensibility so as to curb the pretenses of a primacy of perception. For Ricoeur, reason posits "being" as the pure concept of the thing-in-itself as signified or intended. Reason thus thinks a reality that in part transcends intuition. Hence reason combines the signifying power that is consciousness with the sensible intuition that is perception. "Reason" so understood checks the claim that intentions must solely refer to sensible intuitions. The ability to intend beyond intuition is precisely the ability to signify in speech some objectivity as a unification of a manifold.[13] This ability presupposes the positing of "being" as a limit-concept that we must *think* but do not *know*.

Ricoeur resists Husserl's idealism on a second ground, that his doctrine of the "other subject" is mistaken. The idealist presupposition that all phenomena are constituted in, by, and for the ego was deduced from analysis of perceptual objects. But when applied to other egos, the consequence is that even other egos are constituted in the subject's transcendental ego as an object in, by, and for the ego. Ricoeur found this position defective. To repair it he appeals to Kant's practical feeling, which posits the other person as an end-in-itself. My respect for the other as one who is not to be subordinated to my own ends limits my freedom to act.[14] This view of the other as an end-in-itself is made possible by Ricoeur's having preserved reason as a function of the mind that posits limit-concepts.

Ricoeur's phenomenology thus takes its uniqueness over against Husserl by virtue of the Kantian elements he has appropriated in order to avoid "idealist" tendencies in Husserlian phenomenology. These elements are (1) the inclusion of reason's limit-concepts within the Kantian framework of a distinction between reason *(Vernunft)*, understanding *(Verstand)*, and sensibility; and (2) the incorporation of the other subject as an end-in-itself who commands respect and who limits my freedom to act. Reason remains for Ricoeur as in Kant a function of the unconditioned in that reason has only itself as object of thought. Objective knowledge (or what Kant calls understanding), on the other hand, is the correlate of conditioned experience in that knowledge reflects given experience. The Kantian notion of "limit" is put to work by Ricoeur to ensure avoidance of idealism insofar as "the concept 'limit' implies not only and even not primarily that our knowledge *is* limited, has boundaries, but that the quest for the unconditioned *puts limits* on the claim of objective knowledge to become absolute."[15] Reason prohibits any absolutizing tendencies on the part of objective knowledge (which might forget that its own principles are a matter of reason, not knowledge) just as it precludes sovereignty for itself (reason knows itself as competent to justify objective knowledge yet incompetent to speak about things in themselves apart from the forms of knowledge).

Ricoeur also defends his use of the Kantian notion of limit against the ontological development of phenomenology represented by Heidegger. Heidegger's creation of a new language of ontology by which the formal and empty concepts of reason are given content is resisted by Ricoeur on the grounds that the distinction between the figurative and the literal ought not to be collapsed. Ricoeur agrees with Heidegger that the Kantian notion of limit ultimately requires the creation of a new indirect language of ontology that can picture and present what things *are like* even when it is prohibited from saying what things objectively *are*. According to Ricoeur, Heidegger's ontological language transcends the strict limits of knowledge through creation of an indirect speech that is in the end figurative. But this new ontological language poses as objective language and thus surrenders the tension between the literal and figurative. Ricoeur puts it this way:

> We are free to create such terms as Advent, Retrieve, Resolution, etc., but we must preserve the philosophical awareness that this kind of language is indirect, figurative, that it draws its strength from its hermeneutical potential, therefore that it is *not* objective. The "limit" works here as a warning against a new scholasticism. It reminds us that the "is like" implies an "is not." This is why I do not give up the Kantian vocabulary of the "limit" imposed by Reason on the claims to objective knowledge. In the same way as the "tension" between a literal and a metaphorical interpretation is essential to the meaning of a metaphor, a tension between the *objective* claim of knowledge and the *poetic* presentation of the Unconditioned must be preserved in the new language of Advent, Retrieve, and Resolution. This language is at the same time that of *limit-concepts* and *figurative* presentation of the Unconditioned.[16]

Phenomenology is thus restricted by Ricoeur to the role of a description of experience. It is not initially extended into an ontology either by absolutizing the "I" as in Husserl or in generating an indirect language as in Heidegger. But we shall see below (chapter

5) that Ricoeur is deliberately postponing the ontological task, not denying its necessity or importance. His decision to delay ontological construction is made for the sake of ontology.

In sum, Ricoeur's early reflective philosophy can be characterized through his development of a phenomenology that takes its bearing from the Husserlian doctrine of intentionality but that resists the tendency toward idealism in Husserl by introducing Kantian limit-concepts to phenomenology. Ricoeur's unique version of phenomenology is epitomized by this interplay of Kant and Husserl:

> The merit of phenomenology is to have elevated the investigation of the appearing to the dignity of a science by the reduction. But the merit of Kantianism is to have been able to coordinate the investigation of the appearing with the limiting function of the in-itself and with the practical determination of the in-itself as freedom and as the totality of persons.[17]

Ricoeur's Kantian modification of Husserlian phenomenology is applied as method in *Fallible Man*. Ricoeur sets forth a model of human being in order to disclose the condition of the possibility of fallen existence. The Kantian style of the description extends even to the framework of the model in two ways. The model has three levels, corresponding to the Kantian faculties: the theoretical consciousness, practical consciousness, and affective consciousness. And second, the mediation of understanding and sensibility by the transcendental imagination at the level of theoretical consciousness is taken as paradigmatic for the analysis of the practical and affective domains.

At the outset of the study Ricoeur proclaims that the method he applies here and calls "reflective philosophy" reaches its limits where it isolates the abstract structure of fallibility and recognizes that it is barred from passage into the concretely lived world of the fallen will. Any further disclosure of what it means to be human in the midst of an already disrupted world must rely on "a revolution in method, represented by the recourse to a hermeneutics, that is, to rules of deciphering applied to a world of symbols." Hermeneutics is announced as a second starting point, which is "not of the same nature as the reflective thought which led to the concept of fallibility."[18] Since Ricoeur's hermeneutics is the direct outgrowth of his reflection on the abstract structure of existence in *Fallible Man* and is demanded by the nature of that reflection itself, I propose to concentrate on *Fallible Man* to see why the results of that work prompted Ricoeur's efforts in hermeneutical theory. To do that, I shall compare *Fallible Man* with Heidegger's *Sein und Zeit*. Such a comparison will be helpful in showing in what way *Fallible Man* already *is* a hermeneutical work and in what way it *is not* hermeneutics.

Ricoeur's *Fallible Man* can be compared to Heidegger's *Sein und Zeit* because, despite differences between them, there is a sense in which *Fallible Man* can be called an interpretation of existence or a hermeneutic of *Dasein* even though Ricoeur does not use the term *hermeneutics* to indicate his method here. He instead calls it a work of pure reflection, in that it follows "a way of understanding and being understood which does not come through image, symbol, or myth."[19] Nonetheless *Fallible Man* accomplishes the task Heidegger sets for interpretation: It takes what is already understood in a preliminary and preontological way and puts it into methodical and exact concepts. Just as Heidegger starts from the everyday language of *Dasein* in its fallenness and develops it into appropriate existentialist concepts, Ricoeur works from prephilosophical expressions of the reality he wants to reflect conceptually and takes them as the guide for his meditation.

More specifically, Ricoeur selects certain "excellent expressions" of a primary language, which he calls the *pathétique* of misery, and deliberately analyzes the meaning for the content of those expressions.[20] According to Ricoeur, the myths of the soul as *mélange* in Plato and the rhetoric of man as suspended between two infinites in Pascal give expression to the misery of discord that is endemic to man's ontological constitution. The rule for thought is that "philosophy has to proceed as a second order elucidation of a nebula of meaning which at first has a pre-philosophical character." He says, "Philosophy does not start anything independently: supported by the non-philosophical, it derives its existence from the substance of what has already been understood prior to reflection."[21] Although Heidegger does not focus so explicitly on a set of expressions that contain a meaning that reflection must attempt to equal, he does include in the center of *Sein und Zeit* (section 42) a confirmation *(Bewährung)* of the existential interpretation of *Dasein* as care through a prephilosophical fable.[22] Also, Otto Pöggeler claims that Heidegger's model of authentic factual existence is the conceptual articulation of a meaning already expressed in the New Testament documents of the primitive Christian religion.[23] But despite minor differences in emphasis on the role of a prephilosophical expression as impetus for reflection, both Ricoeur and Heidegger hold that philosophy recovers what is already understood and expressed elsewhere in prereflective language.

The decisive difference between *Sein und Zeit* and *Fallible Man* lies elsewhere; it is that, whereas Heidegger's work is undertaken in the context of asking the question as to the meaning of being, Ricoeur's work is simply a reflection on human being. And since Heidegger's existential analytic is a hermeneutic of *Dasein* in part because it interprets the existential structure of *Dasein* for the meaning of being that it displays, Ricoeur's analysis of human being in this second sense is not a hermeneutic. Ricoeur does not attempt in this text to interpret the structure of human being as a sign with a sense, namely, the meaning of being.

Ricoeur's work also has a more restricted scope than Heidegger's in *Sein und Zeit*, in that Ricoeur's focus is not the being of *Dasein* as such but is the dimension of human being designated by the concept of fallibility. In Ricoeur's view, however, this restriction heightens concentration on what is crucial to the being of man, for fallibility pertains to "the innermost structure of human reality."[24] The hypothesis is that the condition of human fallenness and liability to err can be found in what is ontologically most characteristic of man: that he is a mixture, a living contradiction, because "his act of existing is the very act of bringing about mediation between all the modalities and all the levels of reality within him and outside of him" and because these levels are in some sense discontinuous with each other.[25]

The goal of *Fallible Man* is to manifest the locus of fallibility. It intends to show that man is a creature who is a possibility for evil. The condition of this possibility is that man is noncoincident with himself. Human freedom is so constituted that it must mediate between finite and infinite aspects of itself, and this makes it fallible. Ricoeur begins with analysis of theoretical synthesis, expands to the practical dimension of experience in order to retrieve a bit more of what is implied in the fullness of content of the *pathétique* of misery, and finally includes the affective side of human being. The basic procedure is to reduce experience to a finite and an infinite aspect of the self at each level, and then to trace the relation between the two aspects of the self back to a third mediating term. In the concluding chapter Ricoeur deduces the three categories of fallibility from the three triads that he obtained in the course of his analysis of thinking, doing, and feeling. Those categories of fallibility constitute an existentialist interpretation of the categories

Kant labeled reality, negation, and limitation. Ricoeur renames them originating affirmation, existential difference, and human mediation.[26] These categories are the result of a transcendental deduction in that they specify the conditions of the possibility of a certain discourse on man, that is, that of the *pathétique* of misery.

At the end of his reflection on fallibility, Ricoeur arrives at the limit of the transcendental method of pure reflection. Pure reflection is able to describe in noematic analysis the kind of activity that is "human mediation," but the description remains abstract and does not disclose the meaning of the disruption of existence. Pure reflection is unable to make the transition from fallibility to fault, from the possibility of evil to its actuality in concrete existence,[27] because there is a hiatus between those two that prompts the turn from reflective philosophy to hermeneutics.

The first cycle of the analysis in *Fallible Man* focuses on the transcendental synthesis of theoretical reason, and this section then functions paradigmatically for the subsequent two. Ricoeur's phenomenological method here begins with the object known and discovers with regard to or *on* that object "the specific disproportion of knowing, between receiving it and determining it. *Upon the thing* it apprehends the power of synthesis."[28] Proceeding in that way, Ricoeur refashions the Kantian opposition between sensibility and understanding into the opposition of "finite perspective" to "infinite verb." Beginning with the object, one discovers finite perspective reflectively by accepting the facts of acquaintance with some thing and working back to the elements that make it up. The first element that one notices is that no one percept is sufficient to the object that is given. The object appears through a sequence of *Abschattungen* or profiles. This perspectival feature of perception indicates that the "I" to whom the object appears is a "here" of situated bodily openness and point of view.[29] Infinite verb, the second term of the opposition, is also revealed reflectively as a second aspect of the mediating self. Just as I apprehend the perspectival character of seeing with regard to or, as Ricoeur says, *upon* the object, I also transgress perspective upon the thing itself precisely in the act of expressing that one-sidedness and thereby expressing all the other sides that I do not presently see.[30] If I say, "This is a tree," I transcend the appearing percept in determining the thing itself. According to Ricoeur,

> this transgression is the intention to signify. Through it I bring myself before a sense which will never be perceived anywhere

by anyone, which is not a superior point of view, which is not, in fact, a point of view at all but an inversion into the universal of all points of view.

If I now note that to signify is to intend, the transgression of the point of view is nothing else than speech as the possibility of expressing, and of expressing the point of view itself.[31]

The correlation of perceiving and signifying, seeing and saying, is the primal structure of knowing, and it involves a combination of a finite perspectival receptivity with a linguistic ability to transcend perspective by conveying the *intention*, not the perception, of what is seen.[32] Saying always exceeds what is displayed perspectively, thus "I say more than I see when I signify."[33] The transcendence of nominal signification does not yet specify the infinite moment of speech, however. For this Ricoeur has recourse to Plato's discovery in the *Cratylus*, the *Theaetetus*, and the *Sophist* of the distinction between noun and verb that is "the cornerstone of human discourse."[34] This distinction is picked up by Aristotle in *On Interpretation*, where he says that the verb is a noun-meaning with an added, two-fold signification. The verb both designates the tense, and thus posits existence or some modification of present *time*, and adds attribution to the *subject*. The whole verb bloc accomplishes both functions: "Socrates is walking" means the walk "exists now" and it is "said of" Socrates.[35] Ricoeur adds to this reflection that the soul of the verb is affirmation, the saying of yes or no, and that through this power of assent, the verb has an infinite dimension that transcends the nominal contents. While nouns have a truth-intention to reach their object, verbs add a freedom-intention in their reference to the subject and to time. The "I" is free in expressing sentences to affirm or negate a designated state of affairs with respect to a mode of time.

The discovery of both finite perspective and infinite verb on the same object opens the problem of the third term, which can mediate between the two disporportionate levels. This third term, the transcendental imagination, is not given for scrutiny but must be inferred from the unity of speech with the point of view that is effected externally on the object. The object *is* the synthesis of meaning and appearance, and its subjective correlate remains obscure because the pure imagination "does not exist *for itself*" but completely spends itself in the act of constituting objectivity. Pure imagination is blind, for "this mediating term has no intelligibility of its own."[36]

The one clue that does appear on the object that gives some indication of the nature of the synthesizing activity is the temporal element involved in the connect*ing* of meaning with sequential appearance. This insight reflects the influence of Heidegger's notion of time and his interpretation of Kant's chapter on schematism. But it merely names time as the unity of the disproportionate duality of speech and appearance. "For the third term to be intelligible in itself we would have to show that it is the 'common root' of understanding and sensibility," and that time is a "ground."[37] The enigma of the transcendental imagination remains intact.

The first cycle of reflection on theoretical synthesis does not exhaust the ability of Ricoeur's phenomenology to disclose something about human mediation. So far, noematic analysis of the theoretical synthesis presents reflection with a formal description of consciousness. But "'consciousness' is not yet the unity of a person in itself and for itself; it is not one person; it is no one. The 'I' of 'I think' is merely the form of a world for anyone and everyone. It is consciousness in general, that is, a pure and simple project of the object."[38] As such, the reflection on transcendental synthesis is insufficient to the richness of the prereflective *pathétique* and must be supplemented by reflection on the practical synthesis.

In passing from the "I think" to the "I will," certain differences between the transcendental synthesis and the practical synthesis emerge. In the first place, the point of reference is changed. Whereas the object as a synthesis already given provided the starting point for reflection in the theoretical part, in the practical part the reference is to *works* of human beings.[39] And whereas the object presented a synthesis already accomplished, in this case the synthesis constitutes a *person* and it is something *to be done*. The practical synthesis makes a person be through the specific moral feeling that Kant called respect.[40] Respect for the person synthesizes *character* and *happiness*, which correspond to the finitude of perspective and the infinity of verbal meaning. Respect is the mediating term in the practical synthesis of a person: respect for another person simultaneously constitutes one's own personhood and accords dignity to another person's combination of happiness and character.

Ricoeur approaches the finite dimension of the practical self in three steps. The first is analysis of affective perspective as it functions to limit the will. The will is always "nourished with *motives*" and projects its work as a *pragma* according to its inclinations.⁴¹ Only an inclined, aroused will is moved to determine itself to do something, and the finitude involved in such a pattern is that desire is both a *drive toward* and a *lack of*.⁴² The inclined will is both open to its *pragma* and attached to its own felt individuality. Affective finitude is attachment to one's felt difference from others.⁴³ The second step in marking the limitation of character is a description of habit as a fixing of behaviors, aptitudes, and tastes. Habit can be either acquisition of skills or the mechanization of life, but in either case it contributes to the finitude of doing.⁴⁴ The third step is to delimit character in its totality as "the finite openness of my existence taken as a whole."⁴⁵ One's character is never perceived directly, but it can be caught indirectly through certain revealing expressions that uncover the depth of personal motivations.⁴⁶

The infinite side of the disproportionate polarity in the practical dimension is that of happiness as such. Happiness is a Kantian Idea that "dwells in the human will" and guides action as the horizon and goal of every person's respect. Happiness appears embodied in those human works which open the will to the horizon of unlimited possibilities for fulfillment and which evoke the feeling of the "immense" that accompanies the unrestricted view of an infinity of directions by which to attain the true end of human existence.

The practical synthesis in respect, which connects happiness and character, is not an accomplished one but one to be accomplished by the projection of an image of what the person should be. The projected image is that of a concretely existing person who is an end-in-itself and must not be subjected to use as a means by another will. This synthesis can be explicitly expressed in the Kantian categorical imperative, which is first of all felt as respect: "Act so that you treat humanity, whether in your own person or in that of another, always as an end and never as a means only."⁴⁷

The peculiar fragility of this demand for synthesis in respect is that the will as motivated project is always a *split* will.⁴⁸ The "I" who is motivated to respect the humanness of human being is split from the "I" who carries out the demand. Even when moved by respect I may act so as to degrade the ideal of selfhood.

The final cycle of the analysis of existence in its fallibility concentrates on affective fragility. Here the terms denoting the finite-infinite polarity and their mediation are *epithumia* or vital affectivity, *eros* or spiritual affectivity, and *thumos* or courage that separates and unites the two.[49] According to Ricoeur's analysis, feeling is in its nature paradoxical. Consequently, this level introduces the moment of fragility *par excellence*.

Feeling for Ricoeur is not properly thought of as one function alongside two others (knowing and doing). It is rather a "significant moment of the whole."[50] Just as feeling permeates the practical synthesis insofar as the acting will is always a motivated and inclined will, feeling is bound up with knowing because of its structure of intentionality. The feeling of love or hatred, for example, is always a feeling *of* the lovable or hateful. But feeling both responds to qualities of things or persons and reveals an inward affection of the self. With feeling, "an intention and an affection coincide in the same experience, a transcending aim and the revelation of an inwardness."[51]

Ricoeur holds that feeling is "the manifestation of a relation to the world which constantly restores our complicity with it, our inherence and belonging in it, something more profound than all polarity and duality."[52] Whereas knowing divides and separates self and world, subject and object, in feeling "objects touch me" and reality is interiorized. And whereas discrete things or persons or events, and so on, are felt in certain ways, Ricoeur agrees with Heidegger that beyond the feelings with limited intentions there are also "formless" feelings or moods, which constitute man's very openness to being as such.[53] Ricoeur mentions joy and anguish (*Angst*) as moods attuned to the positive and negative sides of being as such. *Thumos* or courage mediates between these open states of being-attuned in feeling. The object of these three formless moods, however, cannot be named through our felt inherence in it: "One can merely call it the Unconditioned which is demanded by reason and whose inwardness is manifested by feeling."[54]

In affective life, the opposition requiring mediation has to do with noncoincident aims of felt relations. The finite term, *epithumia*, refers to the aims of vital pleasure as perfected in the moment. The infinite term, *eros*, refers to the goal of spiritual beatitude as perfected in the total work of an existence.[55] Pleasure is evoked by a finite pleasurable object, whereas spiritual happiness is the correlate of the infinity of the desirable as such. *Thumos* or courage stands between the two. But the specific character of the mediation in this case is that it is *not* accomplished and cannot be accomplished. Feeling is the field on which the conflict of aims is constantly renewed in the passions bound up with having, power, and worth.[56] This is so because the *thumos* is essentially restless, that is, at no point are motivating tensions completely stilled. Stretched between the finite feelings of organic life and the infinite feeling of the spiritual aspiration, the *thumos* is the locus of the fragility of the indefinite quest of human being: "It seems, then, that *conflict* is a function of man's most primordial constitution; the object is synthesis; the self is conflict."[57]

Fallible Man, then, circumscribes the disproportionate relation of finitude to infinitude at the heart of human existence. Taken as a whole, human existence is a movement of infinite *originating affirmation* through an *existential difference* by *human mediation*. The first terms refers to the "I" whose freedom-intention comes to expression in the aim for happiness as inwardly moved by spiritual aspiration. The second term refers to the "this one here" whose perceptual perspective is riveted to a character and moved by vital desire. And the third term refers to the "am" of "I am this one here" as it denotes the connecting process that is rooted in the primordial conflict of human feeling. Fallibility is the noncoincidence of the self with itself that is mediated with the object in knowing, sensed as the task of becoming a person in doing, and experienced as inner conflict in feeling.

The concept of fallibility so deduced gives abstract and neutral conditions for the possibility of the entrance of evil into the world. But what is more, this concept "includes the possibility of evil in a still more positive sense: man's disproportion is a power to fail, in the sense that it makes man *capable* of failing."[58] No wonder Plato could in myth represent the soul as a mixture and Pascal could speak of the misery of being stretched between two infinites: man *is* the mediator; his act of existing connects the opposites in theoretical consciousness and in intention practically. Deeper down, however, there is conflict. No wonder man finds himself not only fallible but also fallen.

But how to catch sight of that leap from fallibility to fallenness? What about the being of concrete fallen existence? Pure reflection is helpless to proceed further and must seek a second starting point in hermeneutics for two reasons. First, the actuality of evil cannot be derived from its possibility, and the breach or gap between the two demands the abandonment of pure reflection in favor of interpretation of the expressions of humanness that issue out of the fault. Second, the intentions of pure reflection themselves demand the hermeneutic turn, as I shall show presently. At just this point, with the limits of pure reflection in view and impelled by the desire to disclose the being of man as thoroughly as possible, Ricoeur decides to take the leap from pure reflection to the hermeneutical method of understanding, which bears "on the *avowal* that consciousness makes of it (evil) and on the symbols of evil in which this avowal is expressed. The hiatus of method between the phenomenology of fallibility and the symbolics of evil only gives expression, therefore, to the hiatus between fallibility and fault in man himself."[59]

But why does Ricoeur think that reflective philosophy demands the turn to hermeneutics? Why does a philosophical anthropology in line with the tradition through Kant, Fichte, and Heidegger need to incorporate the problematic of Schleiermacher and Dilthey and develop methods for deciphering textual meaning? Ricoeur's answer concerns both the nature of reflective philosophy itself and the setting of the hermeneutical task.

According to Ricoeur, reflective philosophy is ultimately reflexive philosophy or self-reflection because the starting point and foundation of reflection is the positing of the self as *Tathandlung* in reflection. Ricoeur says,

> The positing of the self is a truth which posits itself; it can neither be verified nor deduced; it is at once the positing of a being and of an act; the positing of an existence and of an operation of thought: *I am, I think;* to exist, for me, is to think; I exist inasmuch as I think. Since this truth cannot be verified like a fact, nor deduced like a conclusion, it has to posit itself in reflection; its self-positing is reflection; Fichte called this first truth the *thetic judgment*. Such is our philosophical starting point.[60]

But such is only one aspect of reflection. The "I" posits itself in reflection, but that "I" remains abstract and obscure. In its temporality the "I" is uncatchable in intuition, and in its concrete fallenness it is irrational. Hence Ricoeur says, "the first truth—I am, I think—remains as abstract and empty as it is invincible."

Reflective philosophy is self-grounding but blind to that ground. For self-reflection to proceed, it must recognize with Dilthey that the self is lost, fallen, and alienated in the works, ideas, images, institutions that objectify it. Consciousness of the self is not a given but a task of appropriating what is lost and self-alienated in language. Reflective philosophy must reconstitute itself as hermeneutics in order to recover the meaning of the "I" of "I am" in its act of existing by deciphering the meaning of that self as it has become sedimented in the linguistic tradition.

Hermeneutics as the outgrowth of reflective philosophy is in this sense an ethical practice to the extent that it leads from alienation to freedom and beatitude. Its goal is appropriation, and

> appropriation signifies that the initial situation from which reflection proceeds is "forgetfulness." I am lost, "led astray" among objects and separated from the center of my existence, just as I am separated from others as an enemy is separated from all men. Whatever the secret of this "diaspora," of this separation, it signifies that I do not at first possess what I am. The truth that Fichte called the thetic judgment posits itself in a desert wherein I am absent to myself. That is why reflection is a task; an *Aufgabe*—the task of making my concrete experience equal to the positing of "I am."[61]

Hermeneutics is, for Ricoeur, the way indicated by reflective philosophy itself to heal the rift between the "I" and "this one here." Post-Kantian reflection has always been reflection on experience, and the hermeneutical reflection on language and symbols merely extends the field of inquiry from experience of appearing objects and of thinking to the experience of language. But with such an extension, the first task is to articulate the intelligibility of symbols through semantic theory. Philosophical anthropology here joins hermeneutical reflection on the principles for textual exegesis. With this conjunction we approach the starting point for discussion of Ricoeur's hermeneutical philosophy.

Ricoeur's Notion of Expression

So far we have seen that pure reflection can articulate the mediating activity that is the being of the self as the condition of the possibility of fault. But a gap or hiatus remains between the abstract considerations of pure reflection and the concrete life of existence as fallen. Ricoeur shifts his method to the interpretation of linguistic expressions precisely in hope that he can thereby gain new and fruitful access to the meaning of human subjectivity under the conditions of existence.

In making this turn, Ricoeur can be placed along with Hans-Georg Gadamer and other twentieth-century hermeneutical thinkers who have understood the insight in Heidegger's *Sein und Zeit* that *Rede* or discourse is the place of *Dasein*'s openness. Speech embodies the self-world relation in which *Dasein* exists.

For Ricoeur as for Heidegger, language is the articulation of *Verstehen* and *Befindlichkeit;* it is the medium of any thinking or experiencing. The guiding principle for the hermeneutical turn is that if language is the medium of experience and thought, then we can trace backward from the expression of experience and thought to the kind of self-in-a-world that *"spricht sich aus"* but is otherwise not directly accessible. In a profound sense, man is the animal that has the *logos*, the word, and Ricoeur is willing to wager on that basis that an inquiry into the hermeneutics of expression will repay him with a heightened understanding of the being of *Dasein*.

The basic contrast that makes linguistic expression the starting place for the hermeneutical part of Ricoeur's work is that the expression is not an appearing object. Expression is different from appearance in that with expression we look not for the synthetic unity of a perceptual manifold, but for the thought and experience of the expressing subject. Hermeneutics raises the question as to how to get at what is expressed, and the first step in understanding a hermeneutical theory is to ask what an expression is as an object, a process, and what it implies about the subjective conditions for expression.

Expression as Object

With respect to expression as an object, Ricoeur follows Schleiermacher's conviction that the first reference of expression is to gesture and bodily action rather than to spoken language. This give spoken language a corporeal basis that encompasses it. According to Ricoeur, there are in the free actions of individuals highly revealing expressions, "each of which represents the entire soul, in the sense that the whole content of the soul is reflected in each of them."[62] Such expressions are capable of disclosing the unique way of combining character and happiness that reflects the person who is expressing himself there. But against Schleiermacher's emphasis on the specific individuality as the content of the expression, Ricoeur claims that what is of hermeneutical interest is always the display of an *objective meaning* that does not appeal to the subject's individuality to be understood.

The working out of the notion of objective meaning in linguistic expression is a cornerstone in Ricoeur's hermeneutical theory. For the basic notion of language and logical expression, he relies on the *Logical Investigations* of early Husserlian phenomenology. But Ricoeur does not adopt the Husserlian doctrine of language and logical expression without modification. Indeed, Ricoeur employs Husserl's basic notion of expression to give an integrity and a precision to symbolic expressions, which Husserl had always considered a deficient mode of language. Ricoeur elevates the notion of symbolic expression to a privileged place as the "fullness of language" instead of consigning it to a position of little dignity. After securing the working definition of symbolic expression, Ricoeur is then able to expand his doctrine of expression to include myth as a second-order symbolic expression. With the analysis of myth and symbol, Ricoeur finds himself on the way toward the development of a complete hermeneutical theory of text and in a position to begin to reap some new insight into what it means to be human. This can be explained in more detail.

The Husserlian doctrine of expression is embedded in a theory of language that Ricoeur accepts in basic outline in order to develop a possibility for articulating a definition of symbol. According to Ricoeur, for Husserl

> language is . . . an intermediary between two levels. The first one, as we said, constitutes its *ideal* of logicity, its *telos:* all meanings must be able to be converted into the logos of rationality; the second one no longer constitutes an ideal, but a ground, a soil, an origin, an *Ursprung.* Language may be reached "from above," from its logical limit, or "from below," from its limit in mute elemental experience. In itself it is a medium, a mediation, an exchange between *telos* and *Ursprung*.[63]

Language has its origin in elemental *Erlebnis*, lived experience, and its goal is the univocity and rationality of the logical expression. Language mediates between experience and thought, but in itself it is deficient in expression until the expression reaches the ideal of logicality. For example, expressions of feeling couched in figurative terms (such as "I feel stained") are deficient for Husserl because such an expression lacks ideality of sense.

For Husserl and Ricoeur an expression *(Ausdruck)* is defined as a significative indication in the sense that it announces a meaning.[64] Meaning in the widest sense refers to what can be broken down into sense and reference (Husserl's terms for sense and referent are *Bedeutung* and *Gegenstand*, whereas Ricoeur, following Frege, uses the more common *Sinn* and *Bedeutung*). The key elements are these: 1) expression is borne by a *sign*, a sensory vehicle as "the bearer of a signifying function that makes it stand for something else"; 2) expression carries a *sense;* and 3) expression signifies something through the sense as the *referent*. Ricoeur summarizes: "We say that words, by their sensible quality, *express* significations and that, thanks to their signification, they *designate* something. The term 'to signify' covers the twofold duality of expression and designation."[65]

Ricoeur's alteration of Husserl's doctrine of expression is to reevaluate the Husserlian claim that expressions stemming from the lower threshold of language—what Dilthey would call a *Lebensäusserung*—are deficient in their figurative quality and thus not yet, properly speaking, expressions at all. Ricoeur's view is that the notion of language as a medium with an *Ursprung* and a *telos* shows something about the expressive field not noticed by Husserl. Since there are "upper" and "lower" levels of language, the types of expression are basically two. A basic duality runs through language itself and surfaces in the contrast between the univocal, logical expression and the plurivocal, figurative expression. The field of expression is basically divided between *concept* and *symbol*, since the sense of an expression can be either a notion or an image. And this division is irreducible: symbols are not a defective form of concept, but have a distinct kind of signification that is nonetheless similar enough to that of concept to hold symbolic expression within the field of genuine expression.

The identity of notional and symbolic expressions in Ricoeur's view is that both are significative indications that announce meaning as sense and reference. But the difference is that whereas notional expressions are single-meaning expressions, Ricoeur claims that symbols can be defined as double-meaning expressions.[66] Notional meanings both express an ideal sense and signify an object or state of affairs. In the case of symbolic meanings, however, a second level of signification is added to the first. Symbolic expressions "presuppose signs that already have a primary, literal, manifest meaning." But in addition to that meaning there is a second symbolic meaning, which is suggestive and figurative rather than literal. The literal meaning is what conveys the symbolic meaning: something in the literal meaning signifies a second symbolic meaning.

Consider this passage in which Ricoeur explains what he means by a double-meaning intention through an example.

> Take the "defiled," the "impure." This significant expression presents a first or literal intentionality that, like every significant expression, supposes the triumph of the conventional sign over

the natural sign. Thus, the literal meaning of "defilement" is "stain," but this literal meaning is already a conventional sign; the words "stain," "unclean," etc., do not resemble the thing signified. But upon this first intentionality there is erected a second intentionality which, through the physically "unclean," points to a certain situation of man in the sacred which is precisely that of being defiled, impure. The literal and manifest sense, then, points beyond itself to something that is *like* a stain or a spot.[67]

Now, the above example should properly read, "Take the 'stained,' the 'unclean.' . . . Thus, the literal meaning of 'stain' is 'discolored by a foreign body. . . ,'" because "stain" is the symbolic expression, "discolored" is the literal meaning, and "defiled" as a situation of man in the sacred is the second meaning. Ricoeur's point is nonetheless clear: in symbolic expression the literal meaning points to a second, symbolic meaning on the basis of a resemblance. That second meaning is one of a mode of being or situation in the sacred universe. For Ricoeur's theory, then, symbolic expressions carry the same structure of signification that Husserl identified in his *Logical Investigations*. But symbolic expressions add a level of signification to "being in" the world.

Once Ricoeur has secured the formal definition of symbolic expression, he extends the scope of figurative expression beyond symbol to myth in the following way. Symbols are the basic units of figurative expression. In practice, however, symbols are found already embedded in myths. Interpretation must therefore reduce myth to the primary symbols that it configures sequentially.[68] Ricoeur defines a myth as a second-degree symbolic expression that relies upon primary symbols and adds to them a reference to time in the narrative form of the myth. Myths also refer to the concrete mode of being of a historical community insofar as they characterize the destiny of a community through narration of the struggles of a figure or group of figures who present and make perceptible the community's view on human being.[69] Ricoeur defines myth as a sequential connection between symbols that refers to time and to a concrete mode of existence. Hence the symbol-myth relation recapitulates the noun-verb relation at the level of literal expressions that Ricoeur mentions in *Fallible Man*. And in fact, each of these dualities (noun-verb and symbol-myth) is a linguistic reflection and a sign of the dual structure of the self as *Tathandlung*. At the stage of his theory through the writing of *The Symbolism of Evil* (1960) and *Freud and Philosophy* (1965),

Ricoeur defines hermeneutics as the task of deciphering double-meaning symbolic expressions. The double intentionality of myth and symbol calls for hermeneutics, and hermeneutics is the work of deciphering double-meaning expressions.[70]

The Process of Expression and Understanding Expression

The process of symbolic expression is linked to what Ricoeur calls three great zones of emergence, two of which I shall mention here since the third, poetic imagination, will come up for separate discussion below. The first zone of emergent symbolism is the cosmic dimension of symbols. Symbols are first read *on* the world or some structural elements of the world such as the sky, the sun or moon, the waters, earth, and vegetation.[71] The symbol is in the first place "less spoken *by* men than spoken *to* men"[72] through the expressivity of the living and sacred cosmos. The world speaks to archaic and traditional man. And through his responsive expression of the experience evoked by the cosmic symbol, the matrix of meanings that inspire his further discourse becomes public and perceptible.

Myth places the cosmic symbols into the form of narration of events *in illo tempore* and provides through the narration a paradigm for ritual actions and common forms of thought for those persons who live under the myth and for whom it constitutes the self-understanding of the community. Mythological expression temporalizes the cosmic symbols by placing them in sequence, and it adds reference to the basic form of self-understanding by narrating the destiny of a figure who presents the ideal of the concrete-universal human to the community.[73]

Ricoeur of course focuses on the symbolism of evil and holds that the experience of the fallen will is an even more crucial and disturbing experience of the sacred than is the display of awesome meanings more immediately connected with the central hierophanies of nature such as the transcendence of the sky, and the like, because the experience of evil opens radical questioning concerning the penitant's standing with the sacred.[74] Experience of fallenness provokes symbolic expression in the form of myth. The myth in turn signifies the self-understanding and the experience of time lived out in the concrete context of a historical community. But this is not to say that the myths of the origin of evil are disconnected from cosmic symbols, since the symbols of evil that Ricoeur treats are ultimately derivations of cosmic symbols of evil.

For example, the serpent of Genesis who tempts Eve, and Tiamat, the marine monster vanquished by Marduk in the *Enuma Elish*, are both cosmic symbols of chaos and bad will.

The experience of fallenness that evokes the symbolic expression in the avowal or confession of evil is initially a blind experience, still dominated by the power of emotional anguish. Ricoeur says:

> It is this emotional note that gives rise to the objectification in discourse; the confession expresses, pushes to the outside, the emotion which without it would be shut up in itself, as an impression in the soul. Language is the light of the emotions. Through confession the consciousness of fault is brought into the light of speech; through confession man remains speech, even in the experience of his own absurdity, suffering, and anguish.[75]

But in the context of a linguistic tradition that provides the primary symbols and myth within which one formulates confession of evil, the developing language of fault influences the form of experience itself. The experience of avowal of evil undergoes a transformation that is reciprocal with new expressive renderings of the meaning of the experience. For example, in Ricoeur's study of the expressions of fault stemming from the biblical myth of Genesis that are gathered into the mythological corpus belonging to the Judeo-Christian tradition, he traces the evolution of primary symbols in reciprocity with an emerging consciousness of the meaning of fault. The symbol initially is that of stain as external defilement. Here the symbol expresses the blindness of emotion. At a second level, the symbol of wandering emerges and is understood as the effect of a sinful breaking of a covenant with Yahweh. Here the penitent recognizes his communal complicity. The most advanced level is represented by the symbol of burden representing the guilty conscience. At this stage the symbol of evil is fully subjectivized in avowal of personal guilt. In this last expression, the earlier meanings of defilement and sin continue to sound, but their previous sounding in the language that becomes part of the collective self-understanding provokes a more reflexive symbol, that of burden as figure of guilt.

The second great zone of emergence for symbols is the oneiric dimension, although it is clearly not separated from the process by which symbols appear through nature: "to manifest the 'sacred' on the 'cosmos' and to manifest it *in* the 'psyche' are the same thing. . . . Cosmos and Psyche are the two poles of the same 'expressivity'; I express myself in expressing the world; I explore my own sacrality in deciphering that of the world."[76] Nonetheless, Ricoeur thinks that after the emergence of critical consciousness, which dissolves the self-evidence of myth, it became possible to separate the cosmic and psychic dimensions and to recognize that dreams are symbolic expressions that reveal the private archaeology of the dreamer.

Freud saw in a pathbreaking and convincing way that dream symbolism is the expression of repressed and hidden forces of the unconscious. Dreams are symbolic "texts," which express the "primitive speech of desire" after editing by the work of dream censorship below the level of consciousness. Psychoanalytic theory in fact presents a hermeneutic method that reaches behind the recalled dream account to get at the "text beneath the text" and to decode the messages of the unconscious. It thus offers an alternative hermeneutical program to the "hermeneutics of belief," in which symbol and myth are immediately understood to be transparent to their meaning. According to Ricoeur, the initial impact of the hermeneutic technique offered by psychoanalysis is to divide the hermeneutical field into the "beliefful" interpretation through phenomenology of cosmic symbols in their self-evidence and the "suspicious" interpretation of the systematic distortion of those meanings by the interfering unconscious mind. Ricoeur's response to the split in hermeneutics is to mediate the opposition uncovered there by showing that the symbol is capable of both interpretations. Ricoeur's proposal can be briefly explained as follows.

The Freudian hermeneutic claims successfully to provide a key by which dream symbols and common cultural symbols can be subjected to demystification and removal of illusions adhering to a false consciousness. This form of the hermeneutics of suspicion comes into conflict with the kind of hermeneutics that aims to restore lost meaning through recovery of the naive sense of the symbol taken as truthful voice of the sacred.[77] Ricoeur mediates the opposition by showing how, in the first place, phenomenology of religion and psychoanalysis parallel one another: both are indirect forms of reflection that trace the nature of subjectivity back from the expressions it deciphers. They differ, however, in that phenomenological hermeneutics thematizes consciousness as self-identical, whereas psychoanalysis brackets that self-identity and inquires into the hidden intentions of desire behind the mask of consciousness.[78]

Second, Ricoeur demonstrates how Freudian psychoanalysis as an archaeology of the unconscious points to and finds its completion in one form of phenomenology, that of Hegel's teleology of the Spirit. Hegel's phenomenology in turn points to and is completed by the Freudian theory: the archaeology of desire and teleology of the spirit are two sides of a single phenomenon.[79] Ricoeur shows that whereas both Freud and Hegel aim at developing an authentic self-consciousness from a pale substitute of a self at the outset, each one is the inverse of the other. Freud reads the dream text regressively and analytically to desire as the *Ursprung* of consciousness, and Hegel reads the configurations of spirit progressively and synthetically to absolute knowledge as the *telos* of the Kingdom of God. The nature of language itself, as the mediation between *Ursprung* and *telos*, allows for both hermeneutical programs.

More specifically, what makes this double movement possible is a duality inherent in the symbol itself and the process of its emergence, which Ricoeur calls the "double law of representation": "As standing for objects or things, representation is pretension to truth; but it is also the expression of life, expression of effort or appetite."[80] Symbols themselves have a "mixed texture" that elicits both the regressive hermeneutics of suspicion and the progressive hermeneutics of belief, because symbols are double-vectored and point backward to concealed desire and forward to disclosed truth in hearing the signs of the two great zones of emergence, cosmos and psyche.

Subjective Conditions of Expression

To conclude this chapter I propose to examine what can be traced back to the subject on the basis of Ricoeur's notion of expression. In most general outline, the study of expression reveals three dimensions or successive stages in subjectivity. The three terms that mark out these stages are *first naiveté*, *critique*, and *second naiveté*. Since these are central terms in Ricoeur's hermeneutical theory, I shall elucidate their meaning and interrelation in more detail now.

The initial stage of subjectivity is the one that is the correlate of symbolic and mythic expression. Symbol and myth stand at the birthplace of language, which is "less spoken *by* men than spoken *to* men,"[81] and they constitute a subjectivity of responsive openness to the sacred cosmos. The primary symbols speak directly to the human who stands in immediate and receptive relation to them. Ricoeur acknowledges his ultimate dependence on Heidegger for his notion of symbol in this connection: the speaking of symbol is "like a voice of being."[82] And he adds that in this naive and unquestioning openness to the voice of being, consciousness of self "seems to constitute itself at its lowest level by means of symbolism and to work out an abstract language only subsequently, by means of a spontaneous hermeneutics of its primary symbols."[83]

Consciousness of self is posited in the expressivity of cosmos as it speaks through primary symbols, and it responds by expressing the meaning of being human under the impact of the symbol's direct meaning. The self of first naiveté does this by temporalizing the primary symbols and adding reference to the concrete circumstances of its connection to a historical community by generating myth from the symbols. In his analysis of the symbols and myths of evil, Ricoeur indicates two different expressions of self-understanding in the first naiveté. The distinction is drawn between "speculative" myths of evil such as the *Enuma Elish*, Greek tragedy, and the Orphic myth of the exiled soul and the "reflective" myth of the Judeo-Christian tradition as found in Genesis. Both of the basic types of myth that narrate the origin of evil include reference to a concrete figure who makes the destiny and possibility of the community itself present and perceptible to the group. The principle of division between the two types of myth is whether the fallen condition of the symbolic figure is due to a preexisting structure of being (an evil already there as a symbolic element within the structure of the whole cosmos) as in the speculative myths, or whether fault is due to an act of my deciding in cooperation with an evil already there as in the Adamic myth of Genesis. Both these mythic types make perceptible the meaning of the irrational transition from fallibility to fault, from the essential to the existential, but the meanings differ based on the timing involved. The speculative myths consign the origin of evil to an event past and unrecoverable, for example, the event of creation itself. The reflective myth, however, suggests that the meaning of fault is not merely that man finds himself thrown in the presence of evil, but also that man is *presently* involved in submitting to that evil through actions flowing from the present moment.

Both the speculative and reflective myths represent a naive, precritical structure of consciousness, even though the timing of the primary symbols differs in each case. And for both types the schematization of primary symbols into myth is accomplished just because the display of meaning and plenitude of being expressed in the primary symbols is *not given* to man in his actual existence but must be *aimed at* through mythic expression.[84] Myth restores the lost wholeness of being prior to the rift that separates the self from its essential unity with the world *in intention only*. It does this by way of a reenactment of the primordial drama, which depicts the original plenitude and interprets the fall of man from that wholeness by narrating the events that led to the transition from the essential state of infallibility without fault to the existential condition of fault. First naiveté stands under the immediate self-presentation of meaning by the symbol. But in temporalizing symbols into myth, it expresses its difference from the prelinguistic state of unity with the wholeness of being. Myth now can only indicate that wholeness as *Ursprung* and *telos* of its own expressivity.

The structure of first naiveté in subjectivity has a dynamism to it that ultimately leads to its inversion into critical consciousness. Several steps, however, can be traced en route to the point of inversion. I mentioned in the preceding section how Ricoeur plots three steps of naive consciousness in the Judeo-Christian mythic tradition.[85] On the first level, the symbol of stain as defilement expresses the cry of astonishment at evil as infecting agent there on me. Consciousness here projects the evil deed outside completely and does not yet relate it to the self, though the self is felt as infected. On the second level, the symbol of wandering as sin indicates awareness of failure in a relationship with God. Evil is the result of the broken covenant and is thus subjectivized in part. At the third level, the symbol of burden as the guilt of a servile will brings out the admission of responsibility through the confession "It is I who. . . ." Now for the first time a self-consciousness can refer the symbol of evil to personal responsibility. First naiveté is not exhausted in symbolic expressions of the type just described, however. The primary symbols, the myth that schematizes them, and the symbolic avowals of fault made in response to the mythical meanings in turn give rise to reflective thinking about the symbolic expressions and pave the way for theological and metaphysical concepts or quasi-concepts. Augustine, Aquinas, and Luther, for example, still belong in the first naiveté, in that the conceptuality they develop is worked out under the immediate presence of the unquestioned meaning of effective symbols. First naiveté encompasses the whole movement from original symbolic consciousness through the interpretation of the symbols, which takes the form of metaphysics and precritical theology. Wherever there is some point in consciousness at which the most basic symbol remains unquestioned and unquestionable in its self-evident meaning and truth, there the expression of the symbol and the reality it signifies remain undivided and the first naiveté is intact to that extent.

The second stage of subjectivity is won decisively by Kant, who typifies this structure of selfhood in relentlessly pursuing the peculiarly *critical* question, "*How* do I know what appears to me is as it appears?" This is the question that cuts through the immediacy of naive consciousness by systematically breaking the connection between expression and appearing reality and thereby discovering its power to make the deity appearing in the symbol vanish. It is the subjective correlate to the development of fully literal expression coupled with the demand that all double-meaning expressions be reduced to single-meaning expressions. This demand destroys the immediacy of the symbolic meaning and is effected once any and all appearances are questioned as to the conditions of their possibility. This critical turn, which dislodges the self-evidence of any appearing symbol, can then take the further step toward the suspicious form of critique, which not merely determines to dislodge the self-evidence of symbolic meaning and to question its critical worth but additionally develops alternative hermeneutical programs to unmask the illusion bound up with first, naive reception of symbols by showing some hidden investment of self-interest in the naive consciousness. Feuerbach, Marx, Nietzsche, and Freud all represent extensions of critique into the hermeneutics of suspicion.

The third stage in the progressive actualization of the potentiality of subjectivity, the full emergence of reflexive consciousness in hermeneutics as the "second naiveté," occurs in a restorative hermeneutic that is able to mediate the content of symbolic consciousness through the critical consciousness. This stage represents a new dimension of subjectivity, and is equivalent to a "Second Copernican Revolution" because here is no direct reference to the appearing symbol, either in the naive response or in the critical grasping of symbol. Second naiveté instead has reference to the *consciousness of* the symbol of both the naive and critical forms, so that the agreement or disagreement between those two forms of consciousness can be discerned. Here the "I" self-consciously enters into the naive mode through response to symbolic expressions by reenacting the naive response in "sympathetic imagination," and thereby respects the original, immediate meaning of the symbol. But the "I" also analyzes the symbolic consciousness as revealed in expressions with the tools of critical thought. The subject of second naiveté can play the content recovered through sympathetic imagination and the result of critique off against each other in order to think the meaning of the symbol further. This "I" is no longer the existential self that is in direct relation to the symbol, but is the "I" that synthesizes direct self-world relations. The second naiveté is grounded on the full appearance of reflexivity just because it exists where the naive meaning is mediated through the critical consciousness.

Hermeneutics for Ricoeur at this point involves a return to symbols through a critical mediation of the symbol's direct meaning as it is grasped by the "preunderstanding" that Heidegger articulated in his existential analytic.[86] The recovery of the naiveté through critique proceeds not through discovery of a psychological kinship with the author of symbolic utterance, but demands "a kinship of thought with the thing which is in question" by a reflexive work on the content of the preunderstanding:

> Thus hermeneutics, an acquisition of "modernity," is one of the modes by which that "modernity" transcends itself, insofar as it is forgetfulness of the sacred. I believe that being can still speak to me—no longer, of course, under the precritical form of immediate belief, but as the second immediacy aimed at by hermeneutics. This second naiveté aims to be the postcritical equivalent of the precritical hierophany.[87]

The ultimate aim of hermeneutics for Ricoeur is not simple extension of reflexivity, but a "qualitative transformation of reflexive consciousness."[88] We shall see in the following chapter how Ricoeur advances toward this goal by working out a theory of text.

4 • Ricoeur's Hermeneutical Theory

In the period of Ricoeur's work inclusive of *Symbolism of Evil* (1960) and *Freud and Philosophy* (1965), hermeneutics is defined as "a work of understanding that aims at deciphering symbols."[1] In his mature interpretation theory, however, hermeneutics is initially linked to the more general problem of ordinary language and then beyond that to the theory of text.[2] This extension of the hermeneutical field follows Ricoeur's recognition that double-meaning expressions are not limited to symbols as he defined them, since the qualities of polysemy and ambiguity adhere to the nature of ordinary language at the level of word and sentence. Hermeneutics must attend to the nature of discourse as such and assume the scope of "the decoding of messages based on polysemic words."[3]

But the proposal of a philosophy of discourse by no means exhausts the hermeneutical problem for Ricoeur, who sides with Dilthey in thinking that the true locus of the hermeneutical problem is that of written texts.[4] Discussion of the nature of discourse is conceived as preliminary and foundational for the presentation of a hermeneutical theory focused on the unique problems associated with understanding plurivocal meaning in written texts. I shall follow Ricoeur's pattern of progression in this chapter by describing first the nature of ordinary language as discourse and then the theory of text and its place in Ricoeur's general theory of interpretation.

The Nature of Discourse

It may be recalled how in *Fallible Man* Ricoeur identified the infinite pole of the theoretical synthesis with discourse as language in use, which he said is made up of two basic units, the noun and the verb. The combination of noun and verb forms the sentence by means of which language can be put to use to say something about something. Now, in working out the theory of discourse in more detail, Ricoeur expands this discussion in order to encompass and account for recent developments in linguistic science. Instead of accounting merely for the combination of nouns and verbs in sentences, a reflection on discourse must account additionally for the distinction that has been drawn in recent discussion in linguistics between the production of *sentences* on the one hand and the system of *signs* on the other. The noun-verb duality at the level of the sentence has been eclipsed by a duality of levels of language.[5]

The opening of this duality between levels of language is the result of the advances of linguistic science which, by constituting language as an autonomous object of investigation by a neutralized subject, has successfully isolated the synchronic and closed system of signs (or lexemes) in abstraction from all conditions of language in use. In this way it excludes all reference to time and history as well as to the function of saying something *about* something, in order to concentrate solely on the linguistic codes that govern the combinations of lexemes and thus make the inventory of signs into a *structure*. Thus linguistics has developed an approach to language that does not give a priority to discourse in the classical sense but is antagonistic to it. *Semantics*, as the disciplined inquiry into the principles of discourse, is thereby opposed by *semiotics*, which takes the sign rather than the sentence as the basic unit and attempts to analyze how linguistic signs fit into systems on the basis of codes. *Semiotics* in the broad sense refers not only to linguistic theory with its units of phonemes, lexemes, semantemes, but also to the theory of structuralist analysis of texts, which arises from the success of applying principles of linguistic science to myth and literature. Ricoeur's proposal attempts to restore priority to the semantic dimension of discourse and to prevent its total eclipse by the semiotic by mediating the opposed terms in a renovated concept of discourse that embraces both levels of language.

The semiotic model of language is indebted to the fundamental distinction coined by de Saussure, founder of modern linguistics, between *langue* and *parole*. Briefly, *langue* is "the code—or the set of codes—on the basis of which a particular speaker produces *parole* as a particular message."[6] Code and message are opposites in several key respects. On the one hand, the message is individual, it participates in diachronic (i.e., sequential) temporality as a speech event, it is intended by someone, and it is arbitrary and unnecessary in that message is the product of a free act. The code on the other hand is collective, it exists in time as "a set of contemporaneous elements," that is, in the synchronic dimension of time, it is not intended but anonymous and the product of an unconscious structuring process at the cultural level, and it is systematic and compulsory to the community of speakers.[7] Semiotics brackets the message for the sake of the code and thereby defines language as an empirical object.

The postulates that underlie the semiological approach to language, and beyond that the structuralist approach to texts, are these: (1) synchrony is more fundamental than diachrony because system is always more intelligible than patterns of change; (2) semiotics applies to finite sets of signs (as in a lexicon for a language or a single text); (3) the signs in a system governed by a code are defined purely by their relation to other signs in the same system, and therefore are merely formal and lack any "substantial existence"; (4) the system of signs is closed, in that there are no relations to nonsemiotic realities at all. The system of signs includes the signifier (e.g., a vocable) and the signified (the specified value in the lexical system) but includes no reference beyond the interconnection of signs. Under these postulates, language is a self-sufficient system of inner relationships, a world of its own, and no longer is a mediation between mind and reality.[8] Language as discourse is suppressed in the semiotic subordination of *parole* to *langue*.

Ricoeur's contention is that language cannot be reduced in this way to a system of signs because language in use betrays a synthetic structure that is undissolvable by the postulates of semiotics: "This structure is the synthetic construction of the sentence itself as distinct from any analytic combination of discrete entities."[9] The sentence cannot be reduced to a combination of signs but is an autonomous entity different in kind from the sign. There is a hiatus and change in level between sign and sentence and therefore also between semiotics and semantics. Of the two, semantics has ontological superiority over semiotics because the entities examined by semiotics—signs—are merely virtual entities whereas sentences actualize the virtualities of the system in the meaning-event of discourse.[10]

What, then, are the characteristics of discourse (*parole*) and how is discourse related to the semiotic dimension of language? Here I shall specify the traits that are essential to language as discourse and that distinguish it from language as system according to Ricoeur. I do so because these distinctions carry important hermeneutical implications, which will be developed when the discussion here reaches the level of text rather than that of the spoken sentence. Ricoeur holds that the basic structure of discourse is the same *subject-object structure* that we saw characterizing the nature of the self as *Tathandlung*. The subject-object structure is developed with respect to discourse in two ways: (1) as a dialectic between event and meaning, and (2) as a dialectic between sense and reference. I shall consider these in turn.

The initial distinction Ricoeur draws from the subject-object structure of discourse is that of event and meaning. Subjectively considered, discourse is always the actualization of the codes of *langue* and thus distinct from the ontologically virtual status of the system. Objectively considered, discourse is always the communication of what is said as the propositional content of a sentence. This content is constructed by the combination of functions of the elements of the sentence: the logical subject denotes something relatively singular by means of grammatical devices such as use of proper names, pronouns, demonstratives, and definite descriptions; and the predicate says something relatively universal about the subject. Singular identification and universal predication are intertwined into the objective meaning of the sentence through the verb, which attributes what is relatively universal to the particular and adds reference to existence in time.[11] Event and meaning are abstracted from the sentence as a whole, and the relation between event and meaning is expressed in the axiom "If all discourse is actualized as an event, all discourse is understood as meaning."[12] As event discourse is fleeting and transient, but as meaning it endures in the propositional content.

The subject-object structure of discourse allows a further distinction at the level of meaning: meaning is both subjective as what the speaker intends to say and objective as what the conjunction of identification and predication yields. Reference to the speaker's intention (or "utterer's meaning") can be found within the objective sense (or "utterance meaning") through grammatical devices known as "shifters." The personal pronouns, for example, have no objective meaning but serve to refer the sentence back to the speaker as "I." So too do the tenses of the verb, inasmuch as they focus on the present time of the speech event and speaker, as do the adverbs of space and time as well as the demonstratives. The important points here are that the meaning of discourse is always dialectically related to the event of discourse and that the speaker's intention is not given a psychological interpretation but is defined purely semantically: "No mental entity need be hypothesized or hypostastized. The utterance meaning points back towards the utterer's meaning thanks to the self-reference of discourse to itself as event."[13]

Other dimensions of the event-meaning dialectic include the following. In performative discourse (following J. L. Austin and his analysis of the function of promises) the speaker does something in his saying, and his deed is governed by semantic rules such as the rule to place all promises in the first-person singular. That doing is the *illocutionary* act in the event of discourse, and it is distinct from its objective correlate, the *perlocutionary* effect: what I yield in the doing of a saying. There is also an *interlocutionary* act insofar as discourse is always communication.[14] Through the event-meaning dialectic, the event of discourse is taken up into the propositional content to the extent that the private experience can become public through discourse. The sense becomes public but the experience as lived remains private. But this becoming public of the sense is also an event—the happening of dialogue—insofar as discourse connects the speech-event with the event of hearing.

What is communicated in the event of dialogue is, of course, the sense of the sentences. The sense is transferred to a hearer because the sense is external to the event as such: "This exteriority of discourse to itself—which is synonymous with the self-transcendence of the event in its meaning—*opens* discourse to the other. The message has the ground of its communicability in the structure of its meaning."[15] Propositional content best survives the exteriorization of meaning from event, but the illocutionary act is also indicated objectively through grammatical moods, use of imperatives or optatives, and the like. The perlocutionary dimension is the least exteriorizable of the three, and this points out the potential ambiguity of all discourse in that it always relies on context to screen the multiple senses of words combined in sentences. So far, meaning has been developed in dialectical relation to event where meaning is the objective side of discourse as the propositional content and event is the subjective side. Now the objective meaning can itself be taken in two ways, which together constitute a dialectic that "is so original that it can be taken as an independent guideline" to discourse, and yet in the end is not unconnected with the event-meaning dialectic.[16]

Ricoeur divides meaning or sense into *Sinn* (sense or meaning) and *Bedeutung* (reference). Sense is here specified as the "what" of discourse and reference as the "about what." This distinction is basic to discourse in that sense and reference can only exist for sentences in use and do not pertain to the system of signs in *langue*, since signs refer only to other signs in a system. Whereas the sense of discourse is objective and immanent in the discourse while pointing beyond itself in indicating something outside it as referent, the referent must be given independently of the grasping of the sense, though it is locatable only through the clues in the sense. The referential function of discourse relates language to the world and thereby establishes the correspondence-relation by which discourse can claim to be true.[17]

The sense-reference dialectic can be connected with the event-meaning dialectic in this way. Reference is bound up with the event of discourse in that to refer is what a speaker does in a situation. But this event is structured by the objective form of meaning through which the speaker refers: "The sense, so to speak, is traversed by the referring intention of the speaker."[18]

The hermeneutical implications of Ricoeur's position can now be made clear. This theory of discourse signals the pursuit of a middle path between structuralist and Romantic alternatives at either extreme, while it allows Ricoeur to incorporate aspects of each alternative into his own theory. On one side, the sense-reference dialectic situates the structuralist approach of semiotics as a necessary but insufficient aspect of a hermeneutically significant theory of language. If one proposes to limit the notion of sense to the codification of signs as in the semiotic model, Ricoeur rejoins that language could not be meaningful at all if it were not fundamentally referential in the first place: "The semiotic definition of the sign as an inner difference between signifier and signified presupposes its semantic definition as reference to the thing for which it stands."[19] Semiotics, in Ricoeur's theory, is reserved a place to decipher the sense of discourse, but is insufficient as an alternative approach to language because it neglects the referential side of discourse, which in fact has a status that is ontologically prior to that of the side of discourse which conveys sense. Semiotics is a legitimate hermeneutical tool, but it is limited to a preparatory role.

On the side of the other alternative—the Romanticist tradition of hermeneutics—the event-meaning dialectic allows Ricoeur to overcome the priority given to the speaker's or author's intention by Schleiermacher and Dilthey. Ricoeur's axiom—"if discourse is actualized as event, all discourse is understood as meaning"— preserves a place for the subjective intention (utterer's intention) in the event of discourse while still insisting on the objective exteriority of what is to be understood as such. He thus undercuts the assumption of the psychologizing hermeneutic, which neglects the meaning side of the event-meaning dialectic. For Ricoeur, "the concepts of intention and dialogue are not to be excluded from hermeneutics, but instead are to be released from the onesidedness of a non-dialectical concept of discourse."[20]

Such is Ricoeur's notion of discourse. Now, before we can arrive at the theory of text we must trace how discourse changes in the passage from speaking to writing. The leading thread of Ricoeur's thought on this matter is that written discourse is not a defective form of spoken discourse but rather that discourse comes into its full manifestation when it is inscribed.[21]

We have seen how Ricoeur place the dialectic between the event of language and the meaning of language at the center of this theory of discourse. Discourse is actualized in a fleeting event between interlocutors but understood as objective sense that is exteriorized from the event. In the passage from spoken discourse to text, this dynamic is heightened in importance and altered with respect to the arrangements of elements that make up the structure of discourse. The exaggeration of the event-meaning polarity and the change in the discourse situation give the problem of text its privilege within the framework of Ricoeur's general theory of interpretation. I shall now briefly explain how this is so.

In the first place, the situation of living speech is one in which the interlocutors are present to one another in the sense that the speakers share a world and linguistic milieu out of which the words arise and to which they make reference.[22] Living speech displays the shared horizon of dialogue, and this advantage minimizes the distance and gap between objective meaning and the event of discourse. Utterer's meaning and utterance meaning tend to combine into an inseparable unity, and the exteriorization of the objective sense of the words from the event of speaking them is minimized. With the advent of text, however, the event-meaning dialectic assumes a new dimension. Ricoeur puts it this way:

> What happens in writing is the full manifestation of something that is in a virtual state, something nascent and inchoate, in living speech, namely, the detachment of meaning from the event. But this detachment is not such as to cancel the fundamental structure of discourse discussed in my first essay (i.e., event-meaning dialectic). The semantic autonomy of the text which now appears is still governed by the dialectic of event and meaning. Moreover, it may be said that this dialectic is made

obvious and explicit by writing. Writing is the full manifestation of discourse.[23]

In the case of textual language, meaning is exteriorized and alienated from the event of discourse. The language still shows objective signs of the event of communication in its grammatical references to the "utterer's meaning," but that event is no longer directly accessible.[24] The event of understanding now becomes a task and a goal. To return the alienated meaning to an event of appropriation becomes the specific aim of hermeneutics. Exteriorization of meaning and its distance from the event of discourse in act signals the emergence of the full problem of hermeneutics. In this sense for Ricoeur hermeneutics begins where dialogue breaks off and written text begins.[25]

The second characteristic of textual language as opposed to living speech assures that the writing-reading relation is not a species of the speaking-hearing relation but has a uniqueness that poses the hermeneutical problem in full force. It is that with text the elements in the structure of discourse are not the same as in the case of shared conversation. The "autonomy of the text" is marked not only by the exteriorization of meaning, but also by the dismantling of the shared world and the replacement of the subjectivity of one speaker by the subjectivity of the text. Since the world is not displayed as shared horizon of the dialogue, the text requires an effort of interpretation precisely to work out the kind of world that the text does present.[26] And since there is no speaking subject over against the reader to give gestural and phonic clues as to how the respondent ought to understand the event of the disclosure of meaning, the text itself occupies the position of subject over against the reader. The reader must now decipher in the objective structure of the text itself the code that gives the clue for actualization of meaning as event. In those two ways, the problem of text commands central position for hermeneutical theory. The reason why for Ricoeur text is the full manifestation of discourse, is that with the inscription of meaning and its isolation from event, language displays the full scope of its creative and renewing capabilities. With the substitution of text for conversation, it becomes possible for anyone with the ability to read to interpret the meaning there and to actualize that meaning in a unique event of understanding. The reader is placed in the full openness of language through text, because he or she is able to encounter a new meaning issuing from a world beyond the immediate horizon of shared conversation. The text extends the opportunity for understanding, and it offers the real possibility to broaden one's horizon in unforeseen ways. In addition, the text gives rise to a chain of interpreters, and the history of response to the hermeneutical challenge of actualizing meaning in a new event of understanding itself becomes a text for interpretation. By its heightening of the event-meaning polarity and substitution of text for speaker, textuality uncovers a depth in language that would remain implicit in a tradition of living speech alone.

Now what exactly constitutes discourse as text? Ricoeur's answer is that writing or inscription is the quality that creates semantic autonomy of the text.[27] But this answer might be misleading. It would seem that spoken poetry, legend, or recitation of myth, and so on, even when part of an oral tradition, alone could still exhibit the signs of semantic autonomy. Meaning in these cases would still be exteriorized to a greater degree than with conversation, and the world displayed in the language might require reconstruction. Conversely, a written note from a friend does not necessarily show the characteristics of text just on account of its inscription. It would seem that the peculiar quality of text, whether written or spoken, would be the display of structure that makes a discourse a *work*. The discussion of this notion brings us now to consider Ricoeur's thought on the text more closely.

Theory of Text

Text as Object

Ricoeur's category of text stands under the category of discourse as described in the preceding section. This means that the basic characteristics of discourse—the event-meaning dialectic and the relation between sense and reference—apply to the notion of text. We already saw how text displays a greater distancing of meaning from event than is the case in living speech. In this section I shall examine the reverberations of that objectification of meaning on the two central components of meaning: sense and reference. According to Ricoeur, just as sentences have sense and reference, so too do texts taken as wholes. But because of the alienation of meaning that adheres to the nature of text as such, texts tend to be highly crafted with respect to the configuration of the sense. Since the interlocutor is replaced by the text and the world of that text must be reconstructed, the sense is submitted to a labor of design not found in living speech. In text the sense must be structured so as to enable return of the meaning to an event of understanding. At the level of text, the sense is designated by Ricoeur to be the *structure* of the text as the "immanent design of discourse." The reference of text he claims is twofold: texts refer both to an intended *"world of the text"* and to the "self."[28] Let us look at these two dimensions of textual meaning in turn.

Text as Structured Work

The first step in Ricoeur's consideration of text is to designate its immanent design as work in the literal sense, that is, as a result of labor and the object of a praxis and a technique.[29] The production of a work of discourse is described as the imposition of a form on matter. The matter in this case is the unique message submitted to formal rules of production. These rules concern composition, belonging to a genre, and individual style.[30] This process by which a singular message is formed accomplishes a specific kind of *objectification* of the discourse that makes possible a *structural treatment* of the text (as we shall see in the next section where I shall consider the process of interpreting texts). But at the same time, recognition that the work is formed through the codification of an individual message implies that the modes of discourse as work (e.g., poem, narrative, essay) are fashioned for the sake of the message to be communicated, and not the contrary. The very nature of text as work indicates that a structural treatment that highlights code or deep-structure over message violates its own mode of being. A text intends to signify what the work is about, just as the sense of a sentence presupposes the priority of concern with the reference of that sentence.

The three traits of a linguistic work—composition, genre, and style—play an important role in Ricoeur's theory of discourse and deserve further description now. First, with respect to composition of a work, the rule is that a work is a larger unit of discourse than a sentence; the work must display some higher level of organization than the mere predicational link that constitutes a sentence. Now, the worker with language knows that what Ricoeur calls composition after Aristotle's *taxis* (i.e., composition), is not neutral to the message it is to form, because the orchestration of the sequence of sentences will provide "the first con-text for each partial meaning. As such it delineates a relatively closed space for each individual sentence's interpretation." Ricoeur refers to the composition as the "teleological structure of a work of art as a system of wholes and parts. This structure is similar, to an extent, to the constitution of a living organism."[31] The point here is that the text is a structured whole to the degree that it is not a sum of parts but a "hierarchy of topics" that maps out a "topology" of discourse.

Second, all discourse as work must be submitted to specific codes of production that generate individual pieces. These rules of codification produce essays, narratives, poems as modes of discourse or *genres*. Genres are not in the first place classifications for the diversity of works, but are initially rules of production. Just as a human being cannot be submitted to a taxonomy as a member of a genus with a specific difference such as rational animal, but is the one whose essence is to exist,[32] so too a work of discourse is not an entity with certain properties, but is the result of encoding a message according to genetic rules. The genre has a genetic function, not a taxonomic one: it generates individual messages according to its codes and thus is inseparable from the sense of the text just because "the dynamics of form is at the same time a dynamics of thought."[33]

Third, the work should display a unique *style*; it should exhibit a special way of making connections that allows us to identify it as an individual. For Ricoeur this is the decisive trait if art is indeed the place in human existence where individuality still asserts itself against the expanding and pervasive "anonymity of technological products."[34]

In sum, the three traits of the text as structured work function to *fix* discourse and to provide clues for the disclosure of the meaning carried by the signs. Composition, genre, and style all are devices that serve to close the work in on itself in order to preserve it from distortion. They all work to open the meaning of the discourse to a temporal chain of interpreters who think differently about the sense there in the "immanent design of discourse." In other words, the structure of the work secures the survival of meaning after the work has been generations removed from its author's lifetime, and it presents new possibilities for illuminating situations different from those that surrounded its original intention. It does this in part by the sense carried by the form alone. But additionally the structure of the text fixes a permanent meaning by its function of pointing away from itself to what Ricoeur calls the "world of the text." That brings us to the second dimension of the text as object.

Text as Projection of a World

The "world of the text" is the central category in Ricoeur's hermeneutical program because in the end the text-world is what is to be understood and interpreted. If to understand a sentence is to follow its movement from sense to referent, then in Ricoeur's hermeneutical theory, to understand a text is likewise to follow the direction from what it says as structure to what it talks about as world of the text:

> The structure of the work is in fact its sense, and the world of a work is its reference. . . . Hermeneutics then is simply the theory that regulates the transition from structure of the work to world of the work. To interpret a work is to display the world to which it refers by virtue of its "arrangement," its "genre," and its "style."[35]

The hermeneutically unproblematic case of reference to a world by a text is that of a descriptive or scientific text. Such a single meaning extends the power of ostensive references in spoken discourse to text by use of univocal language. In this instance the sense of the text refers directly to what Ricoeur calls the "world of everyday language,"[36] by which he means the world of sense perception that is designated by way of literal expressions. This first sense of world, then, is the sum of objects available through descriptive accounts of reality. It is in this sense that he speaks of the "Greek world" as the nonsituational reference available, say, through travel accounts, geographical reports, historical monographs, and so on, which recreate the physical setting.

The hermeneutically significant sense of *world* for Ricoeur is enjoined with the interpretation of literary or poetic works, by which Ricoeur means works that refer not to the physical world but to a possible world accessible to the imagination. Ricoeur's claim is that

> die Zerstörung eines primären Verweisungsbezugs durch Fiktion und Poesie die Bedingung der Möglichkeit dafür sei, dass ein sekundärer Verweisungsbezug freigelegt werde, der die Welt nicht mehr nur als Bereich verfügbarer Gegenstände erreicht, sondern als das, was Husserl "*Lebenswelt*" und Heidegger "In-der-Welt-Sein" nennt.[37]

> the destruction of a primary reference through fiction and poetry

is the condition of the possibility for laying open a secondary reference which no longer reaches the world only in the domain of accessible objects, but as that which Husserl calls "lifeworld" and Heidegger "being in the world."

Poetic diction effaces the ostensive and descriptive references in order to redirect attention to "aspects of our being in the world that cannot be said in a direct descriptive way, but only alluded to, thanks to the referential values of metaphoric and, in general, symbolic expressions."[38]

This second sense of *world* is one step removed from the actual world of descriptive language. Fiction removes us from the perceived world in order to open up new possibilities for being-in-the-world accessible to the imagination in that the imagination constructs the fictional text-world as a place in which a new mode of being is manifest. Ricoeur's position on the referential power of fictional texts is expressed in this quotation:

Fiktion und Poesie zielen auf das Sein, jedoch nicht im Modus des gegebenen Seins, sondern im Modus des Seinkönnens. Eben dadurch wird die alltägliche Wirklichkeit mit Hilfe dessen, was man die durch dieLiteratur bewirkten imaginativen Veränderungen des Wirklichen nennen könnte, verwandelt.[39]

Fiction and poetry point to being, however not in the mode of given being, but in the mode of potential being. Just in that way everyday reality is transformed with the help of that which one could call the imagined alterations of the real which are effected through literature.

The "world of text" means the ensemble of references opened up by the power of fictional language to suggest images that are formed in response to the content of the text. The world constructed in the imagination would then be the world of the text for Ricoeur.

But elsewhere Ricoeur uses the same term to indicate a second notion of "world of the text." In this second sense the text-world is not the world formed in imaginative response to figurative meaning, but is formed by intercepting that kind of precritical reading to analyze the structure of the fictional meaning as the code underlying the poetic message and then to follow the significatory power of that structure.[40] Ricoeur's claim is that the structure of the text as uncovered by analysis points to the world of the text as the referent of the objective sense of the text.[41] Ricoeur does not distinguish between these two notions of the "world of the text." They are quite distinct, however, and ought not to be covered by a single term.

The two senses of "world of the text" can be distinguished from each other and set in relation to each other in the following way (although this suggestion will alter Ricoeur's terminology somewhat). The "world of the text" can be used as a term to refer to the set of references formed by the reader's imagination as it works on the content of the story. The "reader" here is the direct and first-order subject and not the reflexive or hermeneutical subject. A second term—*ontological world*—can be used to refer to the world projected *by* the analyzed structure of the text *for* the reflexive subject. The ontological world, as I shall use the term henceforth, is distinct from the text-world because it is not formed by the imagination but is articulated as a work of description undertaken by the reflexive subject.

Ricoeur is explicit in acknowledging that his notion of "world of the text" is adapted from Heidegger's analysis of *Verstehen* and *Befindlichkeit* as structures of being-in-the-world. Ricoeur says that for Heidegger,

> the moment of understanding responds dialectically to being-in-a-situation, as the projection of our ownmost possibilities in those situations where we find ourselves. I want to take this idea of the "projection of our ownmost possibilities" from his analysis and apply it to the theory of the text. Actually, what is to be interpreted in a text is a proposed world, a world that I might inhabit and wherein I might project my ownmost possibilities. This is what I call the world of the text, the world properly belonging to this unique text.[42]

Now if we apply what Heidegger means by *world* to texts in order to bring out the worldliness of fictional texts, we can see that this quality of texts comes out only in what I have above called the "ontological world" and not the "text-world." It may be recalled that Heidegger approaches the articulation of the worldliness of the world by way of the dimension of the world (*Umwelt*) present to *Dasein* in its everyday dealings with things at hand such as tools. The world is charted out by Heidegger as a referential series whose structure is that of *Bedeutsamkeit* or meaningfulness. It is on the basis of world that anything *within* the world can have meaning for *Dasein*. The referential series is one that proceeds from "I" as the originating point of *Dasein*'s thinking and experiencing and links up with a "for the sake of *Dasein*" as the last term in the series. This last term grounds the series in the concrete "this one here" of *Dasein*'s existing, and the series or world-context is the openness of the "this one here" to being as it can be experienced in the world.

Heidegger uses the example of the world of tools to indicate the worldliness of the world, and the principal features of the world in its worldliness are described as follows. Heidegger says that in our prereflective use of tools, a tool is something *in order to*. . . ("*Zeug ist wesenhaft 'etwas, um zu. . .'*").[43] There are various kinds of *Um-zu*, such as *Dienlichkeit* (serving-for), *Beiträglichkeit* (contributing-to), *Verwendbarkeit* (usability-for), and *Handlichkeit* (handiness-for), but common to them all is their having been ordered to an"I" as the source of a projective understanding that is moved to pick up a tool *in order to* do something on the basis of *Dasein*'s preliminary sketch of it. Also common to the types of *Um-zu* is the *Verweisung* or referential structure of the *Um-zu:* the tool refers to something else. Heidegger calls the concrete *Verweisung* of a tool in putting it to use its *Bewandtnis* (from *bewenden*, to leave it at that, and evoking *verwenden*, to use or apply).

Recalling Heidegger's example, let us imagine that "I" pick up a hammer in order to do something. The hammer has its *Bewandtnis* in hammering, and this *Bewandtnis* (a term to designate the *being* of the entity in question) in turn refers ahead to a *Wozu* which in turn is also a referring *Bewandtnis*. In the Heidegger example,

> mit diesem (Hämmern) hat es seine Bewandtnis bei Befestigung, mit dieser bei Schutz gegen Unwetter; dieser "ist" umwillen des Unterkommens des Daseins, das heisst, um einer Möglichkeit seines Seins willen. Welche Bewandtnis es mit einem Zuhandenen hat, das ist je aus der Bewandtnisganzheit vorgezeichnet.[44]
>
> hammering has its *Bewandtnis* in fastening something together, this latter has its *Bewandtnis* in protection against bad weather; this protection "is" for the sake of *Dasein*'s coming under cover, that is, for the sake of a possibility of *Dasein*'s being. Whatever *Bewandtnis Dasein* has with something at hand, that *Bewandtnis* has always been designated on the basis of a totality of such *Bewandtnis*-relations.

The series of *Verweisungen* encompasses the referring of the hammer to hammering, which in turn refers to the securing of protection against bad weather, which refers to *Dasein*'s coming into shelter. This series contributes to a *Bewandtnisganzheit*, a totality of references, on the basis of which any tool can refer in the way it does. The last term in the series is always the *Worumwillen* or "for the sake of *Dasein*," since the context formed by the references is always that within which tools can have meaning for the sake of the concrete projects of *Dasein*.

The totality of references *(Bewandtnisganzheit)* has the structure of meaningfulness *(Bedeutsamkeit)* since it is always on the basis of that totality of references and within that context that *Dasein* can let the tool be what it is in its *Bewandtnis*. The *Bedeutsamkeit*, then, is the world in its worldliness as expressed by Heidegger: "Das Worin des sichverweisenden Verstehens als Woraufhin des Begegnenlassens von Seiendem in der Seinsart der Bewandtnis ist das Phänomen der Welt (The milieu, *in* which we understand ouselves through understanding anything that is, as the *horizon* of the encounter with entities in their being put into activity, is the phenomenon of the world)."[45]

Befindlichkeit and *Verstehen* enter this description in the following way. *Dasein* finds itself there, in the world, through mood and responds dialectically by throwing out or pro-jecting the "I" upon both the *Worumwillen* and the *Bedeutsamkeit*. By letting entities (e.g., a hammer) be, *Dasein* frees the tool for its possibilities and thereby *Dasein* understands itself in terms of possibility through its ontological mode of being-in-the-world. The world of the tool is a series of references that is actualized when *Dasein* places a tool into its *Bewandtnis* by understanding it for the sake of *Dasein*. The so actualized world extends from "I" to "this one here" as the meaningful context within which *Dasein* uses its tools.

Now if we substitute a text for a tool in order to circumscribe the set of connections that make up the "world of the text," the referential series is made in this way between "I" and "this one here": "I" pick up a text that has its *Bewandtnis* in reading. This in turn refers to the gleaning of the sense of the text, which refers to forming images of the world depicted by the content for the imagination, which in turn can refer to a mode of being that I could inhabit, which refers to a possibility for me to appropriate being in a certain way for the sake of self-understanding. The world of the text in the Heideggerian sense would be the network of connections between "I" and my appropriation of meaning. This sense of *world of the text* is equivalent to what I called "ontological world" previously in this section. As the context within which a text can be freed for its possibilities to carry meaning by presenting a possibility for *Dasein* to be, the "ontological world" includes me as the reader as well as the literary world formed by the imagination in response to the language in the text.

In sum, Ricoeur is correct in thinking that I can understand a text in the same way that I understand how to hammer. But it is clear that the one term *world of the text* ought to be restricted to the imagined literary world since Ricoeur uses it in that way, and that a second term—*ontological world*—ought to refer to the context within which "I" am related to "this one here" by way of the imaginative work of reading a fictional text. The ontological world so defined is the world opened for the reflexive subject as it intercepts the prereflective process of reading. It is projected *by* the structure of the text *for* the reflexive reader who bends back to recover in analysis the direct relation to the imagined literary world of the text. The next section will attempt to provide a more thorough analysis of this process and thus to describe more completely the major elements of Ricoeur's hermeneutical theory.

The Process of Textual Understanding

In working out the process of textual understanding, Ricoeur brings his theory of discourse as event and meaning to bear on the dichotomy, inherited from Dilthey, between *Verstehen* and *Erklären*. Ricoeur's theory of textual understanding aims at mediating the conflict between the two opposed procedures on the basis of discourse and at combining understanding and explanation into a dialectical model of textual interpretation.

It is well known that Dilthey saw a *break* between understanding and explanation, which he traced to the ontological discontinuity between the mode of being of nature, which appears to the senses, and the mode of being of *Geist*, which is embodied in linguistic expression. With the subsequent rise of linguistic science, it became possible to see what Dilthey never suspected: that the explanatory attitude is indigenous to the field of linguistic expression and is not an alien. We can indeed constitute language as an object of detached study (de Saussure's *langue*) by abstracting from its function as *parole*. We can do so, Ricoeur claims, because discourse includes the exteriorization of meaning from the event of its being uttered. The linguistic process itself is more original than the difference between *langue* and *parole*. And since both are grounded in the nature of language as such, explanatory and understanding processes (which correspond to *langue* and *parole* respectively) are both legitimately part of the whole hermeneutical process and can both contribute to hermeneutical theory.

Discourse is not only event and meaning, however, but also sense and reference. And this latter dialectic ensures that explanation, insofar as it pertains to the analysis of the objective sense of texts taken as immanent design of the text as structured work, is not on a par with understanding. This is so because understanding is always referred beyond the structure of the text to some extralinguistic reality within a possible world that I might inhabit. The center of gravity in discourse is on the signifying of a referent: sense effaces itself and spends itself in pointing to the referent. Consistently with his reflections on discourse as event and meaning as well as sense and reference, Ricoeur heals the rift between understanding and explanation by preserving an element in a dialectical notion of comprehension that is defined by each. But he also maintains the priority of the understanding process over the explanatory process in understanding texts by subordinating the effort to isolate the objective structure of text to the task of following the movement from what the text says to what it speaks about.

For Ricoeur, the initial moment in reading a text is defined by understanding, although it is at a naive level: we guess at the meaning of the text. The interplay of explanation and understanding begins here: the initial impression can be tested, corrected, and deepened by recourse to the objective structure of the text. A sophisticated understanding must pass through the moment of explanation, and hermeneutics encompasses both procedures. Strictly speaking, Ricoeur says these are not two *methods* of approach, since only explanation is methodic: "Understanding is rather the nonmethodic moment which, in the sciences of interpretation, comes together with the methodic moment of explanation. Understanding precedes, accompanies, closes, and thus *envelops* explanation. In return, explanation *develops* understanding analytically."[46] The two procedures tend to overlap and to interpenetrate each other, but the basic difference is that in explanation "we explicate or unfold the range of propositions and meanings, whereas in understanding we comprehend or grasp as a whole the chain of partial meanings in one act of synthesis."[47] I shall attempt to provide adequate description to each of these steps: (1) structural analysis of the sense of a text through explanation; (2) metaphoric signification: from the literal to the figurative; (3) construction of the text-world in which the referent is identified through understanding. The final step, appropriation, will be the topic of a separate chapter to follow.

From Naive Reading to Structural Analysis

The initial moment in Ricoeur's hermeneutic is that of reading the text and gleaning the apparent meaning. In many cases there is no obstruction in such a procedure and structural analysis as such is not needed. For example, Ricoeur's classification of descriptive texts has them grouped together on the basis of their possession of a single meaning alone. These texts do not evoke sophisticated hermeneutical procedures because there is ordinarily no blockage of understanding as it moves from sense to reference. But the second of the two major groups of texts in Ricoeur's scheme, the literary or poetic texts as defined by their doubleness of meaning, do invite interpretative effort. Poetic texts present a second and indirect sense that points to a second and indirect reference in addition to the literal and direct sense-reference configuration. Literary texts play on the figurative and suggestive power of language in its significative capacity to speak of modes of being in the world, and so a special hermeneutical situation prevails in those cases. When one reads a simple-meaning text, the sense of the text points to a perceivable referent against the background of the perceptual world. Techniques of discourse, such as the use of demonstratives, personal pronouns, definite descriptions, tenses of verbs, and so on, open that discourse to what is not discourse and is given independently of the text. But in the case of literary or poetic texts in which there is a figurative sense in addition to a literal one, the figurative sense is present only as a suggestion made by the literal sense. This figurative sense, which is a construction of the imagination, then points to a referent which is also tied to the literal referent. Whatever the text literally refers to must itself point to a referent in the horizon of a suggested world by virtue of that literal object's signifying capacity.

The pattern, then, for understanding double-meaning texts is to guess the figurative meaning in a naive reading and then to subject that initial understanding to a validation through explanation. The naive reading is then adjusted and corrected in light of the objective sense of the text, that is, with respect to the capacity of the structure of the text to signify and suggest a referent in a possible world. Ricoeur likens the initial guess to what Schleiermacher called the "divinatory" aspect of reading.[48] And as with Schleiermacher, the skilled reader in moving through a text for the first time is aware that he will submit that reading to a "structural" explanation as corrective. What is to be guessed is the meaning of the text as a *whole* (which involves a judgment on the hierarchy of topics), the meaning of the text as an *individual* (which involves a sense for the relation of the surface meaning to a depth structure that is the generic code), and the meaning of the text as a product of *style* (which involves determination of which "horizons of potential meaning" are actualized through the metaphoric-symbolic style of the text).[49]

According to Ricoeur, a logic of probability rather than one of empirical verification rules the procedure for validating guesses.[50] If a text can be construed in various ways, then the best reading of that text is the one that can justify its articulation of the figurative sense with respect to the objective structure of the literal sense in the most *consistent* way and in the *deepest* way. That is, the most probable reading is the one that makes sense of the greatest number of details as they fit into a whole and the one that renders all that can be brought forth by the text. In so constructing a procedure of guess and validation, Ricoeur in effect reformulates the "hermeneutical circle" that he inherited from Schleiermacher along more objective lines: the discourse as text is in dialogue with the discourse of the interpreter. The circle is thus drawn within the wholly semantical space of text-interpretation and not in the psychological space proceeding from the relation between the subjectivity of the author and that of the interpreter.[51]

Ricoeur primarily refers to the results of the French school of structuralism in literary criticism in setting forth the method of structural analysis. For example, he cites the work of Algirdas Greimas, Roland Barthes, Claude Bremond, Louis Marin, and especially Claude Lévi-Strauss.[52] In such analysis, which proceeds according to the postulates of the semiotic model of language that I enumerated above (see p. 76), the aim is to uncover the deep-structure or specific generative code that engenders the surface-structure or message. This deep-structure is often expressed as a set of relations between binary combinations. This is so especially in the case of narrative. Other structural forms are indeed possible, however, especially when one considers poetry and essays.

Ricoeur's favorite example is that of Lévi-Strauss's effort in the essay "The Structural Study of Myth." Here the Oedipus myth is broken down into four columns of mythemes, or sentence-long units of meaning. One column has to do with over-esteemed kinship relations and a second column lists under-esteemed kinship relations. A third column concerns monsters and their destruction, and a fourth entails the use of names to suggest difficulty in walking upright. In Lévi-Strauss's analysis the deep-structure (a code or structural law) of the myth comes out in correlating the columns as follows: one and two in turn reverse the esteem of the kinship relations with respect to positive and negative assignment of value. Columns three and four affirm and negate autochthony respectively. Hence the key to the deep structure is that four is to three as one is to two; or, "The overrating of blood relations is to the underrating of blood relations as the attempt to escape autochthony is to the impossibility to succeed in it."[53] This analysis discloses, to Ricoeur's satisfaction, the structural law of the Oedipus myth. It *explains* the myth but does not yet interpret it. Although Lévi-Strauss's example is used by Ricoeur to illustrate structural analysis, the pattern of combination of binary relations is one that pertains specifically to myth as such and does not necessarily carry over to other forms. Nor does it seem to apply to all myths, especially those for which the diachronic dimension is crucial and cannot be bracketed, such as the Old Testament narrations of Yahweh's intervention in history.[54] So "structuralist" methods in the strict sense of the French schools are not exhaustive.

Another paradigm for structural analysis would be that of isolating the self-world relations in a literary text along the lines of Heidegger's analysis of the *Welt-Sein, In-Sein, Dasein* structure. In this case one could display the pattern of connections within a text between kinds of world-configurations (e.g., spectator world, world recalled, auditory world, world imagined, etc.), kinds of media relating self to world (e.g., sight, memory, sound, imagination), and kinds of self (spectator self, self-remembering self, hearkening self, imagining self, etc.). The point here is that the notion of structure should not be restricted to Ricoeur's repeated reference to the French schools, which concentrate on narrative form, although Ricoeur's hermeneutical writings might seem to suggest that.

Ricoeur's use of structural analysis in hermeneutics carefully disconnects that method from the "structuralist ideology" that often accompanies structural analysis in the French school. For the major figures of structuralism, such as Lévi-Strauss, Barthes, Marin, and others, the legitimate technique of isolating *langue* for analysis is illegitimately extended so as to constitute a decision concerning the ontological status of the text: the meaning of the message is the code and that alone. In other words, texts do not refer outside themselves but are merely presentations of underlying codes.[55] For Ricoeur, explanation of code is at service to understanding the sense and reference and cannot be severed from the hermeneutical task. Ricoeur's claim is that structuralism as ideology misunderstands the essence of code, which is to generate an individual message. Codes to not exist for their own sake.[56] Lévi-Strauss's analysis of the code underlying Oedipus, for example, only makes sense if it serves to point the reader to a mode of being in the world in which an existential conflict is felt in a certain way: "The myth would not even function as a logical operator if the propositions that it combines did not point toward boundary situations."[57] Structural analysis is a necessary stage between naive comprehension and a sophisticated one, but is sorely insufficient as an alternative hermeneutical program.

Metaphoric Signification: From the Literal to the Figurative

In the preceding section I described the first stage of Ricoeur's hermeneutical theory with respect to the process of understanding texts. In brief, Ricoeur proposes that to understand a text is initially to submit a first gleaning of meaning to an explanatory technique that isolates an objective structure so as to validate the meaning first caught. Interpretation involves a dialectic between the prehermeneutical meaning and the results of structural analysis of objective sense. Analysis can confirm and highlight some elements of the prehermeneutical meaning and invalidate and suppress other elements, but in the nature of the case it works on a prereflective grasping of meaning in order to develop that meaning into an explicitly mediated sense.

In so constructing his hermeneutics, Ricoeur is giving methodological specificity to the doctrine of understanding in Heidegger. Interpretation is specified as "*die Ausbildung des Verstehens*."[58] Ricoeur is attempting to show the kind of procedure that would be appropriate to the circular structure of understanding in Heidegger's sense of an explicated comprehension that proceeds out of a preunderstanding. In this section I shall describe how Ricoeur's next stage of hermeneutical theory offers a work of analysis that attempts to provide precision in isolating the process by which the objective sense of a text, once secured through structural analysis, can carry a figurative dimension. The focus here is on the hermeneutically significant case of double-meaning or poetic texts, and the process by which literal meaning opens to figurative meaning Ricoeur calls the *metaphoric process*.[59]

Metaphoric process can unfold at two distinct levels within texts. The first level—that of the *sentence*—is the paradigm for the second level—that of the *text* itself. Just as the literal sense of a sentence can intend a figurative sense, so too can the literal sense of a text intend a figurative sense. For Ricoeur, examination of the way in which the sentence-long metaphors create and discover figurative meaning from the clues in a literal meaning can illuminate the same process by which figurative meanings emerge at the level of texts.[60] Any discussion of Ricoeur's hermeneutical program must note that his theoretical writings analyze metaphoric process at the sentence-level, whereas his only extensive application of the theory of metaphor to actual metaphoric language—the study of the parables in "Biblical Hermeneutics"—unfolds metaphoric process at the level of text. Consequently, the following discussion will assume by *sense* the meaning of that term at the sentence-level, that is, the predicative link between subject and what is attributed to the subject. The ability of an analyzed structure as the objective sense of a text to point beyond itself to a figurative level of sense in texts will not come up for discussion here, because what Ricoeur has had to say about this topic in the context of parable-interpretation will be summarized in the next chapter.

Ricoeur's theory of metaphor finds its most detailed exposition in *The Rule of Metaphor*, where Ricoeur presents a sustained argument for what he calls a *tension* theory of metaphor that can account for *emergent meaning* as a creation of language. Against those leading theorists who present some version of a *substitution* theory of metaphor, which assigns a decorative or emotive role to the figures of speech known as metaphors, Ricoeur claims that the metaphor exposes the very heart of linguistic process. For Ricoeur, metaphor is a matter of semantic innovation by which new information about reality is discovered even as new linguistic meaning is created. The term *metaphoric process* names the activity occurring within a historical language, by which the concepts and insights that illuminate and evoke concrete experience are brought into the light. In the end, the process of writing and understanding metaphor functions as a key for Ricoeur's overall philosophical intention, which is to sustain the query "What does it mean to be human?" This is so because man is the creature with the *word*. And according to Ricoeur, metaphor is a phenomenon of semantic innovation. Metaphor teases the mind into thinking something new by virtue of seeing a resemblance previously unnoticed and unthought: "What is at stake in a metaphorical statement is making a 'kinship' appear where ordinary vision perceives no mutual appropriateness at all."[61] The way this happens is as follows.

When the poet says that "Nature is a temple where living columns . . . ," a tension is set up, which reverberates at three levels and then gives way to and provokes the emergence of new meaning. There is tension within the statement between "nature" and "temple," terminologically designated as tenor and vehicle (I. A. Richards), focus and frame (Max Black), or principal subject and secondary subject. Then there is the tension between two interpretations: between a literal interpretation that succumbs to absurdity and a figurative interpretation "whose sense emerges through nonsense." And third, there is the tension in the copula "to be" itself: in the literal sense of the sentence, "is" means "is not"; but in the metaphorical sense, "is" means "is like." The result is a tension in the relational function of the verb "to be," "between identity and difference in the interplay of resemblance."[62] The new meaning that emerges through this tension is sensed as peculiar because it catches an aspect of reality not brought to light in ordinary use of language. There is the realization that in the metaphor language has organized reality in a different way, and that it has also "made manifest a way of being of things, which is brought to language thanks to semantic innovation."[63] The new meaning is felt as product of creation because it is brought out of the nothing of literal senselessness, but it is also sensed as a discovery since the resemblance previously unnoticed was always there.

How does a living metaphor elicit a new meaning from literal absurdity? According to Ricoeur, in metaphorical language the literal level of meaning abolishes itself in a self-destruction and because of this self-destruction of sense, the literal reference also founders.[64] This is the first and negative step in the process, which conceals a second and positive side: metaphorical meaning emerges with an interpretative "twist" (Monroe Beardsley) on the literal meaning, which extends the meaning so as *to make* sense out of non-sense. And "by drawing a new semantic pertinence out of the ruins of the literal meaning, the metaphoric interpretation *also* sustains a new referential design, through those same means of abolition of the reference corresponding to the literal interpretation of the statement."[65] So "the other reference, the object of our search, would be to the new semantic pertinence what the abolished reference is to the literal meaning destroyed by semantic impertinence."[66] In other words, in a metaphorical statement the literal sense, or some part of the literal sense, can in strict terms be non-sense. But the statement can still elicit a second level of meaning through a metaphorical twist.

One technique for producing the twist by which a figurative meaning emerges is the poetic technique of tying the literal sense to the *sound* of the words in the context of rhythmic cadences, resemblance and opposition between syllables or words, and metric equivalences. New relations of meaning can then be "introduced somehow by the recurrence of phonic form."[67] This proceeds through an interplay that can be set up between the literal level of sense and the sound that takes those two components up into a new and distinct "thingy" substance that seems to possess an "iconic solidity." The further step is that the sense-sound relation can include relations to other sensorial dimensions of meaning through "synaesthetics."[68] The metaphor may synthesize a meaning through sensorial correspondences that form a tangible unity and release a series of images that are let be or "allowed to be by the *epoche* of the (literal) referential relation."[69]

In sum, for Ricoeur metaphoric process involves negation of literal meaning as the condition of a recreation of sense on the basis of a "verbal icon" suggested by the literal language. At the sentence level we can see this process at work in the metaphor "Nature is a temple where living pillars. . . ." Literally, nature is *not* a temple; but the calculated category mistake may allow the reader to see a dimension in both nature and temple that *is like* the other. At the level of text, the reference would be to the literal non-sense of fiction, which nonetheless works on the reader to build a tangible world in the imagination, that is, the "world of the text."

Unfolding the Text-World: From Metaphoric Sense to Metaphoric Referent

So far I have outlined two stages in the process of understanding texts. The first is the submission of a first reading to structural analysis in order to determine the literal sense. The second is the explication of the metaphorical process through which the literal sense suggests a figurative sense. One element in this second step is the suspension, through the non-sense of literal sense, of the literal referential power. But this does not imply that figurative language carries sense without reference. The third stage of this process of understanding textual meaning pertains to the manner in which figurative sense points to a figurative referent on the ruins of the collapse of literal sense and reference. The question is "How does a metaphorical sense signify a metaphorical referent?"

Three terms must be carefully distinguished in order to develop Ricoeur's answer to this question. In the first place, the released images that make of the metaphoric sense a "verbal icon" or a literal "figure of speech" suggest or evoke a *mood*, which is initially felt as an objective state of affairs rather than as a state of the reader's being.[70] Ricoeur refers explicitly to Heidegger's *Befindlichkeit* to specify his meaning.[71] On the basis of this mood as a way of being attuned, the reader forms connections between the images that belong to the metaphoric sense and articulates the *world of the text*, the second key term, which contextualizes the flow of images. Interpretation then has the task "to elaborate the design of a world liberated, by suspension, from descriptive reference."[72]

Now, while Ricoeur often explicitly identifies the world of the text as the referent of figurative sense,[73] the referent of the text is a distinct element from the text-world although profoundly interrelated with it. The referent or *Sache* of the text is not the mood *per se* or the text-world as interconnection of images, but is the self as understood through interpretation. The referent of the text is always found within the text-world and on the basis of the showing or disclosing power of metaphoric sense as it evokes a mood as the attunement to some nonlinguistic reality. That nonlinguistic reality is what Ricoeur calls the *mode of being* signified by metaphor. *Mode of being* is the third element here, and it is the proper referent of a poetic text for Ricoeur. It is a way of connecting "I" and "this one here," happiness and character, or a form of self-understanding.

How, then, does a metaphoric sense signify a mode of being on the basis of a mood within a text-world as the horizon within which one is open to that referent? The requirement of this question is that the distinction be clearly maintained between understanding the metaphoric sense, which points to the metaphoric referent, and the givenness of the referent independently of understanding the sense. The contemporary model for this relation between sense and referent is Heidegger's discussion of *Dasein, Erschlossenheit,* and *Wahrheit* (*Dasein,* Openness, and Truth) in section 44 of *Sein und Zeit*. Heidegger illustrates the relation between saying and showing by means of a literal statement, and Ricoeur deals with the same relation at the level of metaphorical sense and reference. Reference to Heidegger's distinction can, I think, help illuminate the more difficult case of metaphoric signification.

Heidegger gives the example of the statement "Das Bild an der Wand hängt schief" (The picture on the wall is hanging crookedly). This statement conveys a literal sense that in its *Entdeckend-sein* (saying as a pointing to) projects a place of manifestation within the literal, perceivable world. But the same statement also expresses the appearance of the referent, the crookedly hanging picture, within the perceptual world and thus has a dimension of *Entdecktheit* (showing as an appearance of).[74] The sense points to the actual picture, which shows itself independently of the sense. Heidegger's point here is that where one language unites both activities so that there is a correspondence between the saying and showing, we have a manifestation of truth.

Ricoeur's problem is not initially that of truth, but of indicating how a metaphoric sense can say and show in similar fashion. The set of relations would work like this. This literal sense, which would ordinarily point to a place of manifestation in the perceived world where a literal referent could show itself, breaks down in literal non-sense. But the figurative quality of the language releases images that get synthesized into a "verbal icon" (such as "nature *as* a living temple" or "time *as* a beggar"). The central meaning here evokes a mood or state of attunement as the place of manifestation within the text-world or horizon of the imagery where a possible mode of being can show itself as something within the world of the text to which the reader is open. Something in the metaphoric language must allow a way of being, a possible self-understanding, to show itself on the basis of mood and within the context of the evoked imagery.

How can a metaphoric sense, for example a grove of trees seen as a temple, signify a mode of being for Ricoeur? The comparison here is with literal language, where use of demonstratives, shifters, descriptions, and so on, opens the sense of the language to what is outside it in the perceptual world. In the case of metaphoric or figurative language, the literal level of meaning is given a "twist" so that it is clear there is more meaning than the literal level alone. The literal sense must take on a second figurative quality as symbolic language, which opens expectations for the signifying power of literal objects to show something more than their perceptual being. Literary works signify modes of being by creating and discovering them *on* the states of affairs, persons, things described in the fictional world of the text. In the end, the signifying capacity of the described objects allows language to point metaphorically. The metaphorical process projects the figurative sense for the understanding in the form of an image or verbal icon, and the image as symbol shows the reference of that sense. For example, the word *nature* can be knit into a metaphor (e.g., "nature is a living temple") that elicits the image of a grove of trees as living columns in a sacred place. And this in turn evokes a mood as a place of manifestation. Now, as a symbol the image of nature presents or manifests the mode of being projected. Nature as living temple shows itself as a mode of being in the sacred universe, a mode of openness to the sacred as it illuminates the natural world.

Ricoeur's claim is that in metaphoric language, the opening of the language to possible being is marked by the connection between metaphor and symbol. Metaphor and symbol can be distinguished by saying that metaphor is purely a semantic innovation, whereas symbols bring together a linguistic and a nonlinguistic order.[75] Metaphor occurs in the purified air of the *logos*, but it never loses its connection with symbol and is always capable of manifesting the nonsemantic order of symbol. Symbol, unlike metaphor, is engendered in the first place either in the power of the cosmos to signify or in the unconscious as expression of desire in dream. Metaphor, however, is tied to the third zone of emergence, the poetic imagination, which may draw on cosmic and psychic symbols, but subjects them to the poet's craft of semantic work. So while metaphor has the refined quality of being the product of linguistic structuring at a sophisticated level, it preserves its symbolic depth and thus can "show" from the place of manifestation or mood where symbol "testifies to the primordial rootedness of Discourse in Life."[76] Due to the symbolic depth of metaphor, when metaphor projects symbolic meaning, "showing is at the same time creating a new mode of being."[77] The symbol shows what *is like* the image or figure there.

Ricoeur is very clear that the figurative level of meaning in a literary work is not an allegorical meaning. To move from literal to metaphorical sense is not to advance from one set of images to a second set that is already known to carry a traditionally religious or ethical message. Nor is it to move from the imagistic words of the poem or narrative to a "thought" or "proposition" that could be written down in juxtaposition to the poem or narrative as pregiven moral messages. Such allegorical meanings are independent of the language of the poem or narrative and do not contribute to the properly metaphorical sense and reference of the work. They may help in prying out the figurative meaning by indicating that there is more than the surface alone indicates. But the metaphorical meaning is given nowhere but through the literal sense as it is subjected to the "twist" of the process through which meaning emerges. The poem alone manifests that new world of the text and it points, from within that text-world, to the *Sache* as the referent in human experience.[78] How, then, does the interpreter *specify* the metaphorical sense and the referent it shows within the text-world?

In strictest terms, one cannot specify the text-world or referent exactly. But in less than strictest terms, one *can* designate what the poem manifests through the interpretative language of existential analysis. Ricoeur says the metaphorical meaning liberates a world that is to be unfolded in the effort of interpretation at the level that Husserlian phenomenology has designated as the *Lebenswelt* and that Heidegger has called "being-in-the-world."[79] In other words, to interpret the reference of the text as what the poem manifests within the text-world involves some use of the independent language of existential analysis. Without such language the poem manifests its sense and reference to the naive reading alone. But if one leaves it at that, the poem can have *meaning* only and not *truth*. The language of being-in-the-world allows the truth-relation to be established because it is a different language from that of the poem and so gives an independent perspective on the meaning of the poetic language. Through this second language of being-in-the-world, the interpreter can measure the correspondence between what the poem discloses and what the existential categories refer to. If the poetic meaning corresponds with the existential language, we have meaning with truth, which only comes from comparing the meaning presented in the poem with the analysis of existence.

Subjective Conditions for Understanding Texts

In treating the subjective conditions implied by Ricoeur's interpretation theory, I shall focus on three distinct levels of subjectivity. Of these, two levels correspond to the two types of world that I have distinguished above: the world of the text and the ontological world. The form of subjectivity that is the correlate of the world of the text can be called the subjectivity of the direct reader. This is the subject who produces or constructs in the imagination the literary world depicted in a text while reading the text for a first and naive understanding. The second form of subjectivity is the correlate of the structure of the text. It accomplishes a suspension of the referential function of language in order to analyze the formal relations embedded in the text. This "critical subject" takes a step back from naive understanding to trace the structural connections. The third form of subjectivity is the correlate of the ontological world and can be called the reflexive subject. This reflexive subject tests the validity of the initial understanding by comparing it with the structure taken as norm. It is the subject that unfolds the text-world and specifies the referent of the text on the basis of the structure of the text. Reflexivity is a subjectivity that *understands its own understanding* and could just as easily be called the hermeneutical subject. In this section I shall consider each in turn.

Direct Reader as Correlate of Text-World

Ricoeur has concentrated his attention on the understanding of poetic texts, which he grasps as a process of creation and discovery of new meaning beyond the closure of ordinary linguistic patterns, and his specific contribution to hermeneutical discussion at this level circulates around his extension of the Kantian problem of schematism into the area of our understanding of figurative texts. The initial area, then, in which Ricoeur's hermeneutic sheds some light is that of the poetic level of understanding. In effect, Ricoeur is asking about the conditions of the possibility of understanding texts that carry a double meaning.

Ricoeur's presentation of this problem shapes up as follows. In *Fallible Man*, Ricoeur accepts the Kantian theoretical synthesis as an adequate *Erkenntnistheorie* and then models the practical and affective domains on the basis of the map of the cognitive dimension of subjectivity. Kant himself of course remained strictly within the bounds of scientific knowledge in the first *Kritik* and Ricoeur is interested in extending his Kantian model into the area of poetic understanding. I said earlier that what Heidegger and Ricoeur call *Verstehen* takes the place articulated by the transcendental imagination by Kant. What Ricoeur wants to do is to supplement that Kantian doctrine of the imagination in such a way as to allow for the peculiarly poetic level of understanding. In brief, the depiction of the elements of a poetic imagination for Ricoeur looks something like this when set in comparison with Kant.

The topic of the imagination arises in Kant's first *Kritik* in the context of asking how concepts and intuitions could be combined to form theoretical knowledge. Kant referred those opposite terms back to a "third thing," the transcendental image that is generated by the imagination as it takes a schema for a rule of formation in producing images. Ricoeur's aim is to specify the activity in the same productive imagination that generates images for "emergent meanings" in the mode of possible or projected being, rather than the Kantian images for the application of the categories to the perceptual being attributed to sensible intuition. The imagination is to be described not only as the birthplace of a concept, but also as the birthplace of meaning in the metaphorical and symbolic senses. For Kant, the transcendental image holds together or combines a sameness and a difference between intuition and concept. For Ricoeur, the poetic image (and in expanded form, the imagined world of the text) is a holding together of a sameness and difference between a feeling or mood and an emergent and preconceptual meaning that can then give rise to new linguistic meanings with no previous basis in language. Imagination, then, is extended from an activity hidden behind scientific thinking to one also hidden behind the construction of new meanings. These are projected images of possible modes of being.

The analogy that Ricoeur suggests between poetic understanding and the theoretical synthesis is this. The metaphoric process, by which literal signification breaks down at some point so as to give way to the emergent yet constructed figurative signification, is the "schematism" of the poetic imagination. Just as the schema is the rule for production of a transcendental image, the iconicity of poetic language acts as schema for the production of images that make possible the creative synthesis of emergent meaning. The synthesis here is not between the sensible and the intellectual per se, but is a synthesis taking place wholly within language between the affective and the projective. The imagery on the basis of which I am attuned in mood to a text-world is also the imagery on the basis of which I project a way of being in the world. The sequence of operations runs as follows.

I read a literary text and understand it in a figurative way. Behind this we have the pattern in which I read the words that at certain places make semantic non-sense, but because of a planned category mistake, or in the specific case of poetry because of a reverberation of sense in sound, the words are presented as a work of art, a sculpted and tangible work, and they carry a suggestive or evocative power to awaken images in the reader. The icon or sense-sound combination acts as the rule for the arousal of those images.

For Ricoeur the language can be said to play on the reader's subjectivity just as the game transforms the player's subjectivity in

Gadamer's famous analysis of play in *Wahrheit und Methode*.[80] Reading is ludic in that the verbal icon plays on the imagination of the reader, urging him to respond to it by undergoing the imaginative variations expressed in writing and thus by undergoing the corresponding subjective variations at the same time. The text appeals first to the imagination, which pictures the world of the text as the connecting pattern uniting the released images. Those images combine into the text-world, then invite the reader to be attuned in a certain way, to place himself before the imagery in a mood (Heidegger's *Befindlichkeit*) and to project (Heidegger's *Verstehen*) himself into the situation with respect to a possible mode of existence. The emergent reference is designatable as a new mode of being previously hidden behind more accustomed manners of self-understanding. How exactly does this happen in reading?

For this point Ricoeur relies on Marcus Hester's work on the notion of "seeing as" (which is Wittgensteinian in origin).[81] The idea is that the verbal icon is the concrete basis for the reader's making the connection between the terms in a metaphor. The "seeing as" reflects the intuitive relationship that makes the sense and image hold together. That relationship, presented concretely in the icon, guides the seeing of this as that (e.g., to understand "Time is a beggar" is to see time *as* a beggar). Ricoeur says, "Thus, 'seeing as' quite precisely plays the role of the schema that unites the *empty* concept and the *blind* impression; thanks to its character as half thought and half experience, it joins the light of sense with the fullness of the image. In this way, the non-verbal and the verbal are firmly united at the core of the imaging function of language."[82] The "seeing as" designates the preconceptual mediation of new meaning, the activity in which words give birth to new projections of being on the basis of *Befindlichkeit*, so that "What was a 'new being in language' becomes an 'increment to consciousness,' or better, a 'growth of being.'"[83]

All of this takes place as a matter of course in our naive understanding of texts as direct readers. The poetic imagination is meaning-creative in our ordinary dealings with literary texts insofar as they function, as they can, to arouse that imagination to a new vision of the possible, a vision that is "a veritable ontological exploration" of possible being.[84] Since these new meanings subsequently appeal for conceptual elaboration, we can say that the metaphorical schematism indicates the point of emergence of conceptual thinking: "Far from being a part of conceptual thinking, such semantic innovation marks the emergence of such thought."[85]

Critical Subject as Correlate of Structure

The second form of subjectivity invoked by Ricoeur's hermeneutics is the subject of critique. This subject stands in opposition to the direct reader. It brackets the immediacy of response typical of the naive understanding and dislodges the self-evidence of the meanings discovered there. The proper correlate of such subjectivity in the text is the formal structure of the text. In isolating the formal structure, the critical subject suspends the referential power of the language. The natural tendency to follow the movement from sense to reference is interrupted in favor of concentrating on the sense alone. The task of critique is to outline the structural features of the text that control the specific text-world. The critical subject grasps the structure as "code" governing production of the text-world. This level of subjectivity is superseded by the hermeneutical or fully reflexive subject when that structure or code is consciously taken as a sign of the reference. At that point the *epochē* of the referential function of language is ended, and the properly hermeneutical reflection begins.

Reflexive Subject as Correlate of the Ontological World

We have just seen how Ricoeur views the process of understanding poetic meaning as one of productive imagination as it works within the boundaries of affective situations and projective thinking (rather than between sense perception and conceptual thinking). By placing my description of that process under the heading "Direct Reader as Correlate of the World of the Text," I do not mean to suggest that it is an activity cut off from the reflexive subject. As Kant deduced the transcendental ego as the condition of the possibility of the synthesis of the intuited manifold, so too in Ricoeur the reflexive subject is implied as the agent of the connecting activity in the poetic imagination. The reflexive dimension of consciousness is effective wherever there is continuity of consciousness and an ability to ascribe the synthesized experience and thought to the same centered self, even if it does not concentrate its own attention upon the process of the collaboration of itself as reflexive subject with the particular self as the one immediately related to the impressions that each person receives by virtue of possessing sensation and feeling.

Only when the reflexive subject thinks itself, however, does that reflexive dimension of the self actualize itself in an independent way. Whereas the direct subject is the one most immediately involved with forming the images of the world of the text in the naive understanding of texts, the reflexive subject is the one that actualizes itself when the specifically hermeneutical stage of reading begins. Hermeneutics in the narrow sense is *reflexive interpretation of poetic texts*. The interpretative moment takes its first step when one bends back on the direct reading of the text and thinks it as one possible relation to the content of the text. In other words, the reflexive interception of the naive understanding process tries to retrieve in conceptual terms what that primary relation was. And with this attempt the relation between the direct reader and the text-world becomes the subject matter of interpretation and one is removed from the direct involvement in the text-world and placed in the position of reflexivity.

From the reflexive viewpoint, the hermeneutical subject is able to mediate between the naive understanding on one side and the critical explanation on the other side. It has a view of the first relation as one in which the reader constitutes the meaning of the text-world as it immediately presents itself, without questioning whether or not the appearing text-world is the "true" one. It also has a view on the critical relation taken up by the reflexive bending back to isolate the structure of the text. Structural analysis is the work of a detached, reflexive subject who brackets the referential intention of the text in order to discern the design immanent in the text. That "I" then can take that design as a pointer to the text-world and make the comparison between the text-world as constituted in naive understanding and the text-world indicated by the structure. The structure itself, however, primarily points out the horizon of the ontological world in which the reflexive subject places itself. And in the end, it is the meaning of being in that ontological world that becomes the subject matter of hermeneutics. How so?

As the understanding of an understanding in each of two cases, that of the retrieved first understanding and that of the structural analysis, the reflexive subject finds itself free to identify either with the naive relation on the one side or with the critical relation on the other. Thus it realizes itself not simply as a form of awareness, but as a finite *floating subject*. It recognizes that what is presented to structural analysis represents a second dimension of the total meaning there. As for itself, it can either participate directly or step back for critical distance, or it can relate the results of either of those with the other. As floating subject, the "I" recognizes that the meaning there includes all three dimensions: the naive meaning, the critical dissolution of meaning to a design of immanent signs, and the meaning opened up by comparison of the two.

Now, what this further means with respect to the reflexive subject of hermeneutics is that the "I" as floating subject is free, within the limits of one's situation at the present, to actualize itself not only as the neutral form of consciousness, which marks the unity of the subject-pole over against the imaginatively constructed text-world or the analytically displayed structure of the text. The "I" is not merely in the position where it unfolds the text-world according to the way the naive understanding is structured by the text. Rather, the floating nature of reflexive subjectivity points to a deeper possibility. That possibility is that the "I," the hidden and elusive self of self-consciousness, can find itself represented and displayed in the self-world relations presented in a text. The "I" is free to judge, of the self-understanding that ultimately surfaces as the *Sache* of the text, whether that self-understanding is one *for me* in the sense that the text-world presented there provides a context of meaning in which "I" can be the one "I" really am. The deeper possibility of hermeneutics, in other words, is that of self-discovery through texts.

With the articulation of this latter possibility of the *appropriation* of what it means for me to be human through the hermeneutical encounter with texts, we approach a separate topic. It will be the center of explicit discussion in the final chapter of this study. Prior to addressing that issue, however, I wish to determine whether a religious dimension of the text and of the understanding process can be discerned on Ricoeur's hermeneutical principles. If so, the consideration of appropriation will be able to incorporate the specifically religious dimension of textual meaning.

5 • The Religious Dimension of Text and Understanding

At this point my analysis of Ricoeur's hermeneutical theory has advanced through three stages: (1) in the second chapter a historical review of the two lines of thought that intersect in Ricoeur was presented; (2) in chapter three the development of Ricoeur's thought from reflective philosophy to hermeneutics is described prior to an exposition and analysis of the meaning of expression in Ricoeur's hermeneutics. With this latter section of the chapter, the systematic portion of the study begins. With the notion of expression we consider the first topic generated by the systematic principle that directs the succession of topics and forms the subject matter at least in part for the study as a whole. That principle—the self goes out of itself (in expression) and returns to itself (in appropriation)—is derived from the linguistic process itself and orients the discussion of expression as an initial moment in the process of alienation and recovery of meaning in language. (3) In the fourth chapter the systematic principle traces the linguistic process from the level of the spoken to the textual, where the focus is on the theory of text within the context of a theory of discourse. For Ricoeur the text is the place of full manifestation of the potentialities of language as the openness of human being, and the place where expressions of what it means to be human find greatest distance from the event of unobstructed understanding. With text the hermeneutical problem of deciphering meaning on the basis of structure comes into its full form: the world of the text, within which the referent is projected by the structure of the text, must be worked out by methodical procedures. Ricoeur's suggestion is that in the case of poetic texts the best method for discovering the second sense and reference is to reproduce the pattern by which the mind makes sense emerge from the tensions resident in sentence-long metaphors and to apply that pattern to the poetic text as a whole. The reader lets the figurative language of the text work on the imagination so that kinships and resemblances can form a text-world within which a referent may appear to the reader who is attuned to the text-world through mood. Discovery of meaning by following the metaphoric process in reading literary texts is simultaneously a creation of language itself, the emergence of new meaning in the figure of a referred-to "mode of being" as a possibility for being human.

In this fifth chapter, the systematic principle brings the discussion to the extreme moment in the linguistic process. The theme of this chapter is that with the specifically religious dimension of text, the self enters a boundary situation. The self recognizes itself as alienated in a meaning of being human that is first encountered as *not* the self and *other* than I. The self finds its extreme moment of self-distancing through language just where it discovers in what *is not* the self an authentic figure of the self as it *should be*. The extreme moment of alienation through text is also the opening of the possibility for gathering that alienated meaning back into the self by encountering the self in what is, on the surface of things, "not-I," and in responding to a power in the language of self that imparts the authentic selfhood from which one was separated. This chapter, then, is antecedent to description of the stage of appropriation, in which the self returns to itself in the hermeneutical consciousness. This last stage will be treated in the sixth and final chapter of this volume, and it will complete the movement of thought engendered by the systematic principle.

In the present chapter attention will be concentrated on the specifically religious dimension of text and understanding through three sections. In the first part Ricoeur's discussion of the specificity of religious language will be summarized and assessed. In the second and third parts, a possibility for delimiting the religious level of text and understanding that Ricoeur has not recognized will be developed in two steps. Both steps will involve utilizing the sign-sense-referent distinctions to articulate this proposal. In section two a way of defining religious language will be indicated through those distinctions: in brief, the "mode of being" that Ricoeur says is the referent of poetic language can be considered a religious referent, evoking religious understanding when it is itself read as a sign with a sense and reference to the self and, beyond that, to God. In the third section the central trait of such "religious signification," namely, its presentation of reference together with the sense, will be isolated for the purpose of articulating a formal typology of texts by which religious texts both within and without the Bible can be identified without respect to content. These two steps in the specification of religious text and understanding will then allow a formulation of theological hermeneutics consistent with Ricoeur's general interpretation theory. The intention here is to construct this possibility for thought by taking Ricoeur's principles for a guide and thus thinking along with the hermeneutical program that he has authored.

Ricoeur on Religious Language and Theological Hermeneutics

The first difficulty in presenting Ricoeur's thought on the specificity of religious texts is that he has released only occasional studies. We lack a systematic treatment of the topic, although Ricoeur's readers have every reason to anticipate such a work in the planned poetics of the will (vol. 3 of *Philosophy of the Will*). Ricoeur's recent statements on the subject reveal the following orientation: hermeneutical bearings are taken not on the "derived" expressions of religious experience as they might be found in the theological tradition, but on what he calls the "originary level" of the discourse in the confession of religious faith.[1]

The initial task for a hermeneutic of the confessions of faith is to identify the concrete modes of discourse in which the religious consciousness comes to stand, and to situate these modes within the theory of discourse as text.[2] Ricoeur's point is that the confession of faith is inseparable from the mode of discourse in which it is embodied, and that because of the linguistic forms that faith assumes, religious language bears a structure as objective sense, which in turn opens a text-world for the sensitive reader. The procedure for interpreting religious discourse, then, is (1) to read the text in sympathetic imagination, letting the meaning there open what I have called (correcting Ricoeur) the world of the text for the direct and naive subject; (2) to intercept that process through a structural analysis of the objective *sense* of the text and to determine what marks in that sense "open" the sense to a referent; (3) to lay out the referent of the text, within what I have called the ontological world opened now for the reflexive or hermeneutical subject, as an experience of some nonlinguistic reality indicated by the text. This step entails the full comprehension of the text on the semantic level. The fourth step is appropriation and will be treated in the next chapter.

Ricoeur's own interpretative work on the parables of Jesus begins with a naive reading of the language, which he follows with the explanatory moment of structural analysis: the parabolic mode of discourse is considered as genre in the sense of a rule for production of meaning, and this genre is scrutinized for its structural components and for the significatory capacity of those components as now autonomously distanced from their author and his *Sitz im Leben*.[3] As a matter of practice, Ricoeur has chosen only biblical texts for consideration in developing a theological hermeneutics by which to identify religious texts. And of the biblical genres that he has identified, he has done interpretative work on the parables only. Although he does not say that the biblical texts encompass religious texts without remainder, he nonetheless has shown no inclination to stray outside the biblical corpus in identifying religious texts. For Ricoeur to date, a religious text is a biblical text, and the genres that generate religious meaning, understanding, and interpretation are the genres contingently found operative in the Bible. At this point I shall offer some observations concerning the generalized results of Ricoeur's specific interpretations of biblical modes of discourse before I give some indication of how these principles are discerned in the biblical language.

Ricoeur's analysis of biblical genres shows that the religious texts are poetic texts in kind. That is, they display the characteristics of the metaphoric process at the level of text: the "is not" of the literal meaning evokes an "is like" of figurative meaning, which projects a network of meaningful connections at the level of possible being—the "world of the text" as horizon for a possible "mode of being." The poetic text is a *model* that has the capacity to redescribe reality in the mode of possibility through the semantic innovation that results from the presence of metaphoric functioning in language.[4] Religious texts function as poetic models for the imagination, and are subject to the general philosophical hermeneutics of double-meaning expressions. But Ricoeur goes on to say that religious texts reveal a specificity precisely on the basis of a theory of poetics, and this specific characteristic reveals something more about poetic texts in general. This trait in turn inverts the relation of specific to general between religious and poetic texts, turning philosophical hermeneutics of poetic texts into an *organon* of theological hermeneutics of religious texts.[5]

Religious discourse for Ricoeur is similar to poetic discourse in that its referent is not to be sought in the everyday world of perceptual objects as an item subject to definite description, but is available only through the world of the text as a world distanced from everyday reality. Religious discourse is unique within the poetic type because the various genres individually and collectively in polyphonous ensemble refer to the unnamable name of God, a name that has become bound up with the meaning-event preached as Resurrection.[6] "It is the naming of God by the biblical texts that specifies the religious at the interior of the poetic."[7] The reverberation back on the notion of poetic text might be put this way: whereas poetic texts intend new modes of being in the register of the possible, religious texts intend the infinite background of any possible mode of being. Religious texts say something more than poetic ones because the God-referent in the last analysis escapes the project of the poetic imagination, even while jarring it to the limit of semantic innovation. The "God-referent is at once the coordinator of these varied discourses and the index of their incompleteness, the point at which something escapes them."[8] This openness to the infinite background of any mode of being inverts the hermeneutical relationships. Instead of my interpreting figurative sense through discovery and invention of a new mode of being in the register of the possible, the infinite background—or that which refers to it, the "God-referent"—interprets *my* existence and is revelatory of it.[9]

How, then, does religious language function to modify poetic language in order to perform this inversion? Here Ricoeur has recourse to Ian Ramsey's analysis of models and qualifiers, but relocated from the derived theological discourse to the original expressions of religion.[10] The biblical forms are pieces of poetic language that function as models of redescription, and these forms are modified by the presence of qualifiers that Ricoeur calls "limit-expressions." By "limit-expression" Ricoeur means "an indication or modification that undoubtedly affects every form of [biblical] discourse through a sort of passing over to the limit."[11] Limit-expressions function to "transgress" or overturn the normal course of metaphoric process, and to "intensify" its effect so that the forms of language "converge upon an extreme point which becomes their point of encounter with the infinite."[12] The limit-expressions act as qualifiers of the model and make that model say *more* than it would without it. The religious qualification of the poetic linguistic model brings the poetic capacity for semantic innovation to its completion in a "cosmic disclosure" linked with "total commitment," where it stands before the source and origin of poetic linguistic meaningfulness. What follows is an explanation of how Ricoeur apprehends such modification of poetic language in his analysis of the biblical forms.

Ricoeur's work on the Old Testament modes of discourse is set in the context of his articulation of a concept of revelation as the manifestation of meaning.[13] He identifies five distinct modes of discourse (without claiming that this is an exhaustive or systematic list) and indicates how each mode names God in its own way. *Narrative* discourse (Pentateuch) names God as an actor in founding events for a community. He is in part a figure remembered in the third person, who revealed to himself in the events in their historicity. *Prophetic* discourse names God as the voice behind the prophet, and points to a first-person God of the future. *Prescriptive* discourse names God as giver of the law and adds the practical side of revelation. Law is not merely imperative and menace but also promise and election. God is named as the demand for holiness. *Wisdom* discourse names God as hidden, preexistent wisdom, which addresses individual humans in their boundary-situations in which they are asking the "overwhelming question of the sense or nonsense of existence" while confronting the incomprehensibility, silence, and absence of God. *Hymnic* discourse (Psalms) names God as a "You" in the second person, as one who may respond to praise, supplication, thanksgiving.

The second stage of Ricoeur's analysis is to show how various pairs of forms modulate one another's naming of God. For example, narration is linked with prophecy through time: narrative description founds a certain history, which is undercut by the danger forecast in the Day of Yahweh. Here we have contradition with no triumphant dialectic, but only "a double confession that only hope can hold together."[14] Taken together, the polyphony of meaning that sounds through the intertextuality of the biblical forms should be heard to caution against any uniform theology, say of word-event alone or a theology of the ultimate meaning of history alone, and the like. Since the various forms speak in ensemble through tensions and exchanges between messages, and since in none of the modes is the naming of God dominated by knowledge, the individual and collective forms reveal a hidden God. God is revealed and concealed in those texts. In Exodus 3 there is an epitome of the Old Testament naming of God—the divine name is the *unnamable*. "Yahweh—he is—is not a name that defines God, but one that signifies an act of deliverance."[15]

Ricoeur presents more detailed work on the New Testament forms of parable, proverb, and eschatological saying, especially with respect to giving some indication as to how it is that biblical discourse is able to open its sense to an infinite referent that transcends formulation even as a possible mode of being.[16] After lengthy analyses of "structure" in narrative and of redescription and semantic innovation in poetic texts, Ricoeur turns to the parables, which he defines as "the conjunction between a *narrative form*, a *metaphorical process*, an an appropriate 'qualifier' which assures its convergence with other forms of discourse which will point toward the meaning 'Kingdom of God.'"[17] The focus is on the strategy by which the parables effect the passage from sense to the referent. Ricoeur notes that certain marks at the heart of the structure of the parable open the discourse to a figurative or metaphorical sense, which in turn suggests something other than a literal referent. The persistent use of the qualifier "Kingdom of God" additionally functions to confer a specifically religious usage on the poetic model.[18]

Ricoeur's claim in the case of parables is that the narrative form itself is to be taken metaphorically to yield its referent. What then is the structure of parabolic narrative if it is to act as a sense that signifies, and what are the grounds for passing beyond the structure to the referent? According to Ricoeur, "The plot is the very structure *of* the narrative."[19] The plot itself—in the unfolding of a crisis confronted by the character and the response made to the crisis—structures the metaphoric process. The Kingdom of God is described figuratively "to be like" what happens in the plot. And as to the reason one should take the plot as somehow referring metaphorically to something similar beyond the narrative, Ricoeur's answer is that the plot carries the inner clue of metaphoricity in the element of extravagance, which makes the narrative "odd" by mixing the extraordinary with the ordinary. An ordinary incident is given an extraordinary twist, and the combination of the two precipitates a tension between the *closed* form of the narrative and the dynamic process of opening beyond the form generated by the inconsistency or contradiction within the narrative.[20]

The parables, in other words, do convey a literal sense: the story presents an incident in an ordinary and plausible setting that seems to disguise nothing unusual. But the everydayness of the literal meaning is overturned in its identity by another trait of extraordinariness or extravagance within the plot: the action in the plot is always outlandish when seen in terms of expected behavior. As Ricoeur says of the Laborers in the Vineyard (Matt. 20:1–15) parable, "What employer would pay the employees of the eleventh hour the same wages as those hired first?"[21] Other parables betray similar intrusions of the extraordinary in the everyday scene they depict. The tension between the usual and unusual sets up an unstable structure at the literal level, indicates that the story says something more than its literal sense, and suggests that the literal referent points to a figurative one. The contradiction in the literal meaning tends to break up the narrative form as structure and to open that literal meaning to some nonliteral meaning that *is like* what happens there.

Ricoeur also finds a contextual level of clues for metaphoricity of meaning in the parables. In the first place, the parables make sense when taken together as a corpus. And in this context, the fact that the parables all tell different stories with different foci of extravagance is a strong indicator of metaphoric signification.[22] In the second place, the common horizon of the different parabolic stories—the horizon of meaning designated by the symbol "Kingdom of God"—is shared by the other sayings of Jesus in the Synoptics: eschatological sayings and proverbial sayings. This common dimension indicates that in some sense parable, proverb, and eschatological statement are all translatable into the other forms, hence the reader need not dwell on the literal sense of the words alone:

> The equivalence between parable, proclamation, and proverb helps to break up the narrative structures. It explodes the "closure" of the structure. Then the narrative structure recedes to the background and the metaphorical process proceeds to the foreground. This reversal in the priority between *structure* and *process* could not be achieved without these mutual exchanges between several modes of discourse, since the attention should be drawn beyond the narrative at the same time that it is captured by the plot itself. To think inside and outside the form is made possible by the attraction exerted on one form of discourse by another.[23]

Whereas the sayings of Jesus all share a horizon in the "Kingdom of God" image, the three forms use different techniques to indicate a metaphorical meaning beyond the literal one. The equivalent to the use of extravagance in the parables is the employment of a technique of overturning in the eschatological sayings. Jesus takes up the apocalyptic form in these sayings only to overthrow its temporal structure. In the literal sense, the apocalyptic form asks when in the chronological order of things will it come? But Jesus consistently projects a meaning in which the symbol "the coming kingdom" refuses a literal interpretation (the Kingdom of God is "close at hand").

The proverbial formulae function differently again to shatter the literal meaning against the suggestive power of contradiction. The contradiction in this case comes out either as *paradox* or *hyperbole*, both of which overturn the reader's inclination to settle for a literal meaning. In this case the literal meaning would be sought in line with the Wisdom sayings of the Jewish tradition, but when the proverb is taken as a coherent and repeatable saying that can guide one in daily life and assist "the project of making a continuous whole out of one's existence" (Beardslee),[24] this understanding is undone. Paradox violates such a project through the contradiction of "overturning of fates" as in "Whoever seeks to gain his life will lose it, but whoever loses his life will preserve it" (Luke 17:33; cf. Mark 8:35). This form of meaning-intensification makes it impossible to project a strategy for making a continuous whole out of one's existence (how can you plan to lose your life to gain it?), just as it affirms that "in spite of all, life is conferred through this paradoxical route" (Beardslee).[25] Hyperbole intensifies in the opposite direction: for example, "Love your enemies, do good to those who hate you" (Luke 6:27; cf. Matt. 5:44). Here the normal strategy of rounding off one's existence is challenged and upset, but by the suggestion of an unreachable and different way of life.

The sayings of Jesus all show the signs of surplus meaning through the technique of "transgression" of the form of discourse from within that form. The literal sense-referent signifies a metaphorical sense-referent on the basis of that linguistic twist. To what kind of *figurative* meaning is this religious language opened? The power of signification is provided by the presence in the sayings of Jesus as a whole of the expression "Kingdom of God." This key expression functions (following Ramsey) as a "qualifier" working on the poetic linguistic "model" at the level of original religious discourse. The qualifier "Kingdom of God" directs the reader beyond the poetic dimension to the point where a peculiarly religious situation of "total commitment" is evoked and assumes an appropriately odd logical position for expression in that it functions to elicit "cosmic discernment" within the religious situation.[26]

Ricoeur deviates from Ramsey's use of the model-qualifier structure of the function of religious language, in that Ramsey speaks about the logical "oddness" of the use of "God" as qualifier, where this word is said to "preside over" and "complete" the language of created things.[27] It is well known that Ramsey elucidates this logical oddness through the function of tautology (e.g., "I am I" or "God is God") to state the final reason for some action or state of affairs. The qualifier "God" invokes an intuitively known first principle that drives thought to the limit. Ricoeur, on the contrary, sees the logical structure of the qualifier not to be the "odd" one of Ramsey, but to be one of logical *scandal*, whose function is not to preside over and complete in the manner of first principles, but "to re-orient by disorienting," hence to assume a limit-function of transgressing, overturning, and driving to the limit.[28] The religious qualifier points the reader to the infinite dimension of possibility by dislocating the already-in-place project of securing one's life, and by pointing to the limit-experiences of joy and distress that can reorient life and that Tillich designates by the term *ultimate concern*.[29]

Ricoeur further elaborates the ability of the sayings of Jesus to suggest a poetic and ultimately a religious or deep meaning with regard to the placement of the sayings in the Gospel. Since the parables occur in the Gospel, a narrative within a narrative is set up, in which the teller of the parable is also the hero of the inclusive narrative. The parables unfold within the greater context of the narrative of the Passion, so that the parables of Jesus ae also heard as the parable as such and the Gospel: "Jesus proclaimed God *in* parables, but the primitive church proclaimed Jesus as the Parable of God" (Crossan).[30] We *call* "Jesus" the one whose mode of being is suggested by the conjunction between the hero of the narrative that is the Passion and the speaker of the parabolic stories within the Gospel.

In summary of Ricoeur's stated view of religious language, we can say that for Ricoeur religious language is a species of poetic language in that it functions metaphorically to redescribe reality in terms of possibility, but that it reveals another trait that bursts the genus-species relation. That trait is the added reference of religious language to God beyond the world of the text while it also refers to limit-experiences that open up the self-world relations. Religious language functions in this way because of the presence of limit-expressions, which are used as qualifiers to drive metaphorical semantic innovation to its limit where it can disclose the ultimate ground and goal of poeticizing.

Theological hermeneutics can now be defined for Ricoeur with reference to religious language according to this formula: Religious language is to poetic language as theological hermeneutics is to philosophical hermeneutics. Just as poetic language reveals its limit-function when intensified by a religious qualifier, so too does philosophical hermeneutics discover the limit of all hermeneutics and the nonhermeneutical origin of all interpretation when it interprets the originary forms of religious language.[31] Theological hermeneutics is initiated as a species of a general philosophical hermeneutics, namely, the application of interpretation theory to the Bible. But in encountering the biblical texts and undertaking the task of unfolding the world of the biblical text as the proposition of a world which in the biblical language is called a new covenant, the Kingdom of God, a new birth,[32] the general hermeneutics can encounter the *Sache* of this language as the Word of God, which reverberates upon the meaning of our everyday world and the text-worlds explored in other instances of hermeneutical activity. What is unique about theological hermeneutics is that "das neue Sein, von dem sie redet, für die Welt, für die gesamte Wirklichkeit einschliesslich meiner Existenz und meiner Geschichte *offenbarend* ist (the new being, of which it speaks, is *revelatory* for the world, for all of reality, including my existence and my history)."[33] Theological hermeneutics, then, is defined by its subject matter: it is the interpretation of the new being that is the issue of the biblical texts.

Such is the thought of Paul Ricoeur on religious language and theological hermeneutics. It is necessarily an incomplete and uneven account in some respects because of the occasional nature of his discussion of these issues. For example, Ricoeur never penetrates to a detailed analysis of the "overturning" involved in religious texts. The inclusion of the "limit-expression" as qualifier is intended to show how the poetic reference is redirected to the religious, but the way in which this happens is left unspecified. Can it be that the poetic referent, the possible mode of being signified by the sense, is itself a metaphor for the religious meaning? This is left as an unexplored possibility for Ricoeur.

Also, Ricoeur's use of Ramsey's model-qualifier framework to illuminate the religious metaphoricity of the sayings of Jesus tends to break with his emphasis on the hermeneutical task as one that concentrates on laying out the world of the text within which a mode of being in the world is suggested by the language. Ricoeur does not offer a detailed interpretation of the mode of being signified by the religious text, yet he does define theological hermeneutics with reference to the "new being" that appears in the biblical text-world. But what *is* this new being and what significance does it have for his text-based hermeneutics? These points are left unexplained, along with the connection between new being as a configuration of possible being with a text and the "God-referent" of religious texts. If the presence of new being in a text-world signifies a religious text, what is the relation between new being and the religious reference to God? Ricoeur does not offer answers to these questions, although his hermeneutical theory does, I think, allow the formulation of clear responses to these issues. In the second part of this chapter I hope to develop possibilities in Ricoeur for resolving the items mentioned here.

Other problems to be worked out suggest themselves as well. If the Bible is a religious text because it refers to God by virtue of the modification of a poetic model by a religious qualifier, are we to think that it refers to God as an *infinite term* in a self-world or subject-object relation, or as the *ground* and *abyss* of the self-world relations? It maybe that the world of the text as opened to the imagination of the direct reader may name God as a term of the relation; but for the second naiveté or hermeneutical consciousness as it interprets that naive reading, the text must refer to God within the ontological world as ground and abyss of the self-world relation. The episode of the Burning Bush shows for Ricoeur the impossibility of any direct naming of God, and his use of the model-qualifier structure is an approach to an indirect naming. But it does not adequately treat the issue implied in the unnamability of God. That issue is that if God is not a term of a self-world relation, then the God-reference is not to something that is objectifiable in some way, not even in thought, but is a reference to the identity and difference of self and world or subject and object.

Ricoeur is not clear on the difference between a reference to God as term and reference to God as ground and abyss, but one problem that surfaces when God is thought as ground and abyss is that a contradiction opens in the experience of the religious text that would prohibit naming a religious text *as* a religious text. That contradiction, simply put, is this: if the reader of the religious text follows the sense to referent as a power that transcends the subject-object or self-world split, then the experience of the religious referent will in the nature of the case violate the conditions under which the reference can be identified as a reference to God. If the reader, in other words, finds the relation to the text-world inverted so that no longer does the reader reveal the meaning of the text but instead the referent of the text reveals to the reader what it means to be the one he or she is, the experience strips the reader of the ability to apply a criterion to determine whether the text intends God or not. To be able to determine whether the text intends God as a referent relies on being able to apply a criterion by which to measure a certain object over against a neutralized subject. But the experience of God as ground and abyss of the subject-object relation takes away that critical distance in presenting a power that transcends all duality as the Unconditioned.[34]

At stake in this question is a theme that animates the hermeneutical project itself: Hermeneutics is inspired by the realization that critique is an infinite power of dislodging that which seems self-evident. Critique "de-divinizes" the world and forces out the gods that are present to naive consciousness. Hermeneutics seeks to be called again beyond critique in a second naiveté, and the structure of second naiveté as Ricoeur sketches it can provide the elements necessary to interpret this contradiction and to resolve it at a higher level. In the next section I hope to show how this is so.

Another question can be raised with respect to Ricoeur's discussion of religious language. Ricoeur gives no hint as to how to extend the category "religious language" beyond that of "biblical language" and the category "theological hermeneutics" beyond "biblical hermeneutics." He may choose not to look elsewhere because the Bible remains *the* religious text *par excellence* for one with his biography. That is a noble option shared with Karl Barth in this century, but one that is too restrictive within the global context of contemporary philosophy of religion. Since there is no warrant for such restriction on systematic grounds, can the definition be opened up to encompass religious meaning wherever it occurs?

I hope to show how an undeveloped resource in Ricoeur's hermeneutical philosophy can propose an alternative formulation of religious language that can take the above-named questions into account. The suggestions that follow in the next two sections are intended to work out the outlines of this possibility for the interpretation theory of Paul Ricoeur.

A Second Attempt to Specify Religious Language

In Ricoeur's analysis of the function of religious language and his application of Ian Ramsey's qualifier-model structue to the originary forms of religious discourse, we have an example of Ricoeur's professed aim to communicate with the British and American school of ordinary language philosophy, as a way "of both renewing phenomenology and of replying to the excesses of structuralism."[35] The focus of attention for Ricoeur's thought on religious language is on how the use of limit-language can result in a cosmic disclosure in special circumstances created by the "overturning" quality of metaphoric language. For Ricoeur, religious language is poetic language, in that like all poetic language it self-consciously turns attention away from the actual world of given being and toward a possible mode of being in the world. At the heart of the poetic language, a limit-expression such as "Kingdom of God" or "new being" serves to direct the reader beyond the poetic domain of imagined text-worlds to the infinite dimension. Limit-expressions are "God-referents," which open poetic discourse to its own depth and limit.

Another possibility, however, exists within Ricoeur's structure of thought for delimiting the religious dimension of language. It does not conflict with Ricoeur's explicit description but rather supplements that account because it centers attention not on the use of language to disclose depth through limit-expression but instead on the metaphorical power of language to enable creation of new meaning. This possibility merely explores a central theme of Ricoeur's hermeneutic in another register: it looks at the ability of what Ricoeur calls the referent of poetic language, that is, a mode of being, to present a sign for metaphorical interpretation. Ricoeur does not mention the possibility that the mode of being signified by a poetic text might itself function metaphorically to refer to the religious dimension. But that possibility is consistent with Ricoeur's thought and it does not necessitate recourse to a special "qualifier" of a poetic model. Rather, it shows a basic condition for the use of a qualifier such as "Kingdom of God": the "qualifier" relies on the referential ability of the mode of being intended by the poetic language. A qualifier can modify the reference of poetic language beyond the poetic only if the reference of poetic language itself has referential power.

This second possibility can be very precisely indicated by way of the elements of discourse as Ricoeur defines them. For Ricoeur, poetic language is language with a sign carrying literal sense and signifying a literal referent, yet, due to a non-sense at the heart of literal signification, the literal sense opens up for discovery/invention of a metaphorical sense. So too does the literal referent suggest and evoke the synthesis of a metaphorical referent, namely, a projected mode of being. Now, if the poetic referent—a mode of being—is itself seen as a sign carrying a sense that points to a referent, and that reference were in the nature of the case a reference to the infinite dimension of meaning, then one could call that specific aspect of language the religious dimension. If the mode of being announced by the poetic imagery itself carries a meaning and refers to the source and origin of meaningfulness, then we have religious language. Religious understanding would correlatively be described as the prereflective projection of and response to the ultimate dimension of meaning as it appears through particular modes of being. And theological hermeneutics would be the explication and raising to thematic comprehension of the content of the religious understanding.

This suggestion has the advantage of maintaining continuity with Heidegger's hermeneutical project as well as with the program offered by Bultmann and the post-Bultmannian school of theological hermeneutics.[36] It connects with Heidegger's hermeneutic of *Dasein* insofar as it professes to interpret the referent of poetic language (a mode of being) as a sign with meaning. Ricoeur is explicit about his dependence on Heidegger for his contention that discourse may carry a reference to a mode of existence as a way of connecting "I" to "this person here." And under this suggestion, Ricoeur could modify Heidegger's tactic in *Sein und Zeit*, which is to interpret the mode of being or self-world relation as a sign with a sense that signifies the meaning of being. Like Heidegger, Ricoeur would seek out the pointing capacity of the mode of being; but unlike Heidegger in *Sein und Zeit*, he would not attempt under this suggestion to determine the meaning of being in strict conceptual terms. Otto Pöggeler has shown why Heidegger failed to determine the meaning of being in that fashion: the meaning of being remains hidden in the region of infinite subjectivity, which in its temporality is systematically elusive to thought. Heidegger learned that one cannot make a conceptual progression from the analyzed modes of being, as manifest in being-here, to the meaning of being that grounds them, and he called *Dasein* a *Zeichen ohne Deutung* (a sign without an interpretation) for that reason.

Ricoeur of course is aware of the reason for the failure of *Sein und Zeit* in that limited respect, and like Heidegger after *Sein und Zeit*, he sought a second starting point, which aims not at a conceptual connection between *Dasein* and *Sein*, but which hearkens to any indications concerning the meaning of being as they may issue from *Sein* to *Dasein* through symbol. In seeking this second starting point—the hermeneutical turn initiated by *Symbolism of*

Evil—Ricoeur follows Bultmann, who also works in the framework of taking a mode of being as a sign with sense and reference. In fact, Bultmann's outline of just this possibility could be richly suggestive for Ricoeur.[37]

Bultmann proposed a variant of the Heideggerian hermeneutic of *Dasein*, which runs like this.[38] Existence (here he follows Heidegger) is a sign that points to a sense, and this sense in turn signifies the open background of existence and makes it possible for the interpreter to understand the reference signified there. For Bultmann, such understanding aims not at objectification of the meaning of being, however. Instead, Bultmann intends to think responsively in view of the presence or power that shows itself when we look in the direction signified by the mode of being (or "self-understanding" as he uses the term). When we look at the openness projected by the self-understanding or mode of being there taken as a sense with reference, we may see either a self open to God as the all-determining reality *("die alles bestimmende Wirklichkeit")* or a self open to the presence of nothing. These two references—God or nothing—represent the two appearing powers that correspond to the two basic modes of being: *inauthentic* self-understanding (which projects nothing over against the "I") and *authentic* self-understanding (which responds to the power of the all-determining reality). Neither of these realities can be spoken about directly, hence effort for conceptual determination is wrongheaded. But they can be attested to with respect to the power of what appears in the place of manifestation opened by the mode of being taken as sign with meaning. God or nothing may appear there, and the difference lies in what the language *enables* me to become. Where the mode of being suggested by the language I hear enacts my authentic existence in response to the all-determining reality, the language is religious language for Bultmann.[39]

Ricoeur in his turn could modify the Bultmann suggestion so as to specify religious language more exactly. Ricoeur's most important resources for contribution in this instance are (1) his sustained reflection on the nature of language by which he can specify how a mode of being refers as a linguistic phenomenon (namely, metaphorically), and (2) his articulation of the elements of second naiveté or hermeneutical consciousness, by which he can mediate the contradiction that arises in Bultmann as well as in his own work: the experience of God through language necessarily displaces one from the position of distance that is required in order to judge that one *has* followed a reference to God and not to nothing. I shall try to indicate more specifically how Ricoeur could actualize this possibility for specifying religious language.

The suggestion so far is this. Ricoeur could specify religious language as language whose sign points to a figurative sense and reference (i.e., a mode of being) through metaphorical process, and whose reference—the mode of being—itself is read as a sign/sense that projects a referent against the open dimension of infinite possibility. If the literal meaning of the language suggests a mode of being and if that mode of being then opens to the infinite background, we have religious language. In this way the mode of being that Ricoeur says is the object of interpretation can be shown to signify an inexhaustible or infinite meaning, that is, a religious meaning. A nonreligious literary work would be said on this account to have the capacity to engender a large number of interpretations because each new historical situation could lay down new opportunities to decipher the mode of being projected by the work. That mode of being would not, then, ordinarily bear signs of its own significatory powers (although literary language might be said on this account to be implicitly religious since every human project is done against the openness of *Dasein*). A religious work, on the contrary, would on its own open the reader to that infinite dimension by virtue of the signifying power of the mode of being projected there.

Religious language could be said to open to an infinite dimension of meaning because the mode of being (or "self-understanding" in Bultmann's terminology) has the power to open a new level of signification—one that is latent in any poetic text and manifest in a religious text. The mode of being—defined by laying out the forms of relation between the "I" and "this one here" as concretely in the world, for the "I" as well as for the others—carries the sense either of one who strives inauthentically to secure his or her place in the world through recognition of nothing beyond the "I," whose task it is to calculate the way best to fit into a hostile world, or of one who is empowered authentically to accept existential insecurity and the resoluteness of self-commitment in spite of exposure to the world through the appearance of a countervailing force, *die alles bestimmende Wirklichkeit*, which determines the "I" in all its self-determination and enables authentic care.

Beyond Bultmann, Ricoeur could contend that religious language is not infinite because it is the language enabling authenticity. Rather, the issue is that when the readers of religious language look to the place of openness signified by the mode of being, they may see *either* God as the all-determining reality and find their own resoluteness to remain in openness enabled, *or* they may see nothing at all. In either case, the text is what points beyond the mode of being to that open background. The infinity of meaning lies just in the ability of religious language to elicit *both* responses even though they are contradictory. That the same text can yield opposite and contradictory meanings is the signal that an infinite number of readings is possible. It is part of the meaning of a religious text that it can be understood *either* as a projected mode of being that enables my openness and resoluteness *or* that enables my ongoing closure and need to secure my existence. In either case the text enables a response of immediacy to the origin and source of meaningfulness, and that response *is* the religious relation. It does not compel a recognition of God as the all-determining reality, but allows for that recognition as well as for the recognition of nothing as the final power, that is, of no power to which the "I" is answerable beyond its own subjectivity. The working of religious language elicits both affirmation and negation of an appearing power that is counterpoised to the self. I propose now to explain how something in language itself, as analyzed by Ricoeur in his meditations on metaphoric process, can provoke the reader of a text to understand a literal sense/referent metaphorically (where a "mode of being" is grasped) and then beyond that to understand the metaphorical sense/referent religiously (where the open background appears in the place of exposure signified by a mode of being).

For Ricoeur, the self has no direct intuition of itself but carries the structure of *Tathandlung*. The "I" who performs the self-world connections and is the point of origin of all thinking, acting, and feeling, must be discovered hermeneutically through interpretation of figures in texts that convey a sense of what it means to be human and give some insight into the connecting process, the living mediation that is human being. Hermeneutics seeks to overcome the alienation of the "I" in its mediating process from the situation-bound "this one here." And the central premise for the search for signals of true selfhood in the text-tradition is that a poetic text contains structured expressions of humanness that are themselves lost and alienated from the original event of utterance and communication and now can be mediated into a new situation and brought to life again in a new event of discourse. Text is the full manifestation of discourse, in part because it carries the potential for engendering a new act of understanding. And the point of greatest density in such a potential for text is the possibility of self-discovery through hermeneutics. The systematically elusive selfhood *may* appear through the structured work of text. This possibility can be plotted out in two steps.

In the first stage, the mode of being that the fictional narration intends may carry a sense as a *form of timing* or a way of temporalizing human activity that the reader initially and correctly identifies as *not* that of his or her own temporalizing. For example, the mode of being indicated by the poetic text may be one of timing one's thoughts and activities without regard for reward or punishment. The image of human being in this case would be one who acts and thinks without timing his decisions so as to account for calculations of gain or loss forthcoming from external sources but instead whose world is one in which reward and punishment are disconnected from human labor. The reader may in this example (which is used for illustration) initially recognize that such a world is not his or her own and that the mode of being there is not one that corresponds to the actuality of the reader's selfhood. But beyond such a response, an overturning may occur if, through the metaphoric power of the mode of being, the reader were to discern something else beckoning through that unfamiliarity. If the mode of being, which is unfamiliar and strange is not being that of myself in its actuality, is seen as an image of the self as it *should be* and somehow is capable of, then it may happen that the reader can come to a recognition of the true selfhood of authentic existence in and through the figure that is in the first place not the "I."

The possibility of such self-recognition through poetic texts depends upon the efficacy of a logic of overturning and superabundance,[40] which Ricoeur says is the "logic" of the metaphoric process itself: meaning is discovered/created in the image formed when a kinship has been seen through contradiction. The literal "is" of metaphoric attribution includes a literal "is not," due to the "twist" integral to figurative attribution, and the tension between the two opposites generates an act of synthesis beyond the opposition when a new meaning is made visible in the "is like" of poetic image. The logic of metaphor is a dialectical pattern of movement that has the sequential form of (1) primary meaning posited, (2) primary meaning overturned, (3) new meaning engendered. With regard to the signifying power of a mode of being, we can observe the "logic" of metaphoric meaning in the pattern by which (1) the mode of being is recognized, (2) but as one that is plainly not-mine, in that I initially read the subject matter in the everyday way of assuming it is not about me. Then (3), through the symbolic quality of a literary figure to fuse its image in a text-world with the ability to evoke and assemble the awareness of authentic existence as what I "should be" but in actuality am not, the mode of being concretely presented through the literal text and its metaphoric dimension signifies the "I" in its authenticity.

The mode of being that could appear in literary texts and could signify the true selfhood in the sense of a figure or metaphor for authentic timing would, in Ricoeur's terminology from *Fallible Man*, be called "fallibility without fault" or, as he later puts it (evoking Tillich) "new being." More specifically, new being would be the mode of being in which there is balance and harmony rather than conflict and disruption between happiness and character, or freedom and destiny, or "I" and "this one here." New being is an appearance of "essential being under the conditions of existence, conquering the gap between essence and existence" (Tillich).[41] Such a mode of existence would be exposed to the fragility of existence and the power to fail that constitutes fallibility, but without separation from awareness of the origin and source of the temporalizing process. New being is the mode of being in which the "I" understands the connecting process and temporalizing against the background of open possibility. The "I" understands itself as free within its own situation, and the "I" understands its concrete situation as a revelation of its own meaning. In the new being, the self times its activities authentically, and understands itself as one that already understands itself and displays that understanding in its activities. In such self-recognition through text, the possibility is described for the overcoming of the alienation of the meaning of being human in the text-tradition that expresses it. To the extent that the referent of a poetic text—a mode of being—points to the self in its authenticity as the one timing its activities as they should be, that text displays a religious meaning. The meaning of the text in that case pertains to what it means to be the one "I" am as reader, and such texts as have to do with my being what I am are religious texts.

Religious texts can have an additional dimension beyond that of self-recognition: the metaphorical mode of being can actually enable and empower the authentic existence that it depicts. This would be the significant level of religious text, and it takes its importance from the presence of an enabling symbol of the self that can make it possible for the reader to become an authentic self on his or her side. At this level there is not merely self-recognition through text but also empowerment of authentic selfhood through text.

It should be noted for the sake of completeness that a text need not specifically depict a mode of authentic existence in order for the kind of religious self-recognition indicated here to take place. The concrete mode of being may be one that does not fit Heidegger's analysis of authentic timing but that nonetheless shows what it means to be human authentically by referring to the "is like" under its opposite. Sometimes the imagery of fallenness can best manifest the authentic meaning of fallibility, and this possibility is not ruled out by the description here. What is crucial is the appearance of authentic human being through the "is like" generated through contradiction.

A second step of this description opens up with the connection between recognition of new being as the *Sache* of religious texts and the discussion of "God-reference" in texts. These two are not the same, since one may speak of self-recognition through language without acknowledging anything about the ability of elements in a text to refer to God. A "God-reference" in texts would rely on the presence of a symbol or symbolic dimension of metaphor in the broad sense. For a text to refer the reader to God, it would have to provide the symbolic material through which God as ground and abyss of self-world relations can appear. Any use of "Kingdom of God," or rather of limit-expressions as qualifiers of a poetic model that provoke discernment of God, relies on the symbolic power of some image or words that are intended to point to the deity.

The symbol of God obviously need not appear through an image of human being. But any religious text would be able to refer to God only through the pointing power of some metaphorical meaning. If the "mode of being" discerned through the text is also the determined reality through which the all-determining reality of God makes its appearance, then the text could be said to have a theological dimension to it. For example, a mode of being such as new being can symbolize God if a power is presented through that figure which overcomes the division between self and world. The split and conflict between self and world constitutes the fault of existence, and so any text-figure that imparts to my understanding the character of existence against the openness of being and that empowers my overcoming the conflict between "this person here" and the "I" could make present the power of God to the degree to which it overturns fault and establishes authentic fallibility, at least in intention.

In the context of Ricoeur's philosophical anthropology in *Fallible Man*, the specific moods a text must engender on the basis of which the reader might imagine a text-world with a God-referent would be the "formless" moods of joy, anguish *(Angst)*, and courage. Joy and anguish *(Angst)* respond to the presence of being and the absence of being respectively, and they are mediated in terms of content by the mood of courage *(thumos)*. The character of these moods is that they are each attunements not to this or that mere possibility or actuality, but instead to the whole of things. In these moods the belongingness of self and world is still undisturbed by division and, as a consequence, in these moods the ultimate identity of the identity and difference of self and world can make its approach in the symbol of God. God, conceived as the depth of unity that underlies the togetherness and separateness of self and world, can come to stand as a symbol of this depth. When such a symbol of God *is* present, the response is that Ricoeur calls "faith" as the authentic act that is the limit of all hermeneutics and the nonhermeneutical origin of all interpretation.[42]

Is it contradictory to say that some religious texts display a mode of being that points to the self and beyond that to God through a symbolic dimension of metaphoric process? This possibility was raised earlier, and although Ricoeur does not mention it, the prospect of a contradiction deserves notice now. The problem is this: A reader could say a text has a God-referent if a mode of being signified there made the ground and abyss of self-world relations present and perceptible through a symbol. Such an experience would be one felt in the dimension of a formless mood, in which some power crossed the line of division between self and world even while distinct subjectivity and objectivity were maintained on either side. The symbol of God would break down the subject-object distinction in a display of ultimate belongingness. But in just this breakdown of distinction the reader would lose the critical distance that is necessary in order even to raise the question whether the language *is* religious language. Either one experiences the power of God through a symbolic dimension of text ecstatically and loses the distance necessary to judge, or one judges the content of the experience to determine whether the text does indeed refer to God and inevitably turns up the negative response because the power uniting subject and object is lost in the act of judging.[43]

The hermeneutical consciousness as reflexive awareness of some primary relation is able to distance itself from both primary responses—the naive and the critical—having experienced them both. And it is able to compare the content of each with the other. In so doing it can apprehend the identity of the two and can thus claim that a text allows the appearance of God precisely where judging and experiencing correspond to one another. When my critical thinking about God is the response to the presence of the power that transcends subject and object, then I can know that the text refers to God. In such an instance of interpretation, the symbolic experience gives rise to thinking and the thinking accords with the content of the experience.

Notice how there is an overturning at the heart of metaphorical God-reference just as much as there was in the earlier case of self-reference. Just as the "I" recognizes itself in a text by overturning an identification of the subject matter as "not-I," the reader can identify God through text only through a contradiction. What I experience as the power of God to overcome existential opposition is always thought *not* to be God. Any judgment about the presence of God is negative just in the attempt to apply a criterion because it forecloses the presence of the identity between self and world. The thought of God objectifies God and thereby loses the experienced presence of God. But if God is thought as present just where that contradiction between experience and thought appears, then the reflective activity of asking whether the symbol of deity is what it seems to be does not necessarily drive out the presence of God but can affirm that presence. Reflection can affirm that presence if there is something in the symbol of God that elicits the critical question even while it impresses the reader with the power of God. This conflict of experience and thought is not soluble, but is the mark of the presence of God in text. Where the reader's most strenuous activity in thinking whether God is present in the text is *also* the response to the impact of a symbolic power, then the reader's experience of the symbol is also the reader's activity of interpretation. The hermeneutical point of view is able to mediate the opposition between naiveté and critique in a second naiveté.

The specific character of the "overturning" involved in the God-reference of metaphoric language can now be examined more closely. On the side of the *object*, the symbolized mode of being, which makes the power of God present, bears a contradiction that is intrinsic to its constitution as a symbol of God. The givenness of this object contradicts the thought. How, then, can one recognize it as symbol of God? If the symbol that does present the power to overcome existential opposition *denies* that it is a symbol of God, then what the symbol is on its own corresponds to what a reader experiences and thinks it to be. A reader reads a text and recognizes the word of God through the text, yet the text denies that it is the literal word of God. In this case the object may be a text with God-reference, because it would correspond with a contradiction on the side of the *subject*, in which the reader responds to the text as a religious text that reveals God, but when the critical question is asked of the text, the reader must say that it does not reveal God.[44]

In sum, a correspondence between pairs of elements can appear in certain texts. These texts can be designated as religious texts with a God-reference on the basis of such correspondence. The pairs of elements that come into such a relationship with one another are (subjectively) symbolic experience of God and conceptual thought and (objectively) appearance of a symbol of God and what the appearance says of itself in denying that God appears through it. This correspondence is based on a shared structure of contradiction that is intrinsic to the experience of God in text. That contradiction is a trait of both the object and of the subject, and it cannot be eliminated. The contradiction reappears wherever one identifies a manifestation of or reference to God in text, and is the mark of any living symbol of God.

Under this description of a God-reference through the metaphoric process in texts, we can identify a religious text that reveals God as one that presents just that contradiction between experience and thought. The type of understanding process that corresponds to it would also have a contradictory and paradoxical style. Religious understanding through text would be the projective openness to the appearance of God on the basis of mood. More specifically, religious understanding is *an openness to the appearance of God beyond any disappearance of God for thought*. It responds to the presence of God through the contradiction between concept of God and experienced reality.

Religious understanding, as a preconceptual mode of awareness, gives rise to a certain kind of thinking. The thinking that corresponds to religious understanding is one that is involved in an insoluble and unavoidable paradox. Thinking finds that it cannot think the objects of religious understanding (the "I" or "God") directly, since these objects always slip away and in the nature of the case cannot be objectified. Every attempt to grasp the self or God as an object of thought fails, because what is to be thought is precisely the source and goal of thinking. The "I" is impervious to thought because it is always the point of origin of that thinking. God is beyond the thinkable as the unity of the "I" and the universe, that which cannot be turned into an object within the universe.

To think the inability of the human mind to think the religious object as it is on its own *is* the appropriate way to think the religious reality. The earnest attempt to think about the meaning of being-itself is rewarded not by success in grasping these realities, but in the *overturning of the failure* to grasp self and God. Through trying to think God and self and failing to do so, thinking achieves an openness to what is beyond the split of thought and reality. Through thinking the limits of thinking, thinking stands in openness to what is beyond thinking.

This contradiction at the heart of religious thinking is not a violation of the law of noncontradiction or an error in reason. Religious thinking respects the laws of logic and does not lapse from them in thinking the religious reality as a paradox. And nothing in the law of noncontradiction asserts that reality may not appear to thinking in the form of a contradiction. As a matter of fact, the religious reality does appear in contradictory form as a reality that is not confined to the object-side of the subject-object split necessary for knowledge. The religious reality gives rise to thinking that thinks its own boundaries and is thereby open to the announcement and call of what a symbol of God may show.

A Formal Analysis of Religious Texts and Theological Hermeneutics

Earlier in this chapter I have discussed how Ricoeur in practice identifies religious language with biblical language and how he identifies theological hermeneutics with the task of interpreting the subject matter of the biblical text, which he designates as new being. In theoretical discussion Ricoeur has said nothing to break this identification and to open the category of religious language to nonbiblical forms of discourse. But it is obvious that if theological hermeneutics interprets the religious subject matter of new being as it appears through the unfolding of the world of the biblical text, and if the *Sache* there—new being—can be cleanly distinguished from the signs of that text, then any text that discloses new being can be considered religious, and interpretative work on any text in which new being appears can be considered theological hermeneutics. The fact that this *Sache* is found initially in the Bible is incidental.

All this raises the question whether it is possible to identify religious texts on some basis other than that of a content that is tied to one tradition. Would it be possible to classify religious texts and to denote theological hermeneutics on the basis of a purely formal characteristic? If so, there would be a means of classifying texts—biblical and nonbiblical—as religious without reference to subject matter. This section will propose such a formal classification by designating the various possibilities for relations between the elements of discourse.

If we draw the principle of division between types of texts from the structure of language as that of sign carrying sense (either notional or imagistic) signifying a referent, the rule for forming categories could be formulated as "Identify text-types on the basis of relations between sign, sense, and referent." If we follow this rule, these results obtain. In the first place, a group of six types of text can be distinguished by exhibiting six possible relations between sign and sense (excluding reference for the time being):[45]

1. If the sign is accidental to a notional sense, then we have what may be called a *reflective text*.

2. If the sign is accidental to an imagistic sense, then we have a *mythical text*.

3. If sign is inseparable from notional sense, then we have a *literary text*.

4. If sign is inseparable from imagistic sense, then we have *poetic text*.

5. If the sense is accidental to the sign where the sense is notional, we have a *magical text*.

6. If the sense is accidental to the sign where the sense is imagistic, we have an *incantatory text*.

What is common to all these text-types is that the sense, whether imagistic or notional, signifies the everyday world of objects and states of affairs, and in some cases the text also signifies an imagined world of the text within which I entertain a new possibility of relating the "I" to "this one here in the world." What Ricoeur calls the referent or the *Sache* is signified by the sense but is not *presented* by the sense, since it is nonetheless found outside the sense. This is the case even in what Ricoeur calls poetic texts, or texts with double meaning. These texts project a new world, which is found only through the reading, and their referent—the mode of being based on the actual experiences suggested there—is provided through the signifying ability of the sense of the text. But none of the text-types outlined above exhausts the full referential power of language, nor does any of them qualify as a self-actualizing text in the sense specified below. Two text-types can now be added to the list and the similarities and differences between these types and those above can be explained.

The following texts are all distinct from the above ones in that here sign, sense, and referent are all given together. These texts can be called self-actualizing texts, in that they all have the trait that the sign-sense *presents* the referent in the full sense of that term.

7. If the sign and notional sense of a text fully give the referent so that the referent is completely disclosed through the text alone, it is an *ontological text*.

8. If the sign and imagistic sense of a text fully give the referent so that the referent is completely disclosed through the text alone, it is a *religious text*.

Since an ontological text may, under such a typology, also be a reflective or a literary text (just as a religious text may also be a mythical or a poetic text), what is at stake here is the peculiar ability of some texts to present their referents in an eminent way. Now, within the context of such a typology, it is possible to determine the characteristic of the text that signals the potential presence of the religious or ontological dimension of a text. At this point that characteristic could be called a dimension of reflexivity in the sense of the text itself. When that dimension is present in a text, it is not as something "objective" to a subject any more than it is a "subjective" factor alone that reads something into a text. The presence of the religious or ontological dimension of text is a matter of something emerging with the sense of the text that is between subject and object, and that encompasses them both in the dimension of *Zugehörigkeit* or *appartenance,* as Ricoeur calls it. While it is true that this reflective dimension is "hidden" in the direct world of the text, that is, the literal and figurative meaning of the text, it is nonetheless not without objective signals.

The common mark of a religious and an ontological text is that each gives its referent along with the sense of the text. We have also noted that the sense here will display a pattern of overturning by which meaning is engendered through a contradiction. Ricoeur's terms—*intensification, going to the limit, paradox*—can be used to typify the kind of structural arrangement of elements that can be found within the text and that is the objective mark of a process of understanding that creates meaning through contradiction. Obviously, any text that fully gives its referent must be analyzed to determine exactly how a contradiction or tension between opposites is configured there. But the pattern is that the text poses a contradiction, which may provoke an "overturning" by which the text no longer points away from itself to an independent referent but instead presents and manifests that referent.

An example of an ontological text as defined here would be the essay by Martin Heidegger entitled "Das Wesen der Sprache."[46] In this text Heidegger thinks about the nature of language and the peculiar situation of being unable to think that object without already being immersed in it. There is no nonlinguistic relation to language, since language is the medium of our thinking. Thinking about language, moreover, overturns itself as objective thinking. This occurs because the essence *(Wesen)* of language is to point away from itself as language to reality as it is on its own. Language is a medium for showing and pointing out what is not language but being. To think about the being or nature of language is ultimately to think about the form in which being can appear. Conversely, to think about language as it expresses being is to think about the being of language as that which is open to being. To the extent that Heidegger's reflection on the dialectic between language of being and being of language opens the reader's experience to his or her own relation to language and being in their identity and difference, it presents its referent directly. The sense of the text draws the reader into thinking about the linguistic medium of thinking and being that he or she is engaged in through the text. The referent is given fully with the sense of the text to the extent that the sense of the text opens the ontological world by referring the reader to his or her own understanding of language and being against the background of sheer possibility.

Since Ricoeur's analysis of religious language draws largely on the parables, although he nowhere gives a detailed interpretation of any one parable, I shall refer to the Parable of the Great Supper (Matt. 22:2–10; Luke 14:16–24) as an illustration. For the interpretation of this parable I shall rely on that of Robert Funk in *Language, Hermeneutic, and Word of God*.[47] As does Ricoeur's later analysis, Funk's understands the parable as metaphor with the potential for new meaning. Parable reaches the dimension of metaphorical reference that is here called "religious" because the sense presents the referent fully. Funk puts it this way: "The word gives presence to the referent in such a way that the listener is confronted by it; the auditor does not make a distinction between the vocables and the reality to which the vocables give presence.[48] The very sense of the parable as metaphor intends to present the depth of being as such through its figurative language. With the help of Funk's analysis we can see how the objective sense of the parable points to a literal referent and, additionally, through a device of "overturning" at the heart of the sense, points to a metaphoric sense and referent (a mode of being). That mode of being in turn has the capacity not merely to point but to present fully a reference to the "I" in its temporality and to the ground and abyss of the "I" and universe.

Here is one of the two synoptic versions of the Parable of the Great Supper, that of Matthew:

> And again Jesus spoke to them in parables, saying, "The kingdom of heaven may be compared to a king who gave a marriage feast for his son, and sent his servants to call those who were invited to the marriage feast; but they would not come. Again he sent other servants, saying, 'Tell those who are invited, Behold, I have made ready my dinner, my oxen and my fat calves are killed, and everthing is ready; come to the marriage feast.' But they made light of it and went off, one to his farm, another to his business, while the rest seized his servants, treated them shamefully, and killed them. The king was angry, and he sent his troops and destroyed those murderers and burned their city. Then he said to his servants, 'The wedding is ready, but those invited were not worthy. Go therefore to the thoroughfares, and invite to the marriage feast as many as you find.' And those servants went out into the streets and gathered all whom they found, both bad and good; so the wedding hall was filled with guests."(RSV)

Funk, like Ricoeur, locates the structure of the parable in the plot. The objective sense of the text is the structure of the narrative action, and it follows three steps: orientation to an ordinary situation, disorientation through the intrusion of the extraordinary, and reorientation to the extraordinary in the ordinary. Funk lays it out like this:[49]

    I. Introduction
       a. A man
       b. gives a banquet
       c. invites those (socially) worthy

II. Development and Crisis
   a. banquet is ready
   b. sends servant for courtesy remind (Lk. once, Mt. twice)
   c. guests refuse to come and/or offer excuses, go off on pretexts (Lk. three excuses, Mt. two pretexts and the response of "the rest")
III. Denouement
   a. man is wroth
   b. invites those (socially) unworthy (Mt. once, Lk. twice)
   c. table is filled
   d. judgment upon those originally invited

Refusing to be drawn into any form of allegorizing, Funk understands the parable as a narration filled with the metaphoric potential to show some dimension of reality previously hidden.[30] The introduction depicts an everyday scene that prompts no special recognition and allows the mind to understand unobstructedly that this scene is "the way things are." Everyone knows what it means for a king or other prominent person to give a banquet and to invite those socially worthy. The literal meaning is not impeded: the sense is clear and the scene is one that could be reconstructed in typical outline through historical research.

But in the second stage, the everydayness of the text-world is overturned through an unexpected reversal. The excuses and refusals of the guests provoke a crisis and a break in the normality. By this time the reader has already prereflectively understood himself as one of the affluent in the story and in the crisis he is offended because it contradicts his anticipation of the favorable resolution of the parable: *He* would have accepted![51] Or instead the reader has identified with the lowly of the scene, who secretly aspire to the banquet but who cannot openly anticipate inclusion. This expectation of exclusion is overturned as well. The third part brings out the metaphorical quality of the parable. Through what was initially insignificant—the everydayness of the scene—an element of unconditioned seriousness breaks through. The parable has divided the readers into two groups: those who hear judgment and those who hear grace,[52] depending on how the denouement of the parable identifies the reader's mode of being. In each case, the parable shows the self to itself in its act of self-understanding. "I" find myself as recipient of grace or judgment precisely in and through my most everyday actions. The parable shows through the juxtaposition of the two figures just how man's destiny and the depth of his existence are at stake in the commonness of everyday life.[53]

According to Funk, the parable presents its referent by exposing one's fundamental disposition to things at hand by evoking a new relation to reality in its everydayness. "I" am exposed when my anticipation is overturned and then interpreted by the parable as a fundamental mode of being.[54] Either "I" am striving to secure my existence, or I am open to the givenness of the situation and can receive the grace of new understanding. In either case the parable intends to provoke a recognition of the meaning of my existence.

In the scheme of interpretation proposed in the last section, the pattern of recognition might differ slightly from that of Funk. The metaphoric referent is not simply the self who understands himself, either authentically or inauthentically, as graced or judged wanting. The referent is the "I" who can identify with *both* modes of being. The self can recognize itself as capable of both responses and aware of that duplicity in itself. The sense of the text can present as the referent the hermeneutical or reflexive self, which can identify with each of the two responses but not to the exclusion of the other. Such a text would of course be a religious text on account of the direct presentation of the referent—here the concrete relation of the "I" and "this person here." It would add a God-referent to the self-referent if in addition the mode of being that is graced or judged (or capable of both) can symbolize the power of God and show that power. Where the parable presents the power that gives the grace or judgment to the reader through the figure of the parable's metaphoric meaning, the text also has a self-actualizing God-referent.

The parable cited above illustrates the religious text-type according to the criterion that it have a figurative sense that presents its referent fully. As a biblical example, it does not show how this criterion can apply to nonbiblical texts. But application of the criterion to other text-traditions is an open possibility for future attention.

The last example of a self-actualizing text is that of a theological text. A theological text is one that mediates the immediacy of religious figurative language and thus interprets the religious content by developing the image-content into ontological language. It also points out the religious origin of ontological terms. Theological hermeneutics on this account could then be specified as the theory of such mediation between the immediacy of religious understanding and the mediatedness of ontological understanding. It is the theory of the interconnectedness of the religious and the ontological in texts.

6 • Appropriation of Textual Meaning and the Question of Truth

The concluding chapter of this study concerns the topic of appropriation of textual meaning. With this topic we come to the goal of the hermeneutical process as Paul Ricoeur articulates it. In preceding chapters I have attempted to show how Ricoeur's hermeneutical theory displays its inner unity by following his thought through the stages dictated by the systematic principle "the self goes out of itself (in expression) and returns to itself (in appropriation)."

The analysis of the successive stages of Ricoeur's theory has presented in some detail the particularity of Ricoeur's contribution to the line of hermeneutical thought associated with Schleiermacher and Dilthey. We have seen how Ricoeur develops a general theory of interpretation that offers new insight in the debate over methodology. Ricoeur's contribution in this area has been especially noteworthy with regard to the theory of written text and, what is the heart of the enterprise, the theory of metaphoric process as one of "semantic innovation." With the topic of appropriation we come to the final element in the task Ricoeur set for himself to provide a coherent account of the principles for textual exegesis.

With the moment of appropriation, Ricoeur's interpretation theory reaps the harvest of methodological labors, for here the hermeneutical passage from sense to reference is completed. If hermeneutics intends to interpret the text as a projection of a referent by the structure of the text in an ontological world that I might inhabit in order to project one of my possibilities into it, then with the appropriation stage we reach the end of the process, where I take hold of that referent and *actualize* the intention of the text. Appropriation completes the hermeneutical process because at this stage the meaning of the text is brought out of alienation into familiarity.[1] The understanding process here moves from methodical laying out of the sense of the text to a gathering in of that meaning as my own. Ricoeur compares this last moment with the performance of a musical score.² This is a helpful analogy because with appropriation the semantic virtualities of the text—now in a state of readiness after the stages of explanation and comprehension have put the naive understanding to the test by letting the structure of the text speak—are returned to the ground of lived experience from which they arose initially as expression. Ricoeur has never wavered in his contention against the structuralists that appropriation constitutes the "aim of all hermeneutics."³

But insofar as the appropriation stage completes the methodological discussion, which governs the passage from sense to reference by guiding interpretation to its actualization in lived experience, it is also the point where Ricoeur's interpretation theory rejoins the line of thought that initially inspired his work: the line running from Kant through Fichte, Hegel, Husserl, and Heidegger, to Ricoeur. In the end the dominant question for Ricoeur is "What does it mean to be human?" and the development of a text-based hermeneutic is at the service of such inquiry into the being of the self and its position within being-itself.

I documented above how Ricoeur's work in philosophical anthropology came to recognize from Heidegger that understanding the meaning of being human is interpretative through and through. Ricoeur also expropriated from Heidegger the view that *Rede* is the place where *Dasein* is open for interpretation. But there is a difference between Heidegger and Ricoeur. Heidegger pursued the *Seinsfrage* in his attempt to think the meaning of being under the sign of hermeneutics, based initially on interpretation of *Dasein* as situated understanding and then on the linguistic approach of *Sein* to *Dasein*. For Ricoeur, Heidegger's treatment of *Verstehen* as a mode of being rather than a mode of thinking tends to break off epistemological discussion on method even while it places Heidegger on new terrain for ontological thought.⁴ Ricoeur's response to the aporia that he thinks Heidegger opens "*between* ontology and epistemology taken as wholes" is to pursue precisely what Heidegger neglects. Focusing on the methodological issues, Ricoeur holds open and advances discussion with the segment of the scientific community that refuses to accept the Heideggerian reversal of understanding as a mode of thinking into a mode of being and considers questions of method as paramount.

But what is more, Ricoeur pursues interpretation theory in the tradition of Schleiermacher and Dilthey as an indirect form of philosophical anthropology based on the premise that man *is* language. Ricoeur initially turned to hermeneutics in recognition that the *cogito* is a vain and empty starting point for a philosophy asking about the meaning of being human, because there is no content to immediate self-consciousness.[5] Knowledge of the self must be mediated by the objectifications and figures of the self, for the *cogito* gives no insight into the concrete meaning of existence. To gain access to the meaning of human expression of self-understanding, Ricoeur's reflection took the path of hermeneutics conceived as "the appropriation of our effort to exist and of our desire to be, through the works which bear witness to that effort and desire."[6] The merger of the two lines of thought occurs in Ricoeur's project to outline a general theory of text-interpretation and to deduce from the structure of text and text-interpretation the conditions of the possibility for the process of understanding as it is actually mediated through texts. What, he asks, is implied by the given process of interpreting texts about the being of *Dasein* as it belongs to being-itself?

This question can be brought into focus for Ricoeur with consideration of the topic of appropriation, because it is with appropriation that the dynamics of meaning move from sense to reference, from what is said to that about which it is said. With the topic of appropriation the passage is made from semantics and theory of textual meaning and understanding to philosophical anthropology and ontology. Ricoeur's long detour through the literature on symbolic expression, hermeneutics of suspicion, theory of text, and especially the theory of metaphoric creation of meaning, rejoins the primary task of situating the being of *Dasein* in being as such.

Since the intersection of the two lines of thought, "epistemology of interpretation" and "ontology of understanding," occurs in this topic, this chapter will have a dual intention. In the first place, Ricoeur's concept of appropriation will be presented in the context of his text-based hermeneutics. Of particular importance is the appropriation of metaphorical meaning and the role of the productive imagination in constructing and discovering that meaning. The purpose here is to round off and complete the analysis of Ricoeur's contribution to the methodological discussion in the area of semantics of the text. In the second place, the implications of Ricoeur's concept of appropriation for philosophical anthropology and ontology will be articulated. The task here will be to take appropriation of textual meaning as a given object (*noema*) of consciousness from which we can analyze the structure of consciousness presupposed. Ricoeur has managed to make a significant contribution to philosophical anthropology through such a method by shedding new light on the nature of the imagination as the mediating function itself, that is, the being of man. And since in appropriation of textual meaning the object of understanding is always being, the next step is to indicate what his theory implies about the position *Dasein* occupies with respect to being-itself. In this area Ricoeur has been more reticent, but an effort will be made to point out the ontological implications of his hermeneutical theory.

The procedure for this chapter is as follows. I shall consider in turn the object of appropriation (part 1), the event of appropriation (part 2), and the subject of appropriation (part 3), for the purpose of analyzing Ricoeur's basic notion. Within each of the three sections, however, I shall distinguish the surface from the depth level, using the terms *world of the text* and *ontological world* to make the distinction. With the reference to the depth dimension of this process, the implications of Ricoeur's hermeneutics for a philosophy concerned with the being of *Dasein* and being as such will be summarized. Following the three parts on appropriation, I shall more thoroughly discuss his notion of the kind of thinking that is ontological or speculative (part 4). I shall then conclude the chapter with some remarks on the question of truth (part 5) as it is raised in the context of appropriation. The issue here is whether the surface level of truth as correspondence must be sacrificed in appropriation of metaphoric meaning to the depth level of truth as unhiddenness.

The Object of Appropriation

From the beginning of his hermeneutical reflections, Ricoeur has attempted to break the pattern of Romantic hermeneutics with its formation of the circle of understanding between two subjectivities. In Ricoeur's theory, the object of appropriation is not the author as a spiritual entity with whom the reader shares a structure of subjectivity, but is rather defined as the *world* projected by the work: "The coming to language of the sense and the reference of a text is a coming to language of a world and not the recognition of another person."[7] Whereas a descriptive text refers to objects in the perceptual world, poetic language opens new worlds by means of its nonostensive references.[8] According to Ricoeur, then, the circle of understanding is formed between my mode of being and the possible mode of being disclosed by the text as the work's world.[9]

What Ricoeur's account leaves unclear, however, is the difference between (1) the directly imagined *world of the text* as a context of meanings into which the self can project itself in a kind of self-forgetfulness in a first or "naive" reading, and (2) the reflexively articulated *ontological world*, which includes me as the reader and the text-world projected for the direct reader. And Ricoeur also is unclear in distinguishing the *referent* as an extralinguistic object of experience projected into the text-world from the *text-world* itself. The text projects the referent in the opened world of the text, and in surface reading I can identify with the referent in an understanding that is prehermeneutical. Such a prehermeneutical or naive understanding flows with the narrative and may be transformed by it, but lacks reflexive awareness that it understands a text as a sign with sense and reference.

Appropriation in the proper hermeneutical sense is appropriation of a referent within the ontological world, and it presumes that the naive reading of the text has been submitted for interpretation because it was not found to be immediately understandable.[10] At this level the reader attempts to follow the sense to the referent as an experience that can ground a mode of being within an interpreted world. The reader may appropriate that referent by meeting the projection of that possibility by the text with a projection of oneself into that situation. This happens by means of an attunement of the reader to the set of connections forming the text-world on the basis of which the reader can say "I understand what it means to be in the world in the manner presented here." The reader appropriates the referent when the text enables the reader to recognize that mode of being as "my own" and to become what one truly is through that recognition. In appropriation, an imagined *possible* mode of being is made *actual*.

Now, what does show itself in the ontological world so defined? At the level of descriptive texts, *things* in the world, *events, persons* can be disclosed by the language. Poetic texts also have a literal level of meaning and refer to literal objects. But because of the semantics of metaphoric process, in poetic texts the literal level of sense breaks open from some incongruity of predication and something new emerges from the collapse of the merely literal. A metaphorical meaning emerges through some insight into likeness, which involves both a thought-connection and an image-connection (in that something is visualized and "seen as").[11] The new meaning does not discard the suspended literal one but lets itself be read *on* the literal image as a signifier of a mode of being.[12]

A third possibility, beyond the literal and metaphorical, for the reference of a text is *nothing*, literally nothing as it is experienced in the mood of *Angst*. This referent is signified, for example, when the critical consciousness asks of a poetic text, "What *is* the reference here?" and applies standards of verification of falsification as criteria. For the strictly critical consciousness the poetic text can convey no new information about reality and has no referent that can be specified. Yet again a fourth level of referent is possible. If, as was indicated in the last chapter, the referred-to mode of being itself has the significatory power to refer to the very process of situated understanding and to display there the meaning of authentic timing, then the text can refer to *being as such* as the power negating the disruption of existence. Ricoeur does not formulate his hermeneutic theory in that way, and has said very little about the possibility of referring to being beyond nothing. But what he has said can be summarized now.

In the last chapter of *The Rule of Metaphor*, Ricoeur presents his most complete attempt "to propose an interpretation of the ontology implicit in the postulates of metaphorical reference."[13] In this chapter Ricoeur advances the scope of his discussion beyond the analysis of a process that he contends is immanent in language itself. Now his thinking turns from the issues central to interpretation theory and philosophical anthropology to the task of constructing a thought of being as such. Ricoeur's intention was always to enter hermeneutical theory so that he could better reflect on the being of man as it is situated in being-itself. Here he begins to sketch out the notion of being that is implied in his hermeneutics. Hermeneutics approaches fundamental ontology.

The warrant for the ontological discernment that Ricoeur makes can be specified with reference to the nature of language itself. Ricoeur claims that language carries an intrinsic doubleness in it. This doubleness inherent in language is manifest in the various dualities that come to light in analysis of different facets of the phenomenon of language. The dualities of noun and verb, event and meaning, sense and reference, reflection and avowal, and most especially the duality of literal and metaphorical, display that intrinsic doubleness in language. Language cannot in the end be reduced to univocity of meaning, so the pattern of metaphorical emergence of meaning beyond the literal can be considered an ontological characteristic of language itself.

Ricoeur holds further that since the metaphorical process is a characteristic of language itself, it can have clear implications for the ontological reflection on being itself. The "tension" that produces emergence of meaning in a metaphor is ultimately a tension in the copula between *is* and *is not*, which gives rise to a new meaning when the imagination forms a picture and thinks what that image *is like*. This tension in the copula in the metaphorical process is the clue for Ricoeur's ontological statement that "Being (as) . . . means being and not being."[14] Ricoeur's thought of being is the thought of being as it emerges out of nonbeing. His vision of reality is a dynamic one: from the relativization of being by nonbeing, new being appears as "being as." The metaphorical process of gain of meaning out of contradiction signals the dialectical notion of "being as" as the overcoming of nonbeing by being.[15]

The warrant for such an ontological discernment can be further specified with respect to the universal scope of language itself. The principle that Ricoeur applies in this case is that if a characteristic of a certain instance of language in use can be shown to be an ontological feature of language as such, then that characteristic is also demonstrated to be a feature of being as such. The justification of this principle rests on the observation that language is the universal medium of all our thinking and experiencing. Language, as Gadamer argues at length, is the central point where "I" and the world display their original unity even while it is the medium through which the "I" and the world first recognize their difference in the freedom of openness.[16] Language is the *Erschlossenheit* of *Dasein* and the openness of being just because it is the identity of the identity and difference of "I" and universe.[17] Since anything that can manifest its presence *as* something must do so through the medium of language, "Sein, das verstanden werden kann, ist Sprache (Being that can be understood is language)."[18] The linguistic way in which any object of thought presents itself is part of its being, since the object *(Sache)* is always there *in* the word.[19] The fact that we grasp being through language means that there is something about the way being appears that is linguistic. The linguistic nature of being is a condition of the possibility of the understanding-appropriating process itself, just as is the openness of *Dasein* to being through language.

The being of language, however, in turn is to say something *about* something that is *not* language, but the *Sache* there in the words. Language comes into its full being when it presents the being of which it speaks. The speculative structure of language is a second condition of the possibility of understanding. Language is the medium of the self-presentation of what is not language; the word is word just because of what is embodied in it.[20] Language "mirrors" being as the process of the *Selbst-Darstellung* of being.[21] Ricoeur agrees with Gadamer that language has this speculative structure and stands in this dialectical relation to being.[22] The following relations are established as a consequence of that view: Being is being itself only when it is not merely being but becomes a process of self-presentation through language.[23] And conversely, language is language itself only when it is not merely focused on itself as language but becomes a process of the making-manifest of being. Through "being as" as a dimension of language, being-itself is disclosed to the reflexive subject who can listen to the infinity of what is not said resonating with what is said, and can encounter the open space of possibility beyond the actual situation referred to by the language.[24]

How, then, are we *to think* this notion "being itself" if it is the final referent and "object" of appropriation? Ricoeur's implicit answer is that we are to think it through a contradiction. How so? Being-itself appears through the "being as" of metaphorical reference, but in any strict conceptuality, being-itself cannot be specified since it is prior to all objectification. When thought, being is nothing. When encountered through the "being as" of metaphorical meaning, however, being as such is experienced through mood as *not nothing*. A contradiction resides at the heart of the object of appropriation between what is thought as nothing but what is felt and experienced as not nothing. All we can say is that it is *like* what happens in the poem, and be open to its manifestation through contradiction.

Appropriation as Event

There is a surface level of appropriation in which the process of understanding and making what is understood one's own is unmediated.[25] In some conversations we have examples of spontaneous, unmediated understanding. So too does the hearing of myth in traditional societies take on the immediacy characteristic of linguistic processes in which understanding is unimpeded. This surface level of first, naive appropriation is even approached as a limit by the self-conscious interpreter who knowingly opens himself up to a text or art work in order eventually to retrieve the initial experience after it is over and now pierced by the critical eye. But strictly speaking it is a prehermeneutical event that is not yet aware of itself *as* event, but merely follows the movement of image or sound. It is simply passive in receiving the content there.

Once the critical consciousness has broken through this first naiveté, appropriation is recognized as inauthentic to the extent that the reader is absorbed in the direct world of the text and is oblivious to the manner in which he is absorbed there. The second naiveté attempts to recapture this immediateness only as a limit and as mediated immediateness. It retains the awareness of the self's activity in reading even while it suspends the need to separate sense and reference. Mere reflexivity does not guarantee authenticity, however. What Ricoeur seeks from a reflexive viewpoint is a description of authentic appropriation just because the reflexive consciousness is itself so tenaciously enamored of its own powers of reflection that its mode of understanding and appropriation tends to be inauthentic. What is the process of appropriation like at the depth level where an authentic appropriation is a possibility?

Appropriation within the ontological world involves a reader who places himself within the world of the text and understands the literal sense and referent. Beyond this, the reader finds something non-sensical at the literal level that overturns the primacy of literal meaning even while it points to a second, metaphorical meaning that appears "on" or "through" the literal meaning. This new sense and referent is first understood apart from its appropriation by a reader. But when the reader actualizes the "semantic virtualities" in the meaning by identifying with the signified mode of being so that the reader encounters a figure who represents "I" as I *should be*, then we reach the stage of appropriation. Where the reader can see himself reflected in the text so that he can say "I understand my own authentic being through this text-world," the text-world is appropriated.

In Ricoeur's analysis, such an event of appropriation involves two aspects of a single process. In the semantic process by which metaphoric meaning emerges from a significant clash on the literal level, there is both the "gravitational pull exerted by the second referential field, giving the meaning the force to leave its place of origin" and there is the forward-moving motion of the "dynamism of meaning itself."[26] This dual-vectored event, whereby the new reference approaches me while I follow the signification of the metaphorical sense, is actualized as event when I take on the referential situation as my own and orient myself within it. Ricoeur likens this process of actualization to Gadamer's "fusion of horizons" (*Horizontverschmelzung*),²⁷ in that the appropriation takes place within the common horizon of the reader and that projected by the text. Insofar as "I" follow the sense of the text, I bring my world to bear on the meaning; but insofar as I respond to the appearance of the referent, the linguistic world projected by the text redetermines my own world. In the final analysis, Ricoeur holds that of the two aspects involved, the pull of the world projected by the text is dominant over the role of the subject who runs ahead in staking out the contours of that world. For Ricoeur, "it is not the reader who primarily projects himself," but rather the projective power of the texts that can enlarge the reader "in his capacity of self-projection by receiving a new mode of being from the text itself."²⁸ The primacy of the act of the emergent meaning over the reader's projection is a theme in Gadamer's hermeneutic as well as that of Ricoeur, and it is the trait that confers the specifically "event" (*Geschehen*) nature upon appropriation. Something comes into language that has been said and assimilated in the tradition, and the reader "suffers" the act of the *Sache* itself. Appropriation is an event because of the passivity involved in it.²⁹

The event of appropriation is, of course, a linguistic event through and through; and language is the medium of this act of appropriation within the fusion of horizons. Since the emergent meaning approaches the reader through a linguistically fashioned world and is fused with the linguistic world of the reader, the event of appropriation is an event of language that always finds new expression. The linguistic nature of the event of appropriation has other implications: since we are approached by a meaning that emerges in futurity as a real possibility for me, even as it speaks from the past of the tradition, the language-event of appropriation displays the underlying belongingness-to the tradition that is a condition of the possibility of the understanding-appropriation process. We belong to the subject matter from the tradition that reaches us for appropriation.³⁰ The further condition of being reached by the tradition in such a way that something new is concretized by the event of appropriation requires that the reader be capable of what Gadamer calls *Hören*, an ability to listen and to be negative to his or her immediate and surface experience. The reader must be able to disengage his preconceptions by allowing the ontological world to open. The event of appropriation happens only if the text is permitted to speak into the openness of the reader's linguistic world.

The linguistic nature of the event of appropriation also displays the historicity and the finitude of this experience at the end of the hermeneutical process. Since we appropriate potential meanings embedded in the historical linguistic tradition by actualizing them here in this linguistic situation now, the "omnitemporality" of the linguistic meaning—its ability to generate new meaning in time—is the counterpart of a historicity in the appropriative process.[31] The event of appropriation is always one in a series of such events by a succession of interpreters which belong to the work of the text on itself.[32] The work that is appropriated is in turn interrelated with other events of linguistic appropriation backward and forward in time, which continue to influence the present reader by contributing to the formation of his linguistic orientation:[33] All interpretation places the interpreter in the midst, and never at the beginning or at the end, of a language-event. We enter upon a conversation with a history in which we try to make our own contribution.[34] And since we can always make our own contribution only from a situated perspective that is open to the tradition from the finite orientation of this situation, the event of appropriation is marked by its thoroughgoing finitude.

All of the above concerns the structure of the event of appropriation of metaphorical meaning in the sense of a "mode of being" or "possible world." What would a description of the event of appropriation of being as such add to this structure? Here the classical point of reference by which Ricoeur takes his orientation is the later work of Martin Heidegger in which he thinks being as *Ereignis* ("event of appropriation") through "*es gibt*."[35] In the following I shall take Otto Pöggeler's essay "Sein als Ereignis" as my guide to Heidegger's effort in this regard. The problem here is how to think the depth of the event of appropriation from a fully reflexive point of view. Is it possible to speak not only of an appropriation of a new "mode of being" but also of the appropriation of "being as such"? Since Ricoeur concurs with Heidegger's solution to the problem even while he distinguishes his own working out and presentation of that solution from Heidegger, it is helpful to summarize Heidegger on this issue.

Heidegger undertook his existential analytic of *Dasein* for the purpose of working out the *Seinsfrage*—the question of the meaning of being. *Dasein* was the focus of the analysis because it is ontological in its understanding of being and thus in a sense is the foundation of being. Heidegger's foundation was not conceived in Husserlian fashion as pure consciousness that constitutes its objects transcendentally. Rather, *Dasein* was taken as being-in-the-world, a thrown project marked by care, finitude, historicity, and temporality.[36] *Dasein* is "foundation" only in the sense that in understanding itself, inauthentically in terms of *vorhanden* beings, it still understands its own "to be" and comports itself to beings in their being. *Dasein* thus offers a clearing in being. Man finds himself *within* the wholeness of being determined by a mood that is permeated with understanding.

In the fascination and inauthentic comportment with things in *Vorhandenheit*, *Dasein* deals directly with things *in* time as present-at-hand and is unable to grasp temporality as the basis of its own comportments. *Authentic Dasein*, however, even though it can never free itself entirely from everyday inauthenticity, can open a new perspective on the meaning of being by reflexively grasping itself as the temporalization of time even while it continues to exist in the world alongside entities *in* time.[37] The authentic viewpoint arises from the shock at the finitude of *Dasein* when it anticipates the possibility of its own impossibility to be anything at all, "d.h. den Tod als gegenwärtig fühlen (Luther) (that is, to feel death as present)."[38]

References have already been made to Pöggeler's analysis of the reasons why *Sein und Zeit* failed to grasp the meaning of being in a clear concept based on *Dasein*'s preunderstanding of being: Heidegger grasps *Dasein* most essentially as the temporalization of time and the meaning of Being must be articulated against the horizon of time. *Dasein* finds its openness to being in the timing process, yet conceptual thinking cannot take hold of this timing process as the meaning and manifestation or truth of being.[39] The key difficulty, Heidegger claimed, is in the language of the conceptuality of metaphysics which, in a manner similar to inauthentic *Dasein*, thinks beings only in *Vorhandenheit* and is oblivious to the horizon of temporality in which they are grasped as present. Hence metaphysics grounds beings on a highest being conceived as infinite presence, and fails to think the meaning of being as such.

After *Sein und Zeit* Heidegger pursued his question by seeking to overcome the language of metaphysics by returning to its unthought and abysslike ground in time as the openness between *Sein* and *Dasein*. According to Pöggeler, Heidegger succeeds in this task not by thinking in a line moving from *Dasein* to *Sein*—a line characterized only by a double negation with no content and the opening of *Abgrund* of metaphysics—but by tracing the movement from being to *Dasein* as it is characterized by a double "*Übermacht*," which provides the content. From the orientation of authentic *Dasein*, which grasps itself as the temporalization of time and which responds to the disclosure of the difference between being and beings, *Dasein* witnesses the process in which being "grants" beings to *Dasein* and in this way brings about this difference, thus revealing itself in beings while it conceals itself at the same time.[40]

To authentic *Dasein*, being gives itself in the clearing of openness, but only in the determinate and bounded appearance of beings that conceal being while they disclose it. Being shows itself, but only in the finite place of disclosure, as the *Seinsgeschick*—historical sending and fate of being—which appropriates *Dasein* in the event whereby *Dasein* appropriates the meaning of beings as beings. The horizon of understanding in which being is disclosed, that is, the *meaning* of being, can now be articulated as the event of appropriation *(Ereignis)*, where this means "die Vereignung des Daseins in das Sein und die Zueignung des Seins an die Eigentlichkeit des Daseins (expropriating *Dasein* into being and appropriating being into the authenticity of *Dasein*)."[41] *Ereignis* names the meaning of being itself nonmetaphysically, and becomes a key word for thinking, like the Greek *Logos* or Chinese *Tao*, because "im Ereignis ist die Zeit, in deren Lichte das Sein immer schon auf eine verborgene Weise verstanden wurde, eigens mitgedacht" (in the event of appropriation, time in whose light Being has always already been understood in a hidden manner, is thought also at the same time).[42]

Being is thought by Heidegger as *Ereignis* by appropriating in authenticity the meaning of the event of appropriation. Now, this extension of the reflexivity of *Dasein* as finite care to appropriation of the appropriation of the granting of beings by being, can illuminate the suggestion, offered above in the preceding chapter, that Ricoeur take the religious and ontological level of meaning in texts as one in which the mode of being, granted by the text to the reader in appropriation, is itself a sign with meaning. The event of appropriation can itself be appropriated against the background of the disclosure and hiddenness in the *Selbst-Darstellung* of being. The depth-dimension of appropriation, as the appropriation of the meaning of appropriation, responds to the depth-dimension of the text where that object can be being itself or God the holy. And in the depth of appropriation, the distinction between the act of appropriation and the *object* of appropriation falls away to the extent that being as *Ereignis* is the event of the appropriation of the appropriation of the sameness of the granting of beings by being in openness and the openness of *Dasein* in responding to beings. It is the temporal event whereby it is disclosed that "Mensch und Sein sind einander übereignet. Sie gehören einander (man and being are appropriated to one another. They belong to one another),"[43] or as Ricoeur says, "*Ereignis* and *es gibt* mark the opening and the unfolding by reason of which there are objects for a judging subject."[44]

Subject of Appropriation

At the surface of the appropriation process, where the self passively reads and finds itself identified with the meanings projected by the world of the text, the role of subjectivity is lost and hidden. The everyday form of reading is one of entertainment and escape. But Ricoeur's analysis of the understanding-appropriating process shows that much more is occurring in the escapism of the first-order reading than meets the merely introspective eye. By taking a reflexive view of the understanding process, Ricoeur is able to view the event of understanding-appropriation as a constituted object and to read off from that object the subjective conditions of its possibility.

In the direct reading of a poetic text at the prehermeneutical level, the self moves with the narrative or poetic sense without noticing the transformations it undergoes. Separated from itself as the timing activity, it identifies with the meanings projected there *in* time. This alienation of the self from the self is brought to awareness in hermeneutics along with recognition of the alienation of the sense of the text, which is now cut off from the living tradition from which it sprang. Authentic appropriation of textual meaning from the reflexive viewpoint is the event in which the self-alienation and meaning-alienation are overcome in the fusion of horizons, which transforms world as well as subjectivity. What does Ricoeur's noematic analysis tell us about the role of the subject in this process?

For Ricoeur, there are two crucial vectors of interaction between the text and self, and these two elements make it possible to articulate the role of the subject both in an *active* or productive way as the timing function that synthesizes its meaning through a schematizing activity, and in a *passive* and responsive way as the suffering of a transformation in subjectivity initiated not by the self but by the being that appears with the text. Although these two elements are ultimately to be thought together as an identity, the receptive and responsive dimension is given priority. Understanding really begins when something claims and addresses me, thus provoking *my* response. The being of the subject for Ricoeur is thought as the "imagination," and he best defines it as "the [active] capacity to let new worlds build our self-understanding [through response]."[45]

Typically, the imagination is thought of as the faculty of deriving pale-resemblance "images" from sensory experience, but Ricoeur's analysis embarks on a new direction that follows Kant's theory of schematism rather than Hume's notion of weakened impressions.[46] In *Fallible Man* Ricoeur had already made imagination central, in Kantian style, as the activity that mediates between concepts and intuitions on the basis of a transcendental image deduced as a condition of the possibility of the constitution of perceptual objects.[47] Here, at the final stage of his hermeneutical theory, Ricoeur extends the notion of imagination to that of the condition of the possibility of the "emergent meanings" of metaphoric "semantic innovation." And as such he formulates it as a semantic function that is immanent in the subject's use of language.[48]

The key elements of the metaphoric process that indicate characteristics of the subjective correlate are these: (1) Metaphor is an act of predication, (2) in which meaning emerges at the predicative level through the metaphorical congruence apprehended beyond literal incongruence, (3) which in turn generates a second reference on the ruins of literal reference. Ricoeur's claim is that the mediations that bring about metaphoric meaning are accomplished through the imagination in the medium of language.[49] How do these three steps indicate something about the imagination?

In the first place, imagination is responsible for the insight into a new likeness to the extent that it mediates between subject and predicate in the sentence and can assimilate and make semantically proximate the terms included in the metaphor.[50] It does not do this by subsuming two different items under a higher genus as in conceptual work, but rather by "predicative assimilation," in which the similarity is apprehended in spite of and through the difference without abstracting from the difference. Imagination mediates between literal absurdity and metaphorical suggestiveness to discern a new connection that is not part of the current lexicon. This function is one that lies below the general procedure by which concepts that are part of the lexicon were created in the first place.[51] The literal non-sense acts here as the rule for the formation of a new meaning; the literal image in its instability is a schema for metaphorical attribution.[52]

In the second place, the language of metaphor is a schema for the production of the figurative and pictorial dimension of the emergent meaning. Metaphoric language, in its literal incongruence of imagery, provides a formula for the construction of icons. The construction always occurs, as we have seen, as a depiction of some new figure *on* the old and incongruent one. The literal image allows a new image to appear on it through the productive power of the imagination. In this way the images displayed by the text function as schemata for the production of new figures.

In the third place, the metaphoric language provides schemata for the redescription of reality that occurs in the synthesis of a second reference. This function has two sides: the literal incongruity allows the imagination to address itself to what is *not* and to perform an *epoché* on first-order reference, but beyond that the semantic code impels the projection of new possibilities of referential completion of sense by the imagination.[53] The imagination here mediates between the *actuality* of everyday life and the *absence* of the whole of things to synthesize the appearance of the redescribed and ontologically significant reference to new modes of being-in-the-world.

Ricoeur also extends the mediating function of imagination farther, below the threshold of the productive capacities of understanding, to the level of attunement and feeling. Corresponding to the three levels just mentioned, feeling is integral to (1) the schematization of predicative congruence, (2) the iconic picturing, and (3) the projection of new reality beyond nothing: First, feeling acts to interiorize and include the imagining self with the new meaning. The emergent meaning is not fully objectified but is also *felt*, so that the reader is assimilated to the meaning as much as he or she performs the predicative assimilation. This point pertains directly to the role of the subject in appropriation, since it is preeminently in feeling that I make what was foreign my own. "We feel *like* what we see *like*" in metaphor.[54] Second, feelings accompany and complete the *pictured* image in that the produced icon structures a mood according to its own schematic formula. The mood is synthesized in response to the icon.[55] Third, feeling also plays an important role in the imaginative projection of redescribed reality as world of the text. Just as the imagination suspends the first-order referential world, the metaphoric language reverberates on feeling so as to affect an *epochē* of bodily emotions directed to literal objects. And the feeling dimension is also active beyond that negation in that in the clearance of the *epochē* of first-order emotions, the deeper attunement to being as such can come to the fore. The imagination projects the second meaning and then responds in mood as a way of synthesizing the poetic experience so that it can "insert us within the world in a nonobjectifying fashion."[56]

The interaction between insight, imagination, and feeling, in which imagination is the mediating term, must be thought in identity with the thought, imagination, and sensation triad of perceptual object-constitution. Together they make up the self in the register of understanding the described world and the redescribed world through text. In the appropriation of the specifically metaphorical level of meaning—in which the "I" claims the emergent meaning as its own and is restructured along its lines—the self is presented with the positive possibility of transformation.

Although Ricoeur does not focus attention on the timing involved in metaphorical understanding and appropriation, it should be noted that metaphorical language schematizes the temporality of openness. The reader of a poetic text is open to the past tradition that has preceded the language event of appropriation, and he is open to the future designs of meaningfulness through following the signs of metaphoricalness as they intend new meaning. Metaphor temporalizes openness to the depth of language insofar as it draws the subject into the heritage of the past in an act of recovery in order to project possibility of a new meaning approaching from the future, so that the present moment may be illuminated and discerned in its potentialities for being. The temporalizing of metaphor is designed to engage the reader in a process of authentic timing with its marks of *Wiederholung*, *Vorlaufen*, and *Augenblick*.

For Ricoeur, the role of the subject in appropriation is ultimately not to take possession of a new possibility to be itself, but to experience "a moment of dispossession of the egoistic and narcissistic ego" and to open itself to receive an authentic self from the text.[57] The meaning is appropriated not by submitting the text to one's finite abilities, but by exposing oneself to the text in its ability to confer a geniune sense of selfhood. The self is not so much the foundation of understanding-appropriation as it is the constitution effected through the *Sache* of poetic texts.[58]

The self finds itself and gains its true destiny only in the willingness to withdraw itself from the position of constituting consciousness in order to allow the text-tradition to confer that consciousness in belongingness to and dependence on that tradition. As Ricoeur says, "La chose du texte ne devient mon propre que si je me désapproprie de moi-même, pour laisser être la chose du text. Alors j'échange le *moi, maître* de lui-même, contre le *soi, disciple* du texte" (The issue of the text only becomes my own if I disappropriate myself from myself, in order to let the issue of the text be. Then I exchange the *I, master* of itself, for the *self, disciple* of the text)."[59]

At the deepest level of appropriation, that is, when it is a case of the fully reflexive "I" grasping/responding in correlation with being as such, then the situation might be described as follows (although this is by no means Ricoeur's terminology): the "I" who reads hermeneutically encounters in what is initially not-I the figure of "new being" in the sense described earlier as the appearance of essential authentic *Dasein*, and that "I" recognizes its estranged self there in that image insofar as it is the figure on which that mode of being appears. "I" can appropriate that mode of being to the extent that it can bring about my essential being in spite of the condition of existential split and fault. The enabling power is a direct appearance of the self to the self, and the interpretation of this event allows the self's return to the self in conscious self-recognition.

Ricoeur's Proposal for Ontology

In the above paragraphs the results of Ricoeur's proposals for philosophical anthropology were briefly summarized. The focus is on the imagination understood as the subjective correlate of the dialectic of metaphorical utterance. In the earlier paragraphs I discussed Ricoeur's proposal for an interpretation of the ontology implicit in the theory of metaphor, and indicated briefly how Ricoeur's view of "being as" shares a common ground with Heidegger's notion of *Ereignis*. What was discussed there was limited to a shared terrain even though Ricoeur's "being as" is discerned by taking the turn through methodological discussions to isolate in the end the principles of metaphoric meaning, whereas Heidegger's "*Ereignis*" follows upon a single-minded devotion to the *Seinsfrage* that led him through the analytic of *Dasein* to the "overcoming" of metaphysics and the hearkening to the voice of being as language-event. How, then, could Ricoeur's proposal for ontology, as implied in the work on metaphor, be *distinguished* from Heidegger's?

Ricoeur's answer to this question is that his proposal is able to contribute a clarity to ontological discourse with respect to the point of identity and difference between the speculative (or ontological) mode of discourse and the poetic one.[60] Heidegger points to a secret kinship between thinking and poetry while he insists on their distance, but he points to this kinship metaphorically. Ricoeur is adamant that he will not speak of poetic language poetically and hopes that he can specify the difference between poetry and thought purely conceptually. In the essay "Biblical Hermeneutics" (1975) Ricoeur suggests that Heidegger tends to blur the distinction between thinking and poetry and takes his postmetaphysical language as an objective and direct language when it is actually indirect and figurative.[61] And in *Rule of Metaphor*, Ricoeur says that whereas Heidegger's great attempt "to make speculative thought resonate with the poet's utterance" is one from which to draw inspiration, it is a temptation "when the difference between the speculative and the poetic threatens once again to disappear."[62]

Ricoeur puts the spheres of poetic and speculative discourse in connection in this way. The two spheres share a common basis (or more precisely, a basis in groundlessness) in the appropriation of appropriation, which Heidegger calls *Ereignis*. *Ereignis* is the "semantic aim of metaphorical utterance," just as it is that to which ontology orients itself as the event in which being comes into play and blossoms forth from potentiality into actuality.[63] The two spheres of discourse are nonetheless separated one from the other by a break in level or plane: "One can pass from one discourse to the other only by an *epochē*."[64] On one hand, analysis of the metaphoric process as one of emergent meaning isolates the semantic condition of the *possibility* of speculative discourse, in that it is behind the generation of all semantic fields.[65] But on the other hand, speculative discourse has its own *necessity* in that it is a second-order discourse that rises above the figurative and conceptual: it orders the system of concepts that may be initially sketched out in the metaphoric meaning, and thus "finds the principle of its articulation within itself."[66] The speculative level is a reflexive level of thought that fulfills the aims of both the metaphoric or poetic sphere and the conceptual sphere of discourse, and it establishes itself exactly by establishing the difference between the two even while it discerns an identity.

The three levels of discourse—poetic, conceptual, and speculative—are thus ordered by Ricoeur in Kantian style, in that the relations are analogous to those between the spheres of sensibility, understanding, and reason. Reason grasps the blindness of mere intuition just as speculative discourse knows that metaphor on its own may project surplus of meaning yet not understand what it understands. And reason grasps the emptiness of mere concept just as speculative discourse knows that the concept puts a limit on the inexhaustive depth of symbol and its metaphoric expressions. On its own, reason—or the speculative and reflexive consciousness—allows us to say that the determination of a logical expression is *not* the showing of images, just as it allows us to conjoin thought with figure.[67]

In the end, Ricoeur's speculative discourse is hermeneutical discourse in the strict sense: ontology is hermeneutical ontology just because interpretation theory is the theory governing mediation between the poetic semantic field and the conceptual sphere of discourse. It does not seek to eliminate metaphor or figure nor to confuse figurative with conceptual speech. Conceptual understanding is preserved in its difference from metaphorical understanding, but the limits of conceptuality turn the speculative enterprise back to the language of the poets, who are able to *present* what the concept cannot properly *think*. Thinking can think itself as limited and look to the poet for the impetus to think more.

Religious Appropriation and the Question of Truth

Ricoeur claims that speculative or ontological discourse both orders the system of concepts and mediates between the conceptual sphere of discourse and the poetic sphere of discourse. As a discourse that refers to first-order spheres of discourse rather than directly to the perceptual world or to world as "context of meaning," ontology would be the work of the reflexive "I," which is able to identify with any primary mode of discourse while it takes notice of the differences in style, structure, and the like, characteristic of this particular work. It is of course the same "I" that connects concepts and intuitions, thus generating experience of being in the scientific sense (Kant), as it is the same "I" that synthesizes meaning and image in mood, thus structuring experience of "being as" in the poetic sense (Ricoeur).

At issue here in Ricoeur's proposal for an ontological discourse that mediates between metaphorical utterances and univocal concepts is the nature of the split between the poetic and the conceptual. For Ricoeur, that issue is to be understood within the framework of his distinction between first naiveté and critique. What is characteristic of the first naiveté is immediacy of belief, and this immediacy always adheres to poetic texts (and, therefore, most especially religious texts).[68] Characteristic of critique is mediation of the content of assertions through application of the criteria for knowledge established in critical idealism, and once this critical consciousness is aroused it remains in unrestrained relation to the sphere of poetic utterance.

In showing the conditions of the possibility of interpretation and appropriation in the productive imagination, Ricoeur is developing the reflexive awareness of what he calls "second naiveté" in hermeneutics. For Ricoeur, such a consciousness is able to recover the meaning of its poetic language through having developed that poetic meaning into the systematically ordered language of existential concepts. Now, while this second naiveté does possess a system of post-Kantian and critically sound concepts for analysis of *Dasein* and the relation of *Dasein* to being as such, it recognizes the loss of meaning that is incurred when the poetic content is eclipsed by existential description. The second naiveté also wills, and is able to will, that it reidentify sense and reference, word and thing, beyond criticism. The second naiveté, as the reflexive hermeneutical subject, can decide that it need not suspend the "immediacy of belief," but can re-cite the poetic language and reapproach the naiveté of spontaneous understanding as a limit. It is a second naiveté that is transformed and deepened in its appropriation of textual meaning, and according to Ricoeur the transformation and deepening of the self are the correlates to the dynamism and granting of being through metaphor. Being reveals itself to the reflexive consciousness as "being as," a dialectical notion of being.

The question that this raises, however, is whether or not the hermeneutical consciousness can speak of the *truth* or falsity of the poetic or religious language that it interprets. The reason why this is a question is that critical consciousness measures truth as the correspondence between thought and percept, whose locus is in the judgment. And since in poetic language the metaphor suspends reference to the perceived world in order to redescribe reality, it must sacrifice its claim for truth-value in the narrow sense.

Ricoeur has responded to this problem by claiming that the

peculiarity of poetic discourse abolishes truth in the sense of adequation, as it applies to descriptive discourse. But poetic discourse does incarnate a concept of truth, which he calls *manifestation*, that is, letting what shows itself be.[69] In poetic discourse we know that this means manifestation of a referent within a world projected by the text, into which I may project one of my possibilities to be. In this sense poetic language would be true to the extent that the language is able to manifest some reality, that is, lift that sense and reference out of obscurity and hiddenness and place it against that background.

This notion of truth as manifestation or unhiddenness was revived, as is well known, by Martin Heidegger, initially in section 44 of *Sein und Zeit* and in the essay *Vom Wesen der Wahrheit* (1930).[70] A leitmotif of Heidegger's discussion of truth as *aletheia* is that the being of a judgment is revelatory, in that it brings its *Sache* out of hiddenness and into presence. Truth is not so much in the correspondence of what is said with what is so, but in what is presupposed in any such correspondence, namely, the openness of *Dasein* as being-in-the-world, in that *Dasein* draws things out of unhiddenness in its very mode of being.[71] But even more primordially, *Dasein* is determined by the openness into which it is thrown, that is, by the truth that gives itself *to Dasein*.[72] The truth of correspondence rests on a far more basic sense of truth in which *Dasein* is rooted: the unhiddenness of being in beings (even while *Dasein* also stands rooted in the "untruth" of being's concealment in the mystery).

Ricoeur is surely right that Heidegger, in recovering the sense of truth as *aletheia,* has uncovered the supporting ground of truth in the sense of correspondence, and that poetic language does display the concept of truth as unhiddenness. But a hermeneutic theory that distinguishes so clearly between first naiveté, critique, and second naiveté on the subject-side, and sense, reference, and second reference on the object-side ought not so quickly to yield its claim to truth as correspondence. Ricoeur could retain a claim for a correspondence type of truth at the heart of his theory by reference to the elements of second-naiveté consciousness.[73] As a reflexive consciousness it is referred directly either to the critical consciousness or to the naive consciousness of the religious object, but not both at once. Now, in the nature of the case, these two are contradictories in the sense that the presence of one indicates the absence of the other. Naive immediacy in response to the religious symbol signals identification without critical distance; and conversely, the raising of the critical question—What *is* this?—dislodges the immediacy that *is* the being of the symbol to first naiveté.

At the surface of things these two forms of consciousness clash as opposites, thus relativizing themselves against each other. One has the object in immediate presence, the other drives the object out. A yes and a no relativize each other in a contradiction. But from the second naiveté, the reflexive consciousness can see a correspondence there: the religious consciousness is recognized as religious only by going over to critical questioning. The religious consciousness is grasped as the form of consciousness it is just by moving through it to its negation in critique, where it becomes evident that religion is not critique, and in that way manifests religion as religion.

On the object-side of the relation, the appearing object also carries a doubleness. The appearing symbol is felt as an appearance of the Holy, but is thought to be nothing at all (by the critical consciousness). But here again for the reflexive self there could be measurable correspondence between the sense of the interpreted symbol and the referent of nothing. If it is the case that religious symbols carry a contradictory structure in which the sense somehow denies itself as sense in order to manifest its referent, then such a symbolic structure could be tested for its truth as correspondence. For if the *sense* of the religious object, that is, what the signifying mode of being says to the direct viewer, is that it is *not* something to be taken religiously, then the sense would accord with the referent and the object would show itself as a true symbol of the divine: it appears as the Holy, but denies that it is the Holy.

The pair of correspondences, that of (1) religious and critical consciousness and (2) sense and referent of the symbol, can then in turn be shown to agree. Religious and critical consciousness correspond in spite of contradiction by virtue of the reflexive "I," which sees its object through the movement from one to the other. The sense of the symbol and the referent of the symbol correspond in spite of contradiction by virtue of a reflexive dimension of the symbol that appears through the movement from sense to reference. Now the reflexivity in symbolic awareness can be said to correspond to the reflexivity in the religious symbol itself.

Such a test of correspondence in religious symbols would, I think, tighten Ricoeur's analysis of the kind of truth involved in poetic language. It could also sharpen the task of speculative discourse as it generates concepts from the metaphoric action on symbols and provides principles for formation and collection of concepts. The reflexive consciousness is to take its bearings from displays of truth as correspondence between reflexive symbols and reflexive consciousness.

Notes

Chapter 1: Introduction

1. Paul Tillich, *Systematic Theology*, Vol. 1: *Being and God* (Chicago: University of Chicago Press, 1951), pp. 33–39.

2. Martin Heidegger makes this point in the introduction to *Sein und Zeit*, where he proposes to clarify and to interpret the vague understanding of being that we already possess in conducting our activities. The term *Seinsverständnis* and its explication place understanding in correlation to the being of things. See Martin Heidegger, *Sein und Zeit*, 12th ed. (Tübingen: Max Niemeyer, 1972), pp. 5–6.

For a clear and careful analysis of this notion of understanding as the correlate to being, see Robert P. Scharlemann, *The Being of God: Theology and the Experience of Truth* (New York: Seabury Press, 1981), p. 47.

3. For further discussion of Ricoeur's phenomenological method and its application to hermeneutical problems, see Mary Gerhart, *The Question of Belief in Literary Criticism: An Introduction to the Hermeneutical Theory of Paul Ricoeur* (Stuttgart: Akademischer Verlag, 1979), especially chap. 5.

Chapter 2: Ricoeur's Place in the Tradition of Hermeneutical Discussion

1. Gerhard Ebeling, "Hermeneutik," in *Religion in Geschichte und Gegenwart*. 3rd ed. (Tübingen: Mohr 1959), p. 243.

2. Robert Scharlemann, "Critical and Religious Consciousness: Some Reflections on the Question of Truth in the Philosophy of Religion," *Kairos and Logos: Studies in the Roots and Implications of Tillich's Theology*, ed. John J. Carey (Cambridge, Mass.: The North American Paul Tillich Society, 1978), p. 75.

3. Immanuel Kant, *Kritik der reinen Vernunft* (Leipzig: Verlag Philipp Reclam), A xi, A xii. (Hereafter cited as *KrV*.)

4. See Paul Ricoeur, "The Task of Hermeneutics," *Philosophy Today* 17 (1973); 114; Hans-Georg Gadamer, *Wahrheit und Methode* (Tübingen: J. C. B. Mohr, 2. Auflage, 1965), p. 173 (hereafter cited as *WM*); Joachim Wach, *Das Verstehen: Grundzüge einer Geschichte der hermeneutischen Theorie 19. Jahrhundert*, 3 vol. in 1 (Hildesheim: Georg Olms, 1966), 1: 85–86 (hereafter cited as *Verstehen*); and Otto Pöggeler, "Einführung" to *Hermeneutische Philosophie*, ed. Otto Pöggeler (Munich: Nymphenburger, 1972), p. 11.

5. Friedrich Schleiermacher, *Hermeneutics: The Handwritten Manuscripts*, ed. Heinz Kimmerle, trans. James Duke and Jack Forstman (Chico, Calif.: Scholars Press, 1977), p. 183 (hereafter cited as *Hermeneutics*).

6. Ibid., p. 91.

7. Paul Ricoeur, *Symbolism of Evil*, trans. Emerson Buchanan (Boston: Beacon Press, 1967), p. 14 (hereafter cited as *SE*).

8. Ibid., p. 351.
9. Ibid., p. 349.
10. Ricoeur, "The Task of Hermeneutics," p. 116.
11. Schleiermacher, *Hermeneutics*, pp. 97–98.
12. Ibid., pp. 117 f.
13. Ibid., pp. 147 f. For a helpful discussion of the concept of individuality in Schleiermacher, see Heinz Kimmerle, "Das Verhältnis Schleiermachers zum Transzendentalen Idealismus," *Kant-Studien* 51, no. 4 (1959/60), pp. 410–26.
14. Schleiermacher, *Hermeneutics*, p. 77.
15. Ibid., p. 101.
16. Ibid., p. 112.
17. Ibid., p. 117.
18. Ibid., p. 127.
19. Ibid., p. 150.
20. Ibid.
21. Ibid., p. 100.
22. Ibid., pp. 100–101.
23. Ibid., pp. 150–51.
24. Wilhelm Dilthey, "Die Entstehung der Hermeneutik," in *Die Geistige Welt*, vol. 5 of *Wilhelm Diltheys Gesammelte Schriften* (Leipzig and Berlin: B. G. Teubner, 1924), pp. 329–30.
25. Wilhelm Dilthey, *Der Aufbau der Geschichtlichen Welt in den Geisteswissenschaften*, vol. 7 of *Wilhelm Diltheys Gesammelte Schriften* (Leipzig and Berlin: B. G. Teubner, 1927), p. 150 (hereafter cited as *Aufbau*).
26. Ricoeur, "The Task of Hermeneutics," p. 117.
27. Dilthey, *Aufbau*, pp. 297 and 191; see also Gadamer, *WM*, p. 205.
28. Dilthey, *Aufbau*, 161. For a more detailed discussion of *Erlebnis* in the context of a complete analysis of Dilthey's thought, see Michael Ermarth, *Wilhelm Dilthey: The Critique of Historical Reason* (Chicago: University of Chicago Press, 1978), especially pp. 92–131.
29. Dilthey, *Aufbau*, p. 58.
30. Ibid., pp. 277.
31. Ibid., pp. 192–96. Matthew Lamb provides detailed consideration of Dilthey's notion of awareness as a form of consciousness that accompanies our feelings and moods but does not separate itself completely from the object of awareness. See Matthew Lamb, *History, Method, and Theology: A Dialectical Comparison of Wilhelm Dilthey's Critique of Historical Reason and Bernard Lonergan's Meta-Methodology* (Missoula, Scholars Press, 1978), pp. 200–226 and pp. 290–98.
32. Dilthey, *Aufbau*, pp. 83–84.
33. Ricoeur, "The Task of Hermeneutics," p. 117.
34. Ibid., p. 118.
35. Dilthey, *Aufbau*, p. 205.
36. Ibid., p. 212.
37. Ibid., p. 234: "Jede Lebensaüsserung hat eine Bedeutung, sofern sie als ein Zeichen etwas ausdrückt, als ein Ausdruck auf etwas hinweist, das dem Leben angehört."
38. Ibid., pp. 146–47.
39. Ibid., p. 39. The reference is to Edmund Husserl, *Logische Untersuchungen*, vol. 2, pt. 1 (Halle: Max Niemeyer, 1928), p. 39.

40. Rudolf Makreel indicates that Dilthey's use of Husserl here was not so much imitative as adaptive. Husserl's focus in his account of linguistic expression is the intentional meaning alone, whereas Dilthey was also interested in what expressions tell us about the cultural context from which they emerge. See Rudolf A. Makreel, *Dilthey: Philosopher of the Human Sciences* (Princeton, N.J.: Princeton University Press, 1975), p. 293.

41. Dilthey, *Ausgabe*, p. 213.
42. Ibid., pp. 82, 213, and passim.
43. Ibid., p. 216.
44. Ibid., p. 191.
45. Paul Ricoeur, "Hermeneutics of Symbols and Philosophical Reflection," in *Conflict of Interpretations: Essays in Hermeneutics* (Evanston, Ill.: Northwestern University Press, 1974), p. 317. Ricoeur says here, repeating Schleiermacher almost verbatim: "There does not exist a general hermeneutics, that is a general theory of interpretation, a general canon for exegesis; there are only various separate and contrasting theories." (Hereafter this volume is cited as *CI*.)
46. Paul Ricoeur, "Phénoménologie et herméneutique," in *Phänomenologie heute*, ed. Ernst Orth (Freiburg/Munich: Karl Alber, 1975), p. 40; see also Paul Ricoeur, "Philosophische und theologische Hermeneutik," *Evangelische Theologie* (Sonderheft, 1974), p. 26.
47. Paul Ricoeur, "Structure and Hermeneutics," in *CI*, p. 30; see also *SE*, pp. 355–56.
48. Ibid.; *SE*, p. 355.
49. For my interpretation of Martin Heidegger I am indebted to Professor Robert P. Scharlemann, who conducted two seminars at the University of Iowa on the topic of hermeneutics during the Spring 1977 and Spring 1979 semesters.
50. Ricoeur, "The Task of Hermeneutics," p. 120.
51. Ricoeur, "Existence and Hermeneutics," in *CI*, p. 7.
52. Ibid., p. 10.
53. Ibid., pp. 6–7. See also idem, "Phénoménologie et herméneutique," p. 40.
54. Martin Heidegger, *Sein und Zeit*, 12th ed. (Tübingen: Max Niemeyer, 1972), pp. 3–4 (hereafter cited as *SZ*).
55. Ibid., p. 4.
56. Ibid.
57. Ibid., p. 12.
58. Ibid., pp. 13, 42.
59. Otto Pöggeler, "Heidegger Heute," in *Heidegger: Perspektiven zur Deutung seines Werks*, ed. Otto Pöggeler (Cologne: Kiepenheuer and Witsch, 1969), p. 13.
60. Heidegger, *SZ*, p. 182: "Das Sein des Daseins enthüllt sich als *Sorge*."
61. See Martin Heidegger, *Sein und Zeit*, pp. 56 and 192 for references to facticity and the finitude of *Dasein*. In the secondary literature, W. B. Macomber comments upon the finitude of understanding with special reference to Heidegger's interpretation of Kant. See W. B. Macomber, *The Anatomy of Disillusion: Martin Heidegger's Notion of Truth* (Evanston, Ill.: Northwestern University Press, 1967), pp. 157–68. Consult also William J. Richardson, *Heidegger: Through Phenomenology to Thought* (The Hague: Martinus Nijhoff, 1967), pp. 71–76. For a broader discussion of the theme of finitude focused on Heidegger but with references also to Hegel, Kierkegaard, Sartre, and Merleau-Ponty, see Calvin O. Schrag, *Experience and Being: Prolegomena to a Future Ontology* (Evan-

ston, Ill.: Northwestern University Press, 1969), pp. 146–50; as well as Calvin O. Schrag, *Existence and Freedom: Towards an Ontology of Human Finitude* (Evanston, Ill.: Northwestern University Press, 1961), pp. 67–94.
62. Immanuel Kant, *KrV*, B 19.
63. Ibid.; see the "transcendental deduction," A 96–A 130, B 130–B 169.
64. Ibid., A 107–A 108.
65. Ibid., B 180.
66. Ibid., B 146.
67. Ibid., B 157.
68. J. G. Fichte, *Versuch einer neuen Darstellung der Wissenschaftslehre* (1797), in the *J. G. Fichte Gesamtausgabe der Bayerischen Akademie der Wissenschaften*, ed. by R. Lauth and H. Gliwitzky (Stuttgart: Friedrich Frommann Verlag, 1970), 4: vol. 4, p. 221.
69. Ibid., 4, p. 229.
70. Fritz Medicus, "Die Wissenschaftslehre in ihrer ersten Gestalt," *J. G. Fichte: Dreizehn Vorlesungen* (Berlin: Verlag von Reuther und Reichard, 1905), pp. 75–94.
71. J. G. Fichte, *Grundlage der Gesammten Wissenschaftslehre als Handschrift für seine Zuhörer* (1793), in the *Gesamtausgabe* cited in n. 68 above, 2, p. 259. My interpretation of Fichte's 1793 *Wissenschaftslehre* is indebted to Professor Robert P. Scharlemann, who led a reading and discussion of this text in his home during the 1977–78 academic year at the University of Iowa.
72. Ricoeur, "The Task of Hermeneutics," p. 122.
73. Heidegger, SZ, p. 134.
74. Ibid., p. 142.
75. Ibid., p. 145.
76. Ibid., p. 149.
77. Ibid., p. 150.
78. Ibid., p. 151.
79. Ibid.
80. Ibid., p. 161.
81. Ricoeur, "The Task of Hermeneutics," p. 122.
82. Heidegger, SZ, p. 162.
83. Ibid., p. 360.
84. Kant, *KrV*, B 181.
85. Ibid., B 185.
86. Ibid., B 182.
87. Heidegger, SZ, pp. 428–35.
88. Ibid., p. 414.
89. Ibid., p. 350.
90. Ibid.
91. Ibid.
92. Ibid., p. 365.
93. Ibid.
94. Ibid., pp. 160–67.
95. Ibid., pp. 167–80.
96. Ibid., p. 410.
97. Ibid., p. 250.
98. Ibid., p. 252.
99. For a clear discussion of the background of Heidegger's notion of death, see

Calvin O. Schrag, *Existence and Freedom: Towards an Ontology of Human Finitude*, pp. 95–118.
100. Pöggeler, "Heidegger heute," p. 40.
101. See Heidegger, *SZ*, p. 328.
102. Martin Heidegger, "Was heisst Denken?" in *Vorträge und Aufsätze* (Pfullingen: Günther Neske, 1954), p. 136.

Chapter 3: The Development of Ricoeur's Thought
1. Herbert Spiegelberg, *The Phenomenological Movement* (The Hague: Martinus Nihjoff, 1960), 2, p. 536.
2. See the bibliography of Ricoeur's works in *Studies in the Philosophy of Paul Ricoeur*, ed. Charles E. Reagan (Athens: Ohio University Press, 1979), pp. 180–94.
3. David Rasmussen, *Mythic-Symbolic Language and Philosophical Anthropology: A Constructive Interpretation of the Thought of Paul Ricoeur* (The Hague: Martinus Nijhoff, 1971), p. 3; and Donald Ihde, *Hermeneutic Phenomenology: The Philosophy of Paul Ricoeur* (Evanston, Ill.: Northwestern University Press, 1971), p. 20.
4. See Ihde, *Hermeneutic Phenomenology*, p. 23, and chap. 6 passim.
5. Paul Ricoeur, "My Relation to the History of Philosophy," *The Iliff Review* 35, no. 3 (Fall 1978), pp. 5–6.
6. Paul Ricoeur, "Introduction: Husserl," in *Husserl: An Analysis of His Phenomenology* (Evanston, Ill: Northwestern University Press, 1967), p. 6; and idem, "Kant and Husserl," in the same volume, p. 176.
7. Ricoeur, "Phénoménologie et herméneutique," p. 49; and "Kant and Husserl," p. 178.
8. Ricoeur, "Introduction: Husserl," p. 8.
9. Ricoeur, "Kant and Husserl," pp. 192–93.
10. Ricoeur, "Phénoménologie et herméneutique," p. 44.
11. Ibid., p. 35; and idem, "Kant and Husserl," p. 178.
12. Ricoeur, "Phénoménologie et herméneutique," p. 44.
13. Ricoeur, "Kant and Husserl," pp. 186–89; see also Paul Ricoeur, *Fallible Man*, translated by Charles Kelbley (Chicago: Henry Regnery Company, 1965), p. 58 (hereafter cited as *FM*).
14. Ricoeur, "Kant and Husserl," pp. 197–99.
15. Paul Ricoeur, "Biblical Hermeneutics," *Semeia* 4 (1975), p. 142.
16. Ibid., p. 143.
17. Ricoeur, "Kant and Husserl," p. 201.
18. Ricoeur, *FM*, p. xxi.
19. Ibid., p. 3.
20. Ibid., p. 3.
21. Ibid., pp. 8–9.
22. Heidegger, *SZ*, pp. 197–98. See also *SZ*, pp. 4, 23, 220, where Heidegger says philosophy must preserve the force of the most elementary words in which *Dasein* expresses itself.
23. Otto Pöggeler, *Der Denkweg Martin Heideggers* (Pfullingen: Verlag Günther Neske, 1963), p. 38.
24. Ricoeur, *FM*, p. 3.
25. Ibid., p. 6.
26. Ibid., p. 207.

27. Ibid., p. 217.
28. Ibid., p. 28. (italics mine)
29. Ibid., pp. 31–32.
30. Ibid., p. 40.
31. Ibid., p. 41.
32. Ibid., p. 42.
33. Ibid., pp. 43–44.
34. Ibid., p. 49.
35. Ibid., p. 50.
36. Ibid., pp. 63–64.
37. Ibid., pp. 65–66.
38. Ibid., p. 70.
39. Ibid., p. 73.
40. Ibid., pp. 110–11.
41. Ibid., pp. 78–79.
42. Ibid., pp. 80, 82–83.
43. Ibid., p. 86.
44. Ibid., pp. 87–88.
45. Ibid., p. 89.
46. Ibid., pp. 91–92.
47. Ibid., p. 110.
48. Ibid., p. 114.
49. Ibid., p. 123.
50. Ibid., p. 130.
51. Ibid., p. 127.
52. Ibid., p. 129.
53. Ibid., p. 159.
54. Ibid., pp. 161–62.
55. Ibid., p. 140.
56. Ibid., p. 161.
57. Ibid., p. 201.
58. Ibid., p. 223.
59. Ibid., p. 219.
60. Paul Ricoeur, *Freud and Philosophy: An Essay on Interpretation*, trans. Denis Savage (New Haven, Conn.: Yale University Press, 1970), p. 43 (hereafter cited as *FP*).
61. Ibid., p. 45.
62. Ricoeur quoting Bergson in *FM*, p. 91.
63. Ricoeur, "Husserl and Wittgenstein on Language," in *Phenomenology and Existentialism*, ed. Edward M. Lee and Maurice Mandelbaum (Baltimore, Md.: The Johns Hopkins University Press, 1967), p. 209.
64. For a clear account of the Husserlian doctrine of expression, see Jitendranath N. Mohanty, "Husserl's Theory of Meaning" in *Husserl: Expositions and Appraisals*, ed. Frederick A. Elliston and Peter McCormick (South Bend, Ind.: University of Notre Dame Press), pp. 18–37.
65. Ricoeur, *FP*, p. 12.
66. Ibid., pp. 12–13.
67. Paul Ricoeur, *The Symbolism of Evil*, trans. Emerson Buchanan (Boston: Beacon Press, 1967), p. 15 (hereafter cited as *SE*).
68. Ibid., p. 10.

69. Ibid., pp. 162–63.
70. Ricoeur, *FP*, pp. 8–9.
71. Ricoeur, *SE*, p. 10.
72. Ricoeur, "Hermeneutics of Symbols and Philosophical Reflection," in *CI*, p. 319.
73. Ricoeur, *SE*, p. 18.
74. Ibid., p. 8.
75. Ibid., p. 7.
76. Ibid., pp. 12–13.
77. Ricoeur, *FP*, pp. 27–33.
78. I refer the reader to Ihde's excellent presentation of this issue in *Hermeneutic Phenomenology*, pp. 134–55.
79. Ricoeur, *FP*, pp. 459f.
80. Ibid., p. 456.
81. Ricoeur, "Hermeneutics of Symbols and Philosophical Reflection," p. 319.
82. Ibid.
83. Ricoeur, *SE*, p. 9.
84. Ibid., p. 167.
85. See Ihde, *Hermeneutic Phenomenology*, pp. 108–13.
86. Ricoeur, *SE*, p. 351.
87. Ibid., p. 352.
88. Ibid., p. 356.

Chapter 4: Ricoeur's Hermeneutical Theory
1. Paul Ricoeur, *Freud and Philosophy: An Essay on Interpretation*, trans. Denis Savage (New Haven, Conn.: Yale University Press, 1970), p. 9 (hereafter cited as *FP*); see also "Existence and Hermeneutics," in *The Conflict of Interpretations: Essays in Hermeneutics*, ed. Donald Ihde (Evanston, Ill.: Northwestern University Press, 1974), pp. 12–13 (hereafter cited as *CI*).
2. Paul Ricoeur, "From Existentialism to the Philosophy of Language," in *The Philosophy of Paul Ricoeur: An Anthology of His Work*, ed. Charles Reagan and David Stewart (Boston: Beacon Press, 1978), pp. 88–91.
3. Paul Ricoeur, "Creativity in Language," *Philosophy Today* 17 (1973): 102; and idem, "The Problem of Double Meaning," in *CI*, pp. 71–73.
4. See, for example, Ricoeur, *FP*, p. 8, and "Metaphor and the Main Problem of Hermeneutics," in *The Philosophy of Paul Ricoeur*, p. 134; and "Preface to Bultmann," in *CI*, p. 382.
5. Paul Ricoeur, "Structure, Word, and Event," in *CI*, p. 80; and idem, *Interpretation Theory* (Fort Worth: Texas Christian University Press, 1977), pp. 1–2 (hereafter cited at *IT*).
6. Ricoeur, *IT*, p. 3.
7. Ibid.
8. Ibid., pp. 5–6.
9. Ibid., p. 7.
10. Ibid., p. 9.
11. Ibid., pp. 9–11.
12. Ibid., p. 12.
13. Ibid., p. 13.
14. Ibid., pp. 14–16.
15. Ibid., p. 16.

16. Ibid., p. 20.
17. Ibid.
18. Ibid.
19. Ibid., p. 21. Ricoeur's position of the priority of reference over sense agrees with Heidegger's analysis of *Rede* in Martin Heidegger, *Sein und Zeit*, 12th ed. (Tübingen: Max Niemeyer, 1972), p. 164 (hereafter cited as *SZ*).
20. Ricoeur, *IT*, pp. 22–23.
21. Ibid., pp. 25–26.
22. Paul Ricoeur, "Qu'est-ce qu'un Texte? Expliquer et Comprendre," in *Hermeneutik und Dialektik: Aufsätze II*, ed. Rudiger Bubner, Konrad Cramer, Reiner Wiehl (Tübingen: J. C. B. Mohr, 1970), p. 184.
23. Ricoeur, *IT*, pp. 25–26.
24. Ibid., pp. 29–30.
25. Ricoeur, "Metaphor and the Main Problem of Hermeneutics," p. 134.
26. Ricoeur, "Qu'est-ce qu'un Texte?" pp. 184–85.
27. Ricoeur, *IT*, pp. 29–30.
28. Ricoeur, "Metaphor and the Main Problem of Hermeneutics," p. 139.
29. Paul Ricoeur, "Biblical Hermeneutics," in *Semeia* 4 (1975), p. 68.
30. Ricoeur, "The Hermeneutical Function of Distanciation," in *Philosophy Today* 17 (1973): 134.
31. Ibid., p. 135.
32. Heidegger, *SZ*, p. 42.
33. Ricoeur, "The Hermeneutical Function of Distanciation," p. 136.
34. Ibid., p. 137.
35. Paul Ricocur, *The Rule of Metaphor: Multi-Disciplinary Studies in the Creation of Meaning in Language* (Toronto: The University of Toronto Press, 1977), p. 220 (hereafter cited as *RM*); see also "Biblical Hermeneutics," p. 34; *IT*, p. 88; "The Hermeneutical Function of Distanciation," p. 140; and "Philosophische und theologische Hermeneutik," *Evangelische Theologie* (Sonderheft, 1975), p. 32.
36. Ricoeur, "The Hermeneutical Function of Distanciation," p. 141.
37. Ricoeur, "Philosophische und theologische Hermeneutik," pp. 31–32.
38. Ricoeur, *IT*, p. 37.
39. Ricoeur, "Philosophische und theologische Hermeneutik," p. 32.
40. Ricoeur, "Qu'est-ce qu'un Text?, p. 198.
41. Ricoeur, *IT*, p. 87.
42. Ricoeur, "The Hermeneutical Function of Distanciation," pp. 140–41.
43. Heidegger, *SZ*, p. 68.
44. Ibid., p. 84.
45. Ibid., p. 86.
46. Paul Ricoeur, "Explanation and Understanding," in *The Philosophy of Paul Ricoeur*, p. 165.
47. Ricoeur, *IT*, p. 72.
48. Ibid., p. 76.
49. Ibid., pp. 76–78.
50. Ibid., p. 78.
51. Ibid., p. 79; see also "From Existentialism to Philosophy of Language," in *The Philosophy of Paul Ricoeur*, p. 90.
52. For Ricoeur's best analysis of French structuralism, see "Biblical Hermeneutics," pp. 37–74.

53. Ricoeur, *IT*, pp. 83–84.
54. Ricoeur, "Structure and Hermeneutics," in *CI*, p. 45.
55. Ricoeur, "Biblical Hermeneutics," pp. 51–65.
56. Ibid., pp. 70–71.
57. Ricoeur, *IT*, p. 87.
58. Heidegger, *SZ*, pp. 148, 150. Ricoeur acknowledges his alignment with the doctrine of preunderstanding as formulated by Heidegger and appropriated by Bultmann and other Continental thinkers in *The Symbolism of Evil*, p. 351.
59. Ricoeur, *RM*, p. 188.
60. Ricoeur, *IT*, p. 46; and idem, "Metaphor and the Main Problem of Hermeneutics," in *The Philosophy of Paul Ricoeur*, p. 136.
61. Ricoeur, "Biblical Hermeneutics," pp. 78–79.
62. Ricoeur, *RM*, p. 247.
63. Ibid., p. 239.
64. Ibid., p. 230.
65. Ibid.
66. Ibid.
67. Ibid., p. 223.
68. Ibid., p. 120.
69. Ibid., p. 225.
70. Ibid., p. 227.
71. Ibid., p. 229.
72. Ibid.
73. Ricoeur, "Explanation and Understanding," p. 155, and "Philosophische und theologische Hermeneutik," p. 41.
74. Heidegger, *SZ*, p. 218.
75. Ricoeur, *IT*, pp. 53–54.
76. Ibid., p. 59.
77. Ibid., p. 88.
78. Ricoeur, "Biblical Hermeneutics," p. 92.
79. Ibid., p. 87.
80. Hans-Georg Gadamer, *Wahrheit und Methode: Grundzüge einer philosophischen Hermeneutik*, 2d ed. (Tübingen: J. C. B. Mohr, 1965), pp. 97–115 (hereafter cited as *WM*).
81. Ricoeur, *RM*, p. 212.
82. Ibid., p. 213.
83. Ibid., p. 215.
84. Ricoeur, "Language of Faith," in *The Philosophy of Paul Ricoeur*, p. 231.
85. Ricoeur, *IT*, p. 57.

Chapter 5: The Religious Dimension of Text and Understanding
1. Paul Ricoeur, "Philosophy and Religious Language," *The Journal of Religion* 54, no. 1 (January 1974), p. 71.
2. Ibid., p. 73; Paul Ricoeur, "Towards a Hermeneutic of the Idea of Revelation," *Harvard Theological Review* 70, nos. 1–2 (January–April 1977), pp. 2–3 (hereafter cited as "Hermeneutic of Revelation").
3. Paul Ricoeur, "Listening to the Parables of Jesus," in *The Philosophy of Paul Ricoeur*, ed. Charles Reagan and David Stewart (Boston, Beacon Press, 1978), pp. 239–45.
4. Paul Ricoeur, "Biblical Hermeneutics," in *Semeia* 4: (1975), p. 107.

5. Ibid.
6. Ricoeur, "Philosophy and Religious Language," p. 83.
7. Paul Ricoeur, "Naming God," *Union Seminary Quarterly Review* 34, no. 4 (Summer 1979), p. 219.
8. Ricoeur, "Philosophy and Religious Language," p. 83.
9. Paul Ricoeur, "Philosophische und theologische Hermeneutik," in *Evangelische Theologie* (Sonderheft, 1974), p. 40.
10. See Ian T. Ramsey, *Religious Language: An Empirical Placing of Theological Phrases* (London: SCM Press, 1957), pp. 49–89; and Ricoeur, "Biblical Hermeneutics," pp. 119–26.
11. Ricoeur, "Naming God," p. 223.
12. Ricoeur, "Biblical Hermeneutics," p. 109.
13. See Ricoeur, "Hermeneutic of Revelation," pp. 3–19, for Ricoeur's discussion of these Old Testament forms of discourse.
14. Ibid., p. 7.
15. Ibid., p. 18.
16. See the entirety of Ricoeur, "Biblical Hermeneutics," pp. 29–145, as well as the helpful introduction of Loretta Dornisch.
17. Ibid., p. 33.
18. Ibid.
19. Ibid., p. 97.
20. Ricoeur, "Listening to the Parables of Jesus," p. 244; and "Biblical Herrmeneutics," pp. 114–18, for a discussion of extravagance in the parables.
21. Ricoeur, "Listening to the Parables of Jesus," p. 244.
22. Ricoeur, "Biblical Hermeneutics," p. 101.
23. Ibid., p. 102.
24. William Beardslee, quoted by Ricoeur, ibid., p. 113.
25. Ibid.
26. See Ian Ramsey, *Religious Language*, pp. 47, 90–91.
27. Ibid., p. 64.
28. Ricoeur, "Biblical Hermeneutics," pp. 121–22.
29. Ibid., p. 128.
30. Ibid., p. 105.
31. Ricoeur, "Philosophische und theologische Hermeneutik," p. 43.
32. Ibid., p. 40.
33. Ibid.
34. Robert P. Scharlemann poses this issue in the context of discussing the meaning and verification of "God is" in *The Being of God*, pp. 62–64.
35. Ricoeur, "From Existentialism to the Philosophy of Language," in *the Philosophy of Paul Ricoeur*, p. 88.
36. Ibid. Ricoeur has expressed "continuing interest" in the problems raised by the post-Bultmannian theologies of the Word.
37. In Bultmann's writings, see especially "New Testament and Mythology," in *Kerygma and Myth: A Theological Debate*, ed. Hans Werner Bartsch, trans. R. H. Fuller (London: S.P.C.K., 1954), pp. 1–44; and "What Does it Mean to Speak of God?" in *Faith and Understanding*, ed. Robert W. Funk, trans. L. P. Smith (New York: Harper & Row, 1969), 1, pp. 53–65.
38. See Robert P. Scharlemann, "The Systematic Structure of Bultmann's Theology," in *Dialog* 17, no. 6 (Winter 1978), pp. 31–35. My interpretation of Bultmann is largely reliant on this analysis.

39. For an analysis of Bultmann's recognition that language can not only signify a meaning but donate an enabling power for authentic existence by presenting its referent, see Robert P. Scharlemann, *The Being of God*, pp. 98–105. For an analysis of Bultmann's use of Heidegger, see Michael Zimmerman, "Heidegger and Bultmann: Egoism, Sinfulness, and Inauthenticity," *The Modern Schoolman* (November 1980), pp. 1–20.

40. See Paul Ricoeur, "The Logic of Jesus, the Logic of God," in *Criterion* 18, no. 2 (Summer 1979): 4–6. See also Ricoeur, "Freedom in the Light of Hope," in *The Conflict of Interpretations: Essays in Hermeneutics*, ed. Donald Ihde (Evanston, Ill.: Northwestern University Press, 1974), p. 410 (this latter volume hereafter referred to as *CI*).

41. Paul Tillich, *Systematic Theology*, vol. 2: *Existence and the Christ* (Chicago: University of Chicago Press, 1957), pp. 118–19.

42. Ricoeur, "Philosophische und theologische Hermeneutik," p. 43.

43. See Robert P. Scharlemann, "Critical and Religious Consciousness: Some Reflections on the Question of Truth in the Philosophy of Religion," in *Kairos and Logos: Studies in the Roots and Implications of Tillich's Theology*, ed. John J. Carey (Cambridge, Mass: The North American Paul Tillich Society, 1978), for a complete discussion of this issue.

44. Paul Tillich interpreted the symbol of the cross as self-denying and in virtue of that as infallibly true. The cross is a symbol of the symbolic nature of all symbols. See Robert P. Scharlemann, *The Being of God*, pp. 177–82.

45. These terms were presented by Professor Robert P. Scharlemann in a seminar on Ricoeur's hermeneutical theory during the spring semester, 1978, at the University of Iowa.

46. Martin Heidegger, *Unterwegs zur Sprache* (Pfullingen: Günther Neske, Fünfte Auflage, 1975), pp. 157–216.

47. Robert Funk, *Language, Hermeneutic, and the Word of God* (New York: Harper & Row, 1966), pp. 124–99. Funk's work on the parables already anticipates much of Ricoeur's later analysis and is compatible with it.

48. Ibid., p. 140.
49. Ibid., pp. 165–66.
50. Ibid., p. 143.
51. Ibid., p. 191.
52. Ibid., p. 192.
53. Ibid., p. 155.
54. Ibid., p. 196.

Chapter 6: Appropriation of Textual Meaning and the Question of Truth

1. Paul Ricoeur, "Metaphor and the Main Problem of Hermeneutics," in *The Philosophy of Paul Ricoeur: An Anthology of His Work*, ed. Charles Reagan and David Stewart (Boston: Beacon Press, 1978), p. 145.

2. Paul Ricoeur, "Qu'est-ce qu'un Texte?" in *Hermeneutik und Dialektik: Aufsätze II* (Tübingen: J. C. B. Mohr, 1970), p. 195.

3. Paul Ricoeur, *Interpretation Theory* (Fort Worth: Texas Christian University Press, 1977), p. 91 (hereafter cited as *IT*).

4. Paul Ricoeur, "The Task of Hermeneutics," *Philosophy Today* 17 (1973): 125.

5. Paul Ricoeur, "Towards a Hermeneutic of the Idea of Revelation," *Harvard Theological Review* 70, nos. 1–2 (January–April 1977): 28 (hereafter cited as "Her-

meneutic of Revelation"); and Paul Ricoeur, *Freud and Philosophy: An Essay on Interpretation*, trans. Denis Savage (New Haven, Conn.: Yale University Press, 1970), p. 41 (hereafter cited as *FP*).
 6. Ricoeur, *FP*, p. 41.
 7. Paul Ricoeur, "Metaphor and the Main Problem of Hermeneutics," pp. 144–45.
 8. Ricoeur, *IT*, p. 94.
 9. Ricoeur, "Metaphor and the Main Problem of Hermeneutics," pp. 145–46.
 10. Hans-Georg Gadamer, *Wahrheit und Methode: Grundzüge einer philosophischen Hermeneutik*, 2nd ed. (Tübingen: J. C. B. Mohr 1965), p. 319 (hereafter cited as *WM*).
 11. Paul Ricoeur, "The Metaphorical Process as Cognition, Imagination and Feeling," *Critical Theory* 5, no. 1 (Autumn 1978), pp. 148–50 (hereafter cited as "The Metaphorical Process").
 12. Ibid., p. 151.
 13. Paul Ricoeur, *The Rule of Metaphor* (Toronto: University of Toronto Press, 1977), p. 295 (hereafter cited as *RM*).
 14. Ibid., p. 306.
 15. Ibid., pp. 308–9.
 16. Gadamer, *WM*, p. 432.
 17. Martin Heidegger, *Sein und Zeit*, 12th ed. (Tübingen: Max Niemeyer, 1972), pp. 212 f. (hereafter cited as *SZ*).
 18. Gadamer, *WM*, p. 450.
 19. Ibid.
 20. Ibid.
 21. Ibid., p. 459.
 22. Paul Ricoeur, *RM*, p. 304.
 23. Cf. Gadamer, *WM*, p. 450.
 24. Ibid., p. 444.
 25. Ricoeur, "Explanation and Understanding," in *The Philosophy of Paul Ricoeur*, p. 153.
 26. Ricoeur, *RM*, p. 299.
 27. Ricoeur, *IT*, p. 93.
 28. Ibid., p. 94.
 29. Gadamer, *WM*, p. 450.
 30. Ibid., p. 438.
 31. Ricoeur, *IT*, p. 93.
 32. Ricoeur, "Qu'est-ce qu'un Texte?", p. 199.
 33. See Gadamer on "wirkungsgeschichtlich Bewusstsein" in *WM*, pp. 324 f.
 34. Ricoeur, "Phénoménologie et herméneutique" in *Phänomenologie heute* (Freiberg/Munich: Verlag Karl Alber, 1975), p. 43.
 35. Ricoeur, *RM*, p. 309.
 36. See Otto Pöggeler, "Sein als Ereignis," *Zeitschrift für philosophische Forshchung* 13, no. 4 (1959), pp. 610–11.
 37. Ibid., p. 613.
 38. Ibid., p. 614.
 39. Ibid., p. 616.
 40. Ibid., p. 621.
 41. Ibid.
 42. Ibid., p. 622. See also Martin Heidegger, "Identität und Differenz," in

Identity and Difference, bilingual ed., trans. Joan Stambaugh (New York: Harper and Row, 1964), p. 101.

43. Martin Heidegger, "Identität und Differenz," p. 95.
44. Ricoeur, *RM*, p. 309.
45. Ricoeur, "Metaphor and the Main Problem of Hermeneutics," p. 148. The words in brackets are mine.
46. For thorough treatment of the uniqueness of Ricoeur's theory of imagination, see Mary Gerhart, "Imagination and History in Ricoeur's Interpretation Theory," *Philosophy Today* 23, no. 1 (Spring 1979), pp. 51–68; and Mary Schaldenbrand, "Metaphoric Imagination: Kinship through Conflict," in *Studies in the Philosophy of Paul Ricoeur,* ed. Charles Reagan (Athens: Ohio University Press, 1979), pp. 57–81.
47. Paul Ricoeur, *Fallible Man,* trans. Charles Kelbley (Chicago: Henry Regnery Co., 1965), pp. 27–28, 57–71.
48. Ricoeur, "The Metaphoric Process," p. 145.
49. Ibid.
50. Ibid., p. 148.
51. Ibid., p. 149.
52. Ibid.
53. Ibid., pp. 153–54.
54. Ibid., p. 156.
55. Ibid.
56. Ibid., p. 157.
57. Ricoeur, *IT*, p. 94.
58. Ricoeur, "Philosophische und theologische Hermeneutik," p. 33.
59. Ricoeur, "Phénoménologie et herméneutique," p. 43.
60. Ricoeur, *RM*, p. 313.
61. Ricoeur, "Biblical Hermeneutics," p. 143.
62. Ricoeur, *RM*, p. 309.
63. Ibid., pp. 307–9.
64. Ibid., p. 300.
65. Ibid., pp. 296, 300.
66. Ibid.
67. Ibid., p. 301.
68. Ricoeur, *The Symbolism of Evil,* trans. Emerson Buchanan (Boston: Beacon Press, 1967), p. 351.
69. Ricoeur, "Philosophy and Religious Language," *The Journal of Religion* 54, no. 1 (January 1974), p. 72.
70. "Vom Wesen der Wahrheit" (1930) is in Martin Heidegger, *Wegmarken* (Frankfurt am Main: Klostermann, 1967), pp. 175–201.
71. Martin Heidegger, *SZ*, p. 226.
72. Ibid., p. 227.
73. The following remarks on truth as correspondence rely on the article "Critical and Religious Consciousness: Some Reflections on the Question of Truth in the Philosophy of Religion," by Robert P. Scharlemann, in *Kairos and Logos,* ed. John J. Carey (Cambridge, Mass.: The North American Paul Tillich Society, 1979), pp. 74–95.

Bibliography

Bultmann, Rudolf. "New Testament and Mythology." In *Kerygma and Myth: A Theological Debate*, edited by Hans Werner Bartsch. Translated by R. H. Fuller. London: S.P.C.K., 1954. Pp. 1–44.

———. "What Does it Mean to Speak of God?" In *Faith and Understanding I*, edited by Robert W. Funk. Translated by L. P. Smith. New York: Harper & Row, 1969. Pp. 53–65.

Dilthey, Wilhelm. *Der Aufbau der geschichtlichen Welt in den Geisteswissenschaften*. Vol. 7 of *Wilhelm Diltheys Gesammelte Schriften*. Leipzig and Berlin: B. G. Teubner, 1927.

———. "Die Entstehung der Hermeneutik." *Die Geistige Welt*. Vol. 5 of *Wilhelm Diltheys Gesammelte Schriften*. Leipzig and Berlin: B. G. Teubner, 1924.

Ebeling, Gerhard. "Hermeneutik." *Religion in Geschichte und Gegenwart*. 3d ed. Tübingen: Mohr 1959. Pp. 242–62.

Ermarth, Michael. *Wihelm Dilthey: The Critique of Historical Reason*. Chicago: University of Chicago Press, 1978.

Fichte, Johann Gottlieb. *Grundlage der Gesammten Wissenschaftlehre als Handschrift für seine Zuhörer* (1793). *J. G. Fichte Gesamtausgabe der Bayerischen Akademie der Wissenschaften*. Edited by R. Lauth and H. Gliwitzky. Vol. 2. Stuttgart: Friedrich Fromann Verlag, 1970.

———. *Versuch einer neuen Darstellung der Wissenschaftslehre* (1797). *J. G. Fichte Gesamtausgabe der Bayerischen Akademie der Wissenschaften*. Edited by R. Lauth and H. Gliwitzky. Vol. 4. Stuttgart: Friedrich Fromann Verlag, 1970.

Funk, Robert. *Language, Hermeneutic, and the Word of God*. New York: Harper & Row, 1966.

Gadamer, Hans-Georg. *Wahrheit und Methode: Grundzüge einer philosophischen Hermeneutik*. 2d ed. Tübingen: J. C. B. Mohr, 1963.

Gerhart, Mary. "Imagination and History in Ricoeur's Interpretation Theory." *Philosophy Today* 23, no. 1 (1979): 51–68.

———. *The Question of Belief in Literary Criticism: An Introduction to the Hermeneutical Theory of Paul Ricoeur*. Stuttgart: Akademischer Verlag, 1979.

Heidegger, Martin. "Identität und Differenz." *Identity and Difference*. German with English translation by Joan Stambaugh. New York: Harper & Row, 1964.

———. *Sein und Zeit*. 12th ed. Tübingen: Max Niemeyer, 1972.

———. "Was heisst Denken?" *Vorträge und Aufsätze*. Pfullingen: Günther Neske, 1954. Pp. 129–43.

———. "Das Wesen der Sprache." *Unterwegs zur Sprache*. Pfullingen: Günther Neske, 1975. Pp. 157–216.

———. "Vom Wesen der Wahrheit." *Wegmarken*. Frankfurt am Main: Kostermann, 1967. Pp. 175–201.

Husserl, Edmund. *Logische Untersuchungen*. Vol. 2, pt. 1. Halle: Max Niemeyer, 1928.

Ihde, Donald. *Hermeneutic Phenomenology: The Philosophy of Paul Ricoeur*. Evanston, Ill.: Northwestern University Press, 1971.

Kant, Immanuel. *Kritik der reinen Vernunft*. Leipzig: Verlag Philipp Reclam, n.d.

Kimmerle, Heinz. "Das Verhältnis Schleiermachers zum Transzendentalen Idealismus." *Kant-Studien* 51, no. 4 (1959/60).

Lamb, Matthew. *History, Method, and Theology: A Dialectical Comparison of Wilhelm Dilthey's Critique of Historical Reason and Bernard Lonergan's Meta-Methodology*. Missoula, Mont.: Scholars Press, 1978.

Macomber, W. B. *The Anatomy of Disillusion: Martin Heidegger's Notion of Truth*. Evanston, Ill.: Northwestern University Press, 1967.

Makreel, Rudolf A. *Dilthey: Philosopher of the Human Sciences*. Princeton, N.J.: Princeton University Press, 1975.

Medicus, Franz. *J. G. Fichte: Dreizehn Vorlesungen*. Berlin: Verlag von Reuther und Reichard, 1905.

Pöggeler, Otto. *Der Denkweg Martin Heideggers*. Pfullingen: Verlag Günther Neske, 1963.

———. "Einführung." In *Hermeneutische Philosophie*, edited by Otto Pöggeler. Munich: Nymphenburger, 1972. Pp. 7–71.

———. "Heidegger heute." In *Heidegger: Perspektiven zur Deutung seines Werks*, edited by Otto Pöggeler. Cologne: Kiepenheuer and Witsch, 1969. Pp. 11–53.

———. "Sein als Ereignis." *Zeitschrift für philosophische Forschung* 13, no. 4 (1959): 597–632.

Ramsey, Ian T. *Religious Language: An Empirical Placing of Theological Phrases*. London: SCM Press Ltd., 1957.

Rasmussen, David. *Mythic-Symbolic Language and Philosophical Anthropology: A Constructive Interpretation of the Thought of Paul Ricoeur*. The Hague: Martinus Nijhoff, 1971.

Reagan, Charles E., ed. *Studies in the Philosophy of Paul Ricoeur*. Athens: Ohio University Press, 1979.

———, and Stewart, David, eds. *The Philosophy of Paul Ricoeur: An Anthology of His Work*. Boston: Beacon Press, 1978.

Richardson, William J. *Heidegger: Through Phenomenology to Thought*. The Hague: Martinus Nijhoff, 1967.

Ricoeur, Paul. "Biblical Hermeneutics." *Semeia* (1975): 29–145.

―――. *The Conflict of Interpretations: Essays in Hermeneutics*. Edited by Donald Ihde. Evanston, Ill.: Northwestern University Press, 1974.

―――. "Creativity in Language." *Philosophy Today* 17 (1973): 97–111.

―――. *Fallible Man*. Translated by Charles Kelbley. Chicago: Henry Regnery Co., 1965.

―――. *Freud and Philosophy: An Essay on Interpretation*. Translated by Denis Savage. New Haven, Conn.: Yale University Press, 1970.

―――. "The Hermeneutical Function of Distanciation." *Philosophy Today* 17 (1973): 129–69.

―――. *Husserl: an Analysis of His Phenomenology*. Evanston, Ill.: Northwestern University Press, 1967.

―――. "Husserl and Wittgenstein on Language." In *Phenomenology and Existentialism*, edited by Edward N. Lee and Maurice Mandelbaum. Baltimore, Md.: The Johns Hopkins University Press, 1967.

―――. *Interpretation Theory*. Fort Worth: Texas Christian University Press, 1977.

―――. "The Logic of Jesus, the Logic of God," *Criterion* 18, no. 2 (1979): 4–6.

―――. "The Metaphorical Process as Cognition, Imagination, and Feeling." *Critical Theory* 5, no. 1 (1978): 143–59.

―――. "My Relation to the History of Philosophy." *The Iliff Review* 35, no. 3 (1978): 5–12.

―――. "Naming God." *Union Seminary Quarterly Review* 34, no. 4 (1979): 215–27.

―――. "Phénoménologie et herméneutique." In *Phänomenologie heute*, edited by Ernst Orth. Freiburg and Munich: Karl Alber, 1975. Pp. 31–77.

―――. "Philosophische and theologische Hermeneutik." *Evangelische Theologie* (Sonderheft, 1974). Pp. 24–45.

―――. "Philosophy and Religious Language." *The Journal of Religion* 54, no. 1 (1974): 71–85.

―――. "Que'est-ce qu'un Texte?: Expliquer et Comprendre." In *Hermeneutik und Dialektik: Aufsätze II*, edited by Rudiger Bubner, Konrad Cramer, Reiner Wiehl. Tubingen: J. C. B. Mohr, 1970. Pp. 181–200.

―――. *The Rule of Metaphor: Multi-Disciplinary Studies in the Creation of Meaning*. Translated by Robert Czerny. Toronto: The University of Toronto Press, 1977.

―――. *Symbolism of Evil*. Translated by Emerson Buchanan. Boston: Beacon Press, 1967.

―――. "The Task of Hermeneutics." *Philosophy Today* 17 (1973): 112–29.

―――. "Towards a Hermeneutic of the Idea of Revelation." *Harvard Theological Review* 70, nos. 1–2 (1977): 1–37.

Scharlemann, Robert P. *The Being of God: Theology and the Experience of Truth*. New York: Seabury Press, 1981.

———. "Critical and Religious Consciousness: Some Reflections on the Question of Truth in the Philosophy of Language." In *Karios and Logos: Studies in the Roots and Implications of Tillich's Theology*, edited by John J. Carey. Cambridge, Mass.: The North American Paul Tillich Society, 1978.

———. "The Systematic Structure of Bultmann's Theology." *Dialog* 17, no. 6 (1978): 31–35.

Schleiermacher, Friedrich. *Hermeneutics: The Handwritten Manuscripts*. Edited by Heinz Kimmerle. Translated by James Duke and Jack Forstman. Chico, Calif.: Scholars Press, 1977.

Schrag, Calvin O. *Existence and Freedom: Towards an Ontology of Human Finitude*. Evanston, Ill.: Northwestern University Press, 1961.

———. *Experience and Being: Prolegomena to a Future Ontology*. Evanston, Ill.: Northwestern University Press, 1969.

Spiegelberg, Herbert. *The Phenomenological Movement*. The Hague: Martinus Nijhoff, 1960.

Tillich, Paul. *Systematic Theology*. Vol. 1.: *Being and God*. Chicago: University of Chicago Press, 1951.

———. *Systematic Theology*. Vol. 2.: *Existence and the Christ*. Chicago: University of Chicago Press, 1957.

Wach, Joachim. *Das Verstehen: Grundzüge einer Geschichte der hermeneutischen Theorie im 19. Jahrhundert*. Hildesheim: Georg Olms, 1966.

Zimmerman, Michael. "Heidegger and Bultmann: Egoism, Sinfulness, and Inauthenticity." *The Modern Schoolman* (November 1980), pp. 1–20.

Index

A priori, 29, 31, 40
Affective fragility, 57–59
Alienation, 60, 110, 153
Appropriation, 14, 17, 91, 108–11, 140–63; event of, 147–53; object of 143–47; subject of, 153–57
Aquinas, Thomas, 71
Aristotle, *On Interpretation*, 55
Augustine, 71
Austin, J. L., 78
Authenticity, 40–43, 52, 69, 110, 124–26, 128–29, 139, 148, 151–52, 156–57

Beardsley, Monroe, 97, 117
Befindlichkeit, 34–37, 40–43, 62, 87, 99, 105
Being, 12, 26, 45, 49, 70, 107, 136, 141, 143, 146, 150–53, 156, 160; question as to the meaning of, 28, 53, 141, 151; voice of, 70
Being as, 17, 146–47, 157, 160
Bible, 16, 18, 19, 70, 94, 111–19, 121, 133
Black, Max, 97
Bultmann, Rudolf, 123–25

Character, 56–57, 99, 128
Christian religion, 52
Concept, 11, 12, 28, 30–32, 38, 49, 64, 104, 147, 151, 154, 158–60
Consciousness, 47–49, 51; historical, 19; structure of, 47, 56
Courage, 57–59, 130

Critique, 19, 68, 69, 71–72, 121, 130–31, 148, 160, 161; of ideologies, 48; subject of, 106

Dasein, 27–44, 45, 48, 62, 87–89, 146, 150–53, 157, 161; care as being of, 30, 37, 39–42, 60, 152; meaning of being, 26, 38, 141–43, 150. *See also* Existence; Hermeneutics of *Dasein;* "I"; Self
Death, as one's ownmost possibility, 41–43
Dilthey, Wilhelm, 18, 20, 60, 64, 74, 79, 90, 140–41
Discourse, 36–37, 55, 74–82, 90–91, 117, 126; as event and meaning, 77–82, 90; fixing in text, 83–84; modes of, 83, 111, 114–18; as sense and reference, 78–80, 91, 92. *See also* Language; *Rede*

Ecstases, 40
Empiricism, 22
Enlightenment, 19
Epistemology, 26, 141–42
Erlebnis, 23–26, 63
Evil, 53; myths about origin of, 70; symbolism of, 66; transition from possibility of to actuality, 54, 59–60, 70–71
Exegesis, 9, 24, 26, 61
Existence: disruptions of, 46, 51, 59, 61, 70, 129, 131, 157; image of true end of, 57. *See also Dasein;* Fallibility

181

Experience, 10, 31, 62
Explanation, in relation to understanding, 91–95
Expression, 16–21, 24–25, 46, 61–73; as object, 62–66; process of, 66–69; subjective conditions of, 69–73

Facticity, 31, 41
Faith, 130
Fallibility, 46, 51–61, 128–29. *See also* Existence
Fault, 54, 129
Feeling, 21, 23, 57–59, 155–56; expressions of, 63. *See also* Mood
Feuerbach, Ludwig, 72
Fichte, Johann Gottlieb, 31, 32, 39, 60, 141
Finitude, 31, 150; affective, 57; of doing, 56–57; of freedom, 42; of knowing, 55–56
Freedom, 42, 53, 61
Freud, Sigmund, 68–69, 72
Funk, Robert, *Language, Hermeneutic, and Word of God*, 136–38

Gadamer, Hans-Georg, 146–49; analysis of play, 105. Work: *Wahrheit und Methode*, 105
Geisteswissenschaften, 22–24
Genre, 84, 112, 113
God, 71; as referent of language, 113–14, 118–22, 124–27, 129–33, 139, 162

Happiness, 99, 128; as ethical ideal, 56–59
Hegel, G. W. F., 22, 39, 69, 141
Heidegger, Martin, 26–45, 50, 56, 58, 62, 69, 73, 86, 87–89, 94, 95, 99–100, 102, 103, 105, 122–23, 136, 141, 150–53, 158, 161. Works: *Sein und Zeit*, 27–44, 48, 52–53, 99, 123, 151, 161; "*Vom Wesen der Wahrheit*," 161; "*Das Wesen der Sprache*," 136
Hermeneutics, 15, 24, 46, 73, 74, 118–19; of being, 68; circle in, 21, 93; of *Dasein*, 38, 43, 52–54, 60, 73, 123–26, 150–53; definitions of, 18, 74, 85; of linguistic expression, 46; ontological dimension of, 12; problem of, 18, 59–61; process of, 11, 92–108, 140; Romantic, 20–26, 79, 143; of suspicion, 68, 72, 142; of symbols, 51, 68–69; theological, 9, 111–12, 118–19, 133–39. *See* Interpretation
Hester, Marcus, 105
Historical consciousness, 19
Human being. *See Dasein*
Hume, David, 154
Husserl, Edmund, 15, 24, 45–51, 86, 102, 141; doctrine of expression, 63–64. Works: *Cartesian Meditations*, 47; *Ideas*, 47; *Logical Investigations*, 47, 62, 65

"I", 13, 34–40, 50, 54–57, 59–61, 72–73, 77, 87, 89–90, 99, 106–8, 110, 123, 125–28, 130–33, 134, 137–39, 146, 149, 156–57, 159, 162. *See also* Imagination; Reflexive subject; Transcendental ego
Idealism, 47–49, 51
Ihde, Donald, 45
Imagination, 32, 35, 38, 51, 55–56, 57, 73, 86, 103–8, 143, 154–56, 160
Immediacy, 20, 126, 148, 160, 161
Inauthenticity, 40–43, 48, 124, 148, 151
Intention, 55
Intentionality, 47, 50
Interpretation, 18, 35, 48, 52, 68, 95; of existence, 27, 52–54, 60–61; grammatical, 21–22; of myth, 65; psychological, 21–22; of religious texts, 111–39. *See also* Hermeneutics
Intertextuality, 114
Intuition, 30–32, 38, 47–49, 154

Judaism, 18

Kant, Immanuel, 12, 15, 23, 27, 31, 38, 48–51, 56, 57, 60, 72, 103–4, 106, 154, 159
Kingdom of God, 69, 115, 122, 129, 137
Knowing, 54–56, 58

Language, 14, 37, 41, 44, 45, 48, 52, 61–62, 69, 112, 145–47; event of, 75–82, 113, 148–50, 156; figurative, 50, 64–65, 92–93, 95–102, 112–17, 125, 127, 144–45; levels of, 63–64, 75; literal, 50, 64–65, 92–93, 95–102, 112–18,

125, 127, 144–45; meaning of, 77–82, 113; as medium, 10, 63, 136, 146, 149, 154; religious, 111–39; speculative structure of, 146–47
Lévi-Strauss, Claude, 93–95
Limit-expression, 16, 112–13, 118–19, 129
Linguistic process, 10–14, 90, 96, 109–11
Linguistics, 75
Luther, Martin, 71, 151

Marcel, Gabriel, 46
Marx, Karl, 48, 72
Meaning, 9, 25, 36, 62–66, 77–80, 81–82, 90–102, 160; of being, 28, 53, 107–8, 123–25, 152, 157; emergent, 96–98, 104–5, 122, 145, 149–50, 154–56
Metaphor, 16, 50, 95–102, 104–5, 110, 112–13, 115–19, 122–23, 125–27, 128, 130, 132, 136, 138–39, 142, 145–46, 147–48, 150, 154–56, 157, 158, 159, 162
Metaphysics, 11–12, 29, 151, 157
Mode of being, 14, 16, 27, 30, 32, 37, 40–41, 65, 99–102, 110, 112–13, 115, 119, 122–23, 125–31, 134–35, 139, 141, 143–45, 148, 150, 152, 155, 157
Model, 112–13, 120, 129
Mood, 23, 58, 99–101, 104, 130, 144, 155, 159
Myth, 52, 65–73, 75, 82, 93–95

Naiveté: first, 69–72, 147–48, 160, 161; second, 20, 69, 72–73, 120–21, 148, 160, 161
Naturwissenschaften, 23
Negation, 54, 149
New Being, 119–20, 122, 128, 133–34, 157
New Testament, 52, 114–19, 136–39
Nietzsche, Friedrich, 48, 72
Noematic analysis, 54, 56, 153
Nothing, 124–26, 147, 162
Nouns, 55, 74–75, 145

Objectivity, 31, 38, 49, 55
Ontology, 26, 29, 34, 38, 47–48, 50–51, 105, 141–42, 145–46, 157–63

Parables, 114–18, 136–38
Paradox, 132–33, 135
Pascal, Blaise, 52, 59
Percept, 11, 12, 30, 48
Perception, 47–49, 54, 55, 154
Person, constituted in practical synthesis, 56
Perspective, 54–57
Phenomenology, 15, 46, 50, 60, 122; method of, 47, 54; of religion, 68–69. *See also* Ricoeur, Paul
Philosophical anthropology, 15, 26, 44–45, 60, 61, 141, 142
Philosophy, 11, 16, 45, 53
Plato, 52, 59. Works: *Cratylus*, 55; *Sophist*, 55; *Theaetetus*, 55
Pöggeler, Otto, 30, 43, 52, 123, 150–53.
Positivism, 22
Pragma, 57
Principles, 17, 18, 20, 24, 27, 43, 118; of exegesis, 45, 61; of ontological discernment, 46; of systematic thinking, 10, 109–11
Psychoanalysis, 48, 68–69

Ramsey, Ian, 113, 121
Rasmussen, David, 45
Rationality, 10, 12
Realism, 47
Reality, 49, 52, 54, 58
Reason, 49, 159
Rede, 34, 36, 40–43, 141. *See also* Discourse
Reference, 25, 63, 77–80, 85–88, 91, 92, 95, 98, 102, 103, 106, 111, 117, 120, 122–26, 134–39, 140–41, 142–44, 148–49, 155, 160
Referent, 16–17, 64, 86, 91–92, 109–10, 112–17, 120, 122–26, 128, 134–39, 140–41, 143–44, 149, 162
Reflection, 45, 46, 51–54, 61, 68, 71, 131; limits of, 59–61; Ricoeur's philosophy of, 51–61
Reflexive subject, 31, 60–61, 73, 87, 90, 103, 106–08, 131, 139, 148, 152–53, 157, 160, 162. *See also* "I"; Transcendental ego
Respect, 49, 56
Revelation, 9, 113–14, 119, 161
Ricoeur, Paul. hermeneutics of, 15, 25,

45, 46, 51, 61–121, 140–63; phenomenology of, 45–61. Works: *Fallible Man*, 46, 51–61, 74, 103, 130, 154; *Freedom and Nature*, 45; *Freud and Philosophy*, 74; *Rule of Metaphor*, 96, 158; *Symbolism of Evil*, 46, 74, 123–24

Saussure, Ferdinand de, 75, 90
Scharlemann, Robert P., 19
Schematism, 32, 38, 56, 102–4, 154–55
Schleiermacher, Friedrich, 18, 20, 60, 62, 79, 92, 140–41
Selbst-Darstellung, 71, 146–47, 152
Self, 13, 14, 17, 26, 30, 31, 33–34, 48, 61, 70–71, 94, 102–8, 109–11, 124–29, 141–42, 144, 153, 157; as finite, 53, 60; as infinite, 53; practical, 56–57; structure of *Tathandlung*, 31, 39, 60, 77, 126; understood through myth, 66
Semantics, 44, 61, 75–78; innovation through, 96–97, 112–13, 115, 118, 142, 154
Semiotics, 75–76, 79, 93
Sense, 9, 16, 17, 38, 63, 77–80, 82–83, 91, 98, 106, 111, 117, 120, 122–26, 128, 134–35, 139, 140–41, 142–44, 148–49, 160. *See also* Meaning
Sensibility, 54, 159
Sentence, 11, 55, 74–79, 96–98
Sign, 9, 11, 16, 17, 38, 43–44, 53, 63–65, 74–75, 123–26, 134–35, 148
Silence, 13–14
Structuralism, 75–76, 79, 83, 91–95, 122
Structure, in language, 75, 83–84; of text, 86, 91, 93–95, 106, 109, 111, 115, 116, 135, 137
Style, 21
Subjectivity, 69–72, 102–8, 123, 132–33, 143, 153. *See also*, *Dasein*; "I"; Self
Symbol, 52, 61, 64, 66–72, 101, 116, 129, 131–33, 142, 162; cosmic dimension of, 66–67; oneiric dimension of, 67
Synthesis, 30–32, 155–56, 159; practical, 56–58; theoretical, 55–56, 74, 104

Temporality, 15, 34, 38–44, 66, 70, 123, 127–28, 150–53, 156
Text, 12, 14, 15, 16, 24–25, 45, 126, 153; appropriation of, 140–63; interpretation of, 27; meaning of, 60; poetic, 16, 92–102, 112–13, 125, 127, 134, 144–45; reflexivity in, 135; religious, 16, 17, 109–39; Ricoeur's theory of, 80–109, 142, world of, 81, 83, 85–90, 102–8, 112, 118, 133, 143–44, 148–50, 153
Theology, 71, 114; fundamental, 9. *See* Hermeneutics, theological
Tillich, Paul, 10, 118, 128
Time, 38–44, 56, 75–76, 127–28, 151–53, 156; reference of verb to, 55
Transcendental ego, 31–34, 38, 47–49, 55–57, 106. *See also* "I"; Reflexive subject
Transcendental image, 32, 57, 103–8, 154
Truth, 143, 151, 159–63

Unconditioned, the, 50, 58, 121
Understanding, 9, 10, 11, 14, 18, 28, 31, 32, 49, 51, 52, 54, 62, 87, 127, 136, 147, 151–54, 159, 160; historical, 25; as linguistic, 10–14; as projection, 30, 35, 40, 88–90, 144, 149; as religious, 9, 110–39; through text, 45, 90–108. *See Verstehen*

Verbs, 55, 74–75, 77, 145
Vernunft, 49. *See* Reason
Verstehen, 23, 34–37, 40–43, 48, 62, 87, 90, 103, 105, 141. *See* Understanding

World, 40, 66, 81, 87–88, 146. *See* Text, world of